St. Mary's High School

Nail Artistry

D0139434

Hairdressing And Beauty Industry Authority Series – related titles

Hairdressing

Mahogany Hairdressing: Steps to Cutting, Colouring and Finishing Hair
Martin Gannon and Richard Thompson

Mahogany Hairdressing: Advanced Looks Richard Thompson and Martin Gannon

Essensuals, Next Generation Toni & Guy: Step by Step

Professional Men's Hairdressing Guy Kremer and Jacki Wadeson

The Art of Dressing Long Hair Guy Kremer and Jacki Wadeson

Patrick Cameron: Dressing Long Hair Patrick Cameron and Jacki Wadeson

Patrick Cameron: Dressing Long Hair Book 2 Patrick Cameron

Bridal Hair Pat Dixon and Jacki Wadeson

Trevor Sorbie: Visions in Hair Kris Sorbie and Jacki Wadeson

The Total Look: The Style Guide for Hair and Make-up Professionals Ian Mistlin

Art of Hair Colouring David Adams and Jacki Wadeson

Start Hairdressing: The Official Guide to Level 1 Martin Green and Leo Palladino

Hairdressing – The Foundations: The Official Guide to Level 2
Leo Palladino with Jane Farr

Professional Hairdressing: The Official Guide to Level 3
Martin Green and Leo Palladino

Men's Hairdressing: Traditional and Modern Barbering Maurice Lister

African-Caribbean Hairdressing Sandra Gittens

The World of Hair: A Scientific Companion Dr John Gray

Salon Management Martin Green

Beauty Therapy

Beauty Therapy – The Foundations: The Official Guide to Level 2
Lorraine Nordmann

Professional Beauty Therapy: The Official Guide to Level 3
Lorraine Nordmann, Lorraine Appleyard and Pamela Linforth

Aromatherapy for the Beauty Therapist Valerie Ann Worwood

Indian Head Massage Muriel Burnham-Airey and Adele O'Keefe

The Official Guide to Body Massage Adele O'Keefe

An Holistic Guide to Anatomy and Physiology Tina Parsons

An Holistic Guide to Reflexology Tina Parsons

Nutrition: A Practical Approach Suzanne Le Quesne

The Encyclopedia of Nails Jacqui Jefford and Anne Swain

Nail Artistry Jacqui Jefford, Sue Marsh and Anne Swain

The Complete Nail Technician Marian Newman

The World of Skin Care: A Scientific Companion Dr John Gray

Safety in the Salon Elaine Almond

Nail Artistry

Jacqui Jefford, Sue Marsh and Anne Swain

THOMSON

Australia · Canada · Mexico · Singapore · Spain · United Kingdom · United States

HABIA
Hairdressing And Beauty Industry Authority

Nail Artistry

Copyright © Thomson Learning 2004

The Thomson logo is a registered trademark used herein under licence.

For more information, contact Thomson Learning, High Holborn House, 50–51 Bedford Row, London WC1R 4LR or visit us on the World Wide Web at: http://www.thomsonlearning.co.uk

British Library Cataloguing-in-Publication Data
A catalogue record for this book is available from the British Library

ISBN 1-86152-944-9

First edition published by Thomson Learning 2004

Typeset by Meridian Colour Repro Ltd, Pangbourne-on-Thames, Berkshire

Printed in Croatia by Zrinski d.d.

Contents

The business of nail art 1

Anatomy and physiology of the skin and nails 49

Basic nail art techniques 75

Foreword

In 2001 I wrote the foreword for Jacqui Jefford and Anne Swain's excellent textbook *The Encyclopedia of Nails* published by Thomson Learning. I found the encyclopedia a fascinating read – and now here they are again with the superb *Nail Artistry*! The authors have surpassed themselves and, aided by Sue Marsh, this book is an incredibly in-depth perspective on the colourful world of nail art.

For such experienced nail artists I'm sure writing the book was almost as much fun as their regular work on London Fashion Week. The energy they put into their busy and exciting lives comes through in every word; their systematic approach to work ethic and their insight into fashion shows, photographic work and competitions all make the pages come alive. The huge variation of nail art examples coupled with fascinating real-life stories add more than just a shine!

This book perfectly covers HABIA's new standards for nail technicians and complements the new NVQ/SVQ nail qualifications available in 2004. This is a book for every nail professional – congratulations Jacqui, Sue and Anne for another milestone in nail history.

Alan Goldsbro
Chief Executive Officer
Hairdressing and Beauty Industry Authority

Acknowledgements

Creative Nail Design
Designer Nails UK Ltd
Sudo Simair Ltd
Swarovski

Nail technicians:

Sue Marsh	Shar Gazzard
Anne Swain	Melanie
Jacqui Jefford	Katherine Rae
Neil Patrick	Claudine Rowley
Teruko Kobayashi	Kaoru Suzuki

Models:

Chrissy Conn	Kelly Swain
Michelle Hardy	Simone
Kayleigh Butcher	Leah Stanford
Gemma Jones	Kimberley Wrigley
Spencer Bardill	Claudine Rowley

Hair:
Bev at Toni & Guy, Poole
William Ippoliti

Body art:
Sharon Crawford
Jacqui Jefford

Make-up:
Natsumi Watanabe
Sue Marsh
Jacqui Jefford

Photographers:
James Cumpsty for putting up with us
Richard Eccles
Nathan Jones

Special thanks to
Samantha Sweet for the Alternative Nail Awards
Alex Fox for believing in us
Blunt Agency for giving us opportunities

Introduction

Most clients either love it or hate it – nail art that is! Those who dislike nail art have usually only seen really outrageous designs that they could not wear. But nail art is for everyone and can be worn as 'soft' or as 'outrageous' as you wish. The authors have performed nail art treatments on clients as young as 2 and as old as 90. Both genders can, and do, wear nail art, and many use it as a fashion statement. Some believe that it is only the nail technician who likes nail art, but you will find that if you wear it your clients will want it and a good business can be built around nail art treatments. Nail art can therefore bring extra financial rewards into the salon.

There is no other beauty treatment that transforms a part of our body as instantly as a nail treatment, whether it is a simple manicure, a buffing of the natural nails to a shine, or a complicated airbrush design, and all are art forms. There is no other part of the body, except the face, that is on show as much as the hands. Having a nail treatment could not only transform your clients' nails but their personality as well. Many nail technicians started out as clients, so they know what a confidence boost nice nails can bring.

With the growth of the professional nail industry in recent years there has been an increase in the nail art market and there is now a need for a comprehensive manual to guide technicians who wish to add this treatment to their salon services. There are a number of new nail qualifications available and there will be more in the future. We recommend that anyone coming into the industry should obtain recognised qualifications. Nail art skills can be used in the salon or taken a step further in competitions or photographic and catwalk work. Whichever area you decide to enter to use your skills, we wish you luck and hope that some of our designs will inspire you.

The business of nail art

Learning objectives

In this section you will learn about:

- **marketing and advertising your services**
- **how to incorporate nail art into your existing business**
- **who your clients will be**
- **pricing structure**
- **choosing the right courses for your needs**

The professional nail industry is one of the fastest growing industries in the UK today. Nail treatments have traditionally taken second place to hair and beauty services, with technicians renting desks within hair and beauty salons. However, this situation has now changed and there are many successful nail salons and even chains of nail salons opening across the UK. Nail art is a specialised, but growing, part of the nail business and an accomplished nail artist can hope to build a successful career with the right approach – which includes good training, appropriate marketing and a sound knowledge of this area of the hairdressing and beauty industry.

The work of professional nail artists uses specific work practices, chemicals and equipment that are subject to Health and Safety Regulations and nail artists need to be very familiar with those that apply to the nail industry in general. We endeavour to cover as much as we can in the space available here and intend the information to be up-to-date at the time of writing. In this chapter we will look at cross infection and how to avoid it by implementing rules for keeping your work environment as clean and germ free as possible. We touch our clients every hour of our working life and need to be aware of the precautions we should be taking to inhibit the spread of disease causing organisms. We will also look at the dangers of overexposure to chemicals and how to use them safely.

A vital part of a nail art service is the after care advice given to clients. This will extend the life of a nail art treatment, enabling clients to get the best value possible and making them more likely to return to you on another occasion or recommend you to their friends. It is also important for you and your reputation that you give the right advice and keep accurate records of having done so. This can be invauable in the event of any problems arising after the client has left the salon.

In this chapter we will consider the following aspects:

- **setting up**
- **working safely**
  – Health and Safety legislation
  – overexposure
  – cross infection and salon hygiene
- **after care for your client**

Setting up a nail art service

The setting up of a nail art kit can be as cheap or expensive as you want it to be. Many nail technicians have made very expensive mistakes buying equipment that is wrong either for them or for their market. It is always worth researching more than one area before investing your own hard earned cash. This section will guide you through how to integrate nail art into your already existing nail business or, for the complete beginner, will offer some advice on how to set up from scratch.

Marketing and advertising your services

You must ask yourself first whether you personally like nail art and whether you would wear it. If the answer is no, then it is going to be difficult for you to persuade your clients to wear it as they will be influenced by what you are wearing. If you do not like nail art in its outrageous form, then tone it down to suit your own taste, for example a simple airbrush colour fade or one daisy with a rhinestone on the little finger of a natural French look. Remember that you can also display your skills on your toes; many nail artistes do not wear designs on their fingers but show off beautiful creations on their toes.

Before you invest in expensive courses and products make sure that you have a market to sell to.

Who wears nail art?

Anyone and everyone can wear nail art. The keenest group tend to be 14–18 year olds, but teenagers usually have a restricted budget. However, nail art does not have to be outrageous all of the time. You can attract an older and more professional clientele with stunning subtle designs. One of the most popular finishes to entice clients on to the nail art trail is a simple colour fade performed with an airbrush.

Once you have been on a nail art course and have practised your designs, built a collection of samples for clients to view, and have the confidence to sell yourself, where do you go next? Wear it. You are your own best advertisement. Offer discounts to local hairdressers and display samples in their reception area. Ask wedding shops, boutiques and fancy dress hire agencies to display your work and your business cards. Display posters in doctors' surgeries and dentists' waiting rooms. Find out when major functions are being held in local hotels and leave your cards and leaflets in the reception area and the ladies cloakrooms. Find out if there are any local fashion shows that you can become involved in. Newspaper advertising can be quite expensive and only reach your target audience for one week. Yellow Pages and Thomson directories give a free lineage every year, so if you cannot afford a box in these publications at least contact them to get your free entry. Get in touch with local organisations and parish magazines, they are always grateful for news and features. Contact your local paper to see if they will do a press release or editorial on your new treatments, they may send a reporter to take photographs of you and your work.

Try to work out a budget for your advertising and promotion and stick to it for the first year. At the end of that year analyse where most of your clients have come from and invest more in that area than the others. Remember to build in the cost of donating gift vouchers to charities and also your time spent on giving demonstrations. If you find that word of mouth has been the best form of advertising for you keep your newspaper or directory advertising to a minimum and spend your resources on physically reaching a particular audience, perhaps by giving some nail art parties!

Most nail technicians love their job so much that they do not even consider the business side. We know that the three authors have all been in this position. Once you recognise this, you need to plan your business and make sure you look at areas like marketing and advertising. You will then find you can develop a healthy business.

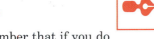

Note

Remember that if you do not value your services your clients cannot be expected to either. Do not give anything away for free: free has no value!

Pricing your services

Initially, it is extremely difficult to decide what prices to charge for a nail art service, as it is basically an add-on to what most professionals are doing already, whether it be a manicure, pedicure or nail extension. You will need to sit down with a pen and paper, perhaps with a friend or member of the family, and work out first of all who your potential clients are, where they live or work and the location where you will be working and use all these factors to determine at which level you will start your pricing. Never undervalue a nail art service, it is a specialist area of work and you should charge accordingly.

As you will see from this book nail art services have developed from the hand painting seen a few years ago and there is now a whole range of services that can be provided for clients, from the very simple to the very intricate and costly. You will need to consider both the cost of materials required and the time it will take you to perform each nail art service. We cannot possibly write your price list for you but we can give you some guidelines for a range of services. If you look at the various chapters in the book you will notice that as you read through, the designs become more intricate and time consuming and therefore the costs to you in terms of equipment, products and time will be higher, so you must build these costs into your pricing structure.

Here are a few sample prices for various designs. These are applicable at the time of writing, and are dependent on the geographic and professional area in which you are working.

- Basic hand painting (daisies, etc.), per set – 10 minutes – £10.00
- Advanced hand painting, per set – over 30 minutes – from £20.00
- Transfers/decals/rhinestones, per set – from £5.00 per nail
- Charms/jewellery – consider the price of products – fitting from £1.00
- Foils/glitters/striping/marbling, etc., per set – from £15.00
- Airbrushing: two colour fade/contour, per set – from £7.50
- Airbrushing: three colour fade/contour, per set – from £10.00
- Airbrushing: detailed stencil design, per set – over 30 minutes – from £20.00 (add more if using rhinestones or other media)
- Embedding lace/material/decals, etc. into nail extensions – add an extra £15 on top of the price of the extensions, or more depending on the difficulty of design and the time it will take
- Coloured acrylics and gels – these designs can be very time consuming and you must charge what you are worth per hour plus the cost of the materials. For example, if a set of nails costs £35 and will take you an hour and a half plus another hour for the design, then you should really add on £20 at least.
- Photographic and fashion work will be determined by your agency

Choosing the right course

You do not have to be a professional nail technician to be a nail artist. There are many people who just provide art services without performing nail treatments. But, if you want to become a full service nail artist then you will have to have mastered nail technology as

---

Remember

The more you practise each design the quicker and more proficient you will become. After you have finished your course, sit and practise on tips for a week or two before attempting to offer your services to clients. This will also give you a selection of designs to show existing and potential clients.

well. Most of the designs in Chapter 2 can be performed by anyone over the age of 14, who has been trained in those media, but for those wishing to progress onto coloured acrylics for instance, a standard of skills as high as an experienced nail technician will be required. If you wish to go into photographic and fashion work, you will need to have done an apprenticeship with an experienced nail technician or have vast experience in all aspects of nail technology.

The types of courses we would recommend, at the outset, would be a Basic Nail Art Course, and perhaps a Basic Airbrushing Course if you can afford the equipment. Once you have built a loyal clientele over a couple of months, the time you take has come down, and your skill has advanced, then you can progress onto other areas.

In our experience, the best teachers are those who have proven experience in the field of nail art and airbrushing. If you can see an artist's work in a trade or consumer magazine, and you like it, then you will have confidence in their abilities. Try to make contact with these professionals and if they do not offer courses themselves, then they will be able to tell you where they did their training, or recommend artists they know who are good at what they do and may be able to mentor you for a period of time. Always choose a training school that has experienced teachers and make sure that you look at their portfolio first before committing yourself to what could be an expensive mistake.

Note

Always choose a centre where trainers know about the equipment as well as the nail art side and where they will share their knowledge and experience and offer after sales support.

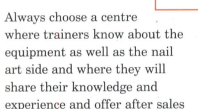

A basic nail art course should not be too expensive and the set up costs should also be achievable. Once you progress onto airbrushing, you will find that the cost of the equipment can run into hundreds of pounds and you will need to be seriously committed to this area of work. There are many nail artists who have bought expensive kits, become demoralised, and given up for a few years, simply through a lack of proper training. Make sure that the training school you choose offers intermediate and advanced classes as well so that you can progress to the next level.

If you are not sure how to find centres that offer nail art courses then try contacting the following:

- trade organisations such as The Association of Nail Technicians
- local art and hobby shops
- colleges
- private nail schools
- trade magazines
- other nail artists
- trade shows
- the internet

Before you commit yourself to your course make sure you know how long it is, whether you will get a certificate, what is in the kit and which designs you will be taking home with you.

There are a number of professional qualifications for nail art and it would be to your advantage – especially if you are paying for a course – if it enables you to gain one of these. It says a lot about you to your clients if you have a professional certificate and it gives them confidence in your dedication and ability as a professional. One of the advantages of nail art is that it is very visual and is easy to collect evidence of your achievements. Make sure that whatever work you do, you take a photograph or do a sample nail and keep it safe. All of this can be used as evidence when gaining a nationally recognised qualification.

WORKING SAFELY

Health and Safety legislation

Learning objectives

In this section you will learn about:

- **the Health and Safety Act 1974 and other relevant acts**
- **Control of Substances Hazardous to Health (COSHH)**
- **First Aid at work**
- **risk assessment**
- **fire regulations**
- **electricity at work**

Because it is such an important issue, there is a great deal of legislation relating to health and safety. Within the service industry, we are legally obliged to provide a safe and hygienic working environment, paying careful attention to health, safety and security.

All Health and Safety regulations are subject to change over a period of time due to national legislation and the influence of the European Union (EU). It is your duty to yourself, your colleagues and your clients to keep yourself up to date on any new legislation that is introduced.

Note

HABIA has produced an excellent Health and Safety pack. For more information, contact HABIA.

Health and Safety at Work Act 1974 (revised 1994)

Health and safety at work relates to the measures designed to protect the health and safety of people while they are at work and also to protect members of the public visiting the workplace – whether they are paying customers or simply passers-by. Most countries in the western world have developed legislation to protect the health and safety of their workforce and in Britain employers must take reasonable care to protect their employees from the risk of disease, injury or death. Employers have a responsibility to protect themselves and those around them from the same risks.

It is a legal requirement for employers either to display an approved Health and Safety poster or to supply employees with an equivalent

Courtesy of HSE

Health and Safety poster

Display

leaflet. This material is updated from time to time in line with changes in legislation.

The factors that affect health and safety can be divided into three main groups:

1 *occupational factors* – people could be at risk from illness or injury from the work they do, e.g. asthma from paint spraying

2 *environmental factors* – the conditions in which people work may cause problems, e.g. noisy environments can cause deafness

3 *human factors* – poor behaviour and bad attitudes can contribute to accidents, e.g. lack of concentration, carelessness and rushing jobs

Your employer has a duty under the law to protect, as far as is reasonably practicable, your health, safety and welfare at work. The Health and Safety at Work Act added further regulations to existing legislation. The Health and Safety Executive (HSE) appoints inspectors to ensure that employers comply with the act. Local authorities are responsible for business premises and shops and they enforce the requirements of the act. In general, employers' duties include making the workplace safe and reducing risks to health by providing proper supervision and training.

The Health and Safety Act 1974 incorporates a variety of legislation and regulations as discussed below.

The Management of Health and Safety at Work Regulations 1992

This act requires a salon owner, for example, to make formal arrangements for maintaining and improving safe working conditions and practices. These arrangements should include providing training for all employees and monitoring working risks. This latter point is known as **risk assessment**.

The Personal Protective Equipment (PPE) at Work Regulations 1992

Through the process of risk assessment, managers should identify activities that require special protective clothing or equipment to be worn. These articles should then be made available to all staff and a good supply kept on the premises at all times.

The Workplace (Health and Safety and Welfare) Regulations 1992

This act provides the employer with a code of practice that can help them to maintain a safe and secure working environment. These regulations cover the legal requirements that relate to the following aspects of the working environment:

● ventilation
● safe and secure salon layout
● sanitary conveniences

- safe flooring, easy access and traffic routes
- drinking and washing facilities
- changing facilities
- staff room facilities
- handling of waste materials
- maintenance and upkeep of windows, doors and walls
- cleanliness of the working environment
- maintenance of all equipment
- maintenance of the workplace in general

The Manual Handling Operation Regulations 1992

A risk assessment should be carried out by an employer of any activities undertaken by employees which involve manual lifting. Evidence should be provided that the following have been considered:

- the capabilities of each individual worker
- any potential risk of injury
- the manual movement involved in the lifting activity
- any action needed to minimise potential risks

The Provision and Use of Work Equipment Regulations (PUWER) 1992

This act requires the identification of any new and old equipment that is used. Specific regulations address the dangers and potential risk of injury that could occur during the operation of certain equipment. They state the duties of the employer, employees and the self-employed. It also identifies the requirement to select suitable equipment and attend to its maintenance. Equipment manufacturers also have a responsibility to provide information on any specific training needed to operate the equipment.

Employers' Liability (Compulsory Insurance) Act 1969

Employers are responsible for the health and safety of their employees while at work. Employees may be injured while at work, and former employees may be eligible to make a claim if they become ill as a result of the work they did whilst in your employment. Both groups may try to claim compensation from you if they believe you are responsible. The Employer's Liability (compulsory insurance) Act 1969 ensures that employers have at least the minimum level of insurance cover against any such claims.

An HSE inspector can check that you have employer's liability insurance with an approved insurer for at least £5m. The inspector can ask to see your certificate and other details and you can be fined up to £2500 for any day you are without suitable insurance cover. If the certificate is not displayed and it is not produced on demand, you could be fined up to £1000. Employers should keep all insurance certificates that have been issued.

Technical Tip

Don't forget about public and product liability insurance.

This addresses the minimum standards required in the following areas for premises to operate:

- sanitation
- cleanliness
- ventilation
- lighting
- overcrowding

This act is linked to the Health and Safety at Work Act. Note that new EU directives will affect this act. It covers each part of shop premises from the shop to the showroom, hall, stair and passageways. Premises are required to have appropriate fire fighting equipment and clean staff toilets and washroom facilities which are easily accessible and suitably lit and ventilated. Halls, floors, passageways and stairs should be properly constructed, free from obstructions and properly maintained. There should also be an area where staff can hang clothing.

Control of Substances Hazardous to Health (COSHH)

Using chemicals or other hazardous substances at work could put people's health at risk. Therefore employers are required by law to control exposure to hazardous chemicals and substances to prevent ill health. Employers have a duty to protect employees and any visitors who may be exposed. All employers must comply with the Control of Substances Hazardous to Health Regulations 1999, but it is a good management tool as it sets out basic steps. If an employer fails to meet the required standards by not adequately controlling hazardous substances or chemicals they can be prosecuted. Adverse effects can range from mild eye irritation to chronic lung disease. Understanding and following the rules of COSHH can not only lead to safer working conditions, but can also improve employees' morale and subsequently raise productivity in the workplace.

The next seven stages will help to guide you through COSHH regulations.

Stage one

Carry out a risk assessment to assess any hazardous substances that may give cause for concern in your workplace.

Stage two

When the risks have been identified, record them and decide what action and precautions – if any – are to be taken. Check with product manufacturers for COSHH or material safety data sheets (MSDSs). You should read and understand all the information you are giving. If you do not, you must ask questions. Ignorance would not be an acceptable excuse if there is a problem.

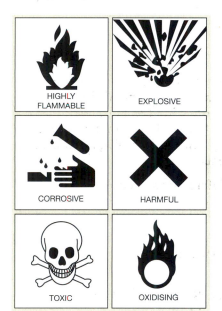

COSHH warning signs

Remember to check that any systems you introduce work effectively. Nail technicians should be aware of the routes of entry into the body. The products that are used in the nail industry can be absorbed through the skin if not used correctly. Checks must be made and regular training put in place to prevent mistakes being made.

Stage three

Under the COSHH regulations there must be adequate control of chemical usage to prevent overexposure. In the nail industry exposure can be greatly reduced by good housekeeping and regularly updated training.

Stage four

Training should be monitored to make sure employees are adopting the techniques they have been taught, and all comments should be recorded.

Stage five

Monitor the exposure level if necessary. Nail technicians must know how to recognise overexposure symptoms and what to do in an emergency. All symptoms should be recorded.

Stage six

Carry out appropriate health surveillance if COSHH regulations have set specific requirements.

Stage seven

Ensure all employees are fully trained, informed about procedures, kept up to date and supervised.

Disposal of chemicals

All chemicals and substances identified in stage one of the risk assessment must have a designated means of disposal. The manufacturers keep COSHH sheets or MSDSs and they will normally be happy to supply you with the relevant information if requested. The activity box will help you to establish good working practices for the disposal of chemicals.

A COSHH or MSDS will give you information about:

- any hazardous ingredients
- safe exposure levels
- possible routes of entry into the body
- emergency First Aid advice
- fire precautions and appropriate fire equipment
- safe working practices and safety precautions
- early warning signs of overexposure

 Activity

- Contact the manufacturer for COSHH sheets or MSDSs.
- Draw up a chart listing all chemicals used in the salon.
- List all safety equipment required and precautions which should be taken.
- List the requirements for disposal of all chemicals in the salon.
- Set and record acceptable standards of safety within the salon.
- Ensure all staff are trained to the required level.
- Record all accidents and their details.
- Review procedures on a regular basis.

First Aid and accidents

Whenever an illness or injury occurs, wherever it may be and whatever its cause, it is imperative that the correct action is quickly taken. The First Aid Regulations 1981 require employers to provide appropriate and adequate equipment and to inform employees of all First Aid arrangements.

Signs should be placed telling staff who the first aider (or appointed person) is and where the First Aid box is kept. There is legislation relating to how many first aiders or appointed persons there must be, according to the type of business and number of employees. The appointed person is someone who can take charge if an injury occurs or if someone falls ill at work. One of this person's duties is to take responsibility for the First Aid box and this includes stocking it and replacing any item that may be used. This person should be available at all times but may not necessarily be a qualified first aider. The first aider is a person who has been trained in the administration of First Aid and who holds a current First Aid certificate. Their training must be approved by the HSE. A first aider can also take the responsibilities of an appointed person.

It is not a nail technician's responsibility to treat an injury or condition. This should be left to a professional such as a doctor or nurse. But it is, however, the nail technician's responsibility to see that help is called and only to apply First Aid if he or she holds a current certificate. Although it is not a legal requirement for nail technicians to have a First Aid certificate it is a good idea for all individuals to gain this qualification. The three main organisations that offer certified training are St John Ambulance (in England and Wales), the British Red Cross and the St Andrews Ambulance Association (in Scotland).

First Aid kit

There is no standard list of items that should be kept in a First Aid box. If there are no special risks in the working environment, the size and contents of a First Aid box can vary according to the number of employees and the nature of the business.

The following is only a list of suggested items:

- First Aid booklet or leaflet giving general advice
- sterile eye dressings
- individually wrapped triangular bandages
- packet of individually wrapped sterile adhesive dressings in assorted sizes
- medium-sized (12 cm × 12 cm) sterile, individually wrapped, non-medicated wound dressings
- large (18 cm × 18 cm) sterile, individually wrapped, non-medicated wound dressings
- safety pins
- disposable gloves

Activity

- Locate the First Aid kit and the accident book.
- Check who is the first aider or the appointed person responsible for the kit.

Consider also the following points:

- because of the nature of the nail business, the kit should also include eye wash and an eye bath
- tablets and medicines should *not* be kept in the First Aid box
- COSHH sheets and MSDSs should be available in case of accidents.

Reporting accidents

Accident book

The reporting of all accidents and near misses must be recorded in the accident book which should be kept with the First Aid kit. Note that all accidents should be recorded, no matter how minor. The following information is required:

- the full name and address of the person/s involved in the accident
- date, time and place of the accident
- circumstances of the accident
- all details of what may have contributed to the accident
- any witness accounts of events
- witness's name and address
- action that was taken, e.g. First Aid, ambulance, etc.

Reporting of Injuries, Diseases and Dangerous Occurrences Regulations 1995 (RIDDOR 95)

Under RIDDOR 95, employers are legally required to report certain injuries, diseases and near misses at work. The information helps the Health and Safety Executive and local authorities to identify how and where risk occurs. This information assists them in their investigations of serious accidents.

Death or major injury

This category includes any accident connected with work, including physical violence. If an employee, visitor or self-employed person working on the premises suffers illness or injury which is work-related and affects the person over a three-day period a fully completed accident form (F2508) must be sent to the enforcing authority within ten days.

Disease

If a doctor reports to you that an employee is suffering from a reportable work-related disease you must complete form F2508 A and forward it to the enforcing authority. Reportable diseases include certain poisonings, some skin diseases such as occupational dermatitis, skin cancer, chrome ulcer and oil folliculitis/acne. Lung diseases including occupational asthma, hepatitis, anthrax and tuberculosis are also notifiable.

Definition of major injuries, dangerous occurrences and disease

Reportable major injuries are any fracture other than to fingers, thumbs, or toes; the dislocation of the hip, knee, shoulder, or spine; amputation; loss of sight – temporary or permanent; a chemical or hot injury to the eye or any permanent injury to the eye; any injury resulting in an electric shock or electric burn leading to unconsciousness or that requires resuscitation or admittance to hospital for more than 24 hours; unconsciousness caused by asphyxia or exposure to a harmful substance or biological agent; acute illness requiring medical treatment, or loss of consciousness arising from absorption of any substance by inhalation, or ingestion through the skin; acute illness requiring medical treatment where there is reason to believe that this resulted from exposure to a biological agent or its toxins or to infected material.

For further information see the HSE leaflet, RIDDOR Explained, or consult http://www.hse.gov.uk/riddor

Risk assessment

There are two types or risk assessment. The first is one which we all do every day of our lives, such as when crossing the road. We stop, look, listen and assess the speed of oncoming traffic; we look at weather conditions and consider if we should be crossing at a zebra or pelican crossing. We then assess the overall risk of crossing at that particular spot and how long we have to do it. This is called an *informal risk assessment*.

The second type is known as a *formal risk assessment* and should be carried out in every workplace where there are people employed or working as self-employed. They are usually carried out by a trained member of staff who is familiar with the task being performed and is aware of the relevant safety issues. External consultants can be employed to conduct a risk assessment for a company which does not have the time or the resources to carry out an assessment. These consultants will usually liaise with managers, supervisors or other members of staff to help in the writing of the risk assessment.

A risk assessment is the process by which staff, supervisors and managers are asked to identify potential risks in the workplace and find ways by which accidents, problems and potential ill health can be prevented. A risk assessment is a legal requirement but can also be useful for companies as it can help to identify problem areas, decide on priorities, highlight staff training needs and help with quality assurance programmes.

It is an examination of the hazards that cause harm to people in the working environment. Once this has been achieved you can ascertain whether your precautions are adequate, or whether more can be done to prevent injury and harm. The object of this section is to guide you through the assessment of the risk in your own business.

Activity

Look at the potential hazards in your place of work. Concentrate on significant hazards, things that could cause harm or injury. Ask questions of your employees to check that all risks have been considered. This information should be recorded, given to all staff and a record kept on site.

What is a hazard?

A hazard is anything that has the potential to cause harm. For example:

- damaged flooring
- damaged equipment
- harmful substances
- sharp tools
- fire
- bad lighting
- noise levels
- inadequate ventilation

What is a risk?

Risk is the likelihood that a hazard could cause harm or injury and can be affected by a variety of factors. For instance, if a salon has a carpet that has a tear or an edge curling up, the risk factors could be:

- the level of lighting in that area
- how bad the damage to the carpet is
- how many people walk over it
- what type of shoes those people wear

Control measures

A control measure can be either an action or an item that will help to remove or reduce a potential risk. Hazards should be removed if possible. If they cannot be removed, then it is important to reduce the risk by making staff and clients aware of the potential problem. In the example of the carpet above, put a barrier or warning sign over it.

Your workplace should be carefully examined for potential hazards, some of which will be very obvious, such as trailing flexes from lamps, and others which are not so obvious, such as dust that could be inhaled. Once all the risks have been identified you can consider the consequences of injury or harm in the long term. Look at the likeliest scenarios first and the less likely ones afterwards, but always remedy all potential risks. You may decide to introduce some personal protective equipment into the salon, but if you do not then you should consider the long-term risk of not doing so for yourself, your staff and your business.

Whatever control measures you put in place, they must be checked on a regular basis to make sure they continue to work efficiently.

Risk assessments themselves should be reviewed at least every six months or when new techniques, products or equipment are introduced into the salon. If a risk is identified records should be updated immediately.

Decide exactly who is at risk from which hazards, for example new personnel, young trainees, visitors, members of the public, etc.

Evaluate all the risks and decide if the precautions are adequate or whether new procedures need to be put in place. Consider what the law says you must do to limit the risk. Have you put the industry standards in place? The law says you must do what is reasonably practicable to keep your workplace safe. Decide whether you can remove the hazard, and if not what will be the best way to control the hazard and make conditions as safe as possible. In the nail industry chemicals and solvents are used, so these need to be assessed and the necessary precautions taken, including the Control of Substances Hazardous to Health regulations (COSHH). Staff must be trained in the use, application, and transportation of products or hazardous substances.

All of the comments and findings derived from the assessment must be recorded. Any changes made should also be recorded. If you have less than five employees, you are not required by law to write anything down. However, the fact that you have less than five employees does not mean there are no risks and it is useful to keep a record. It will show that checks have been made and that precautions are in place. Such information could be invaluable when training new personnel. Your findings should always be shared with your employees.

Risk assessment form

SUGGESTED FORM FOR RISK ASSESSMENT 1

NAME OF SALON	Nails R Us	DATE	02 January 2002
COMPANY ADDRESS	1 High Street	REVIEW DATE	02 April 2002
	Anytown		
POSTCODE	AN1 2YT		

LIST HAZARDS	PEOPLE AT RISK	CONTROLS IN PLACE	ACTION TAKEN
- Wires in a heavy traffic area	- Clients, staff and all visitors	- Technician was responsible for removal of gel machine when not in use	- Trunking placed and wires organised. Further training given to technician
- Boxes in front of fire exit	- Clients, staff and all visitors	- Manager in charge of keeping fire routes clear	- Boxes removed to store room and 'KEEP CLEAR' notice placed. Further training given to staff and manager
- Fire extinguishers not in high-risk areas, such as the chemical store, by the fire exit.	- Clients, staff and all visitors	- Annual check on all fire extinguishers and placement	- Advice was sought on correct placement.
- One fire extinguisher not serviced for the past two years.	- Clients, staff and all visitors	- 1 new extinguisher was acquired after service visit and therefore placed in an unsuitable position	- Fire extinguisher contractor was called in to carry out a service
- Loose carpet tile	- Clients, staff and all visitors	- None	- Door was dragging up carpet tile. Door was rehung and new carpet tiles were fitted.
- Waste bin overflowing causing a problem with vapours	- Clients and staff	- Each technician is responsible for correct disposal of his or her own waste.	- A larger metal bin was provided. Further training given to technician.

NOTES
- Tracey had complained about tripping over wires and loose carpet tiles (pleased with the repairs and actions taken)
- Risk assessor picked up on the fire escape routes being blocked and extinguishers out of service date

| NAME *Claudine Rowley* | SIGNED *CERowley* | DATE *02.01.02* |

SUGGESTED FORM FOR FIRE RISK ASSESSMENT

NAME OF SALON	Nails R Us	DATE	10 January 2002
COMPANY ADDRESS	1 High Street	REVIEW DATE	10 April 2002
	Anytown		
POSTCODE	AN1 2YT		

LIST HAZARDS	PEOPLE AT RISK	CONTROLS IN PLACE	ACTION TAKEN
- Roller shutters on metal cabinets where chemicals are stored were not locked down at night	- Staff	- Manager to close up all cabinets on a nightly basis	- Manager cautioned
- Bins need to be metal	- Staff and clients	- Technicians responsible for own waste and correct disposal of.	- 6 metal pedal bins purchased
- Incorrect extinguisher for chemical and electrical fires	- Staff, clients and visitors	- Inherited from previous tenant	- New extinguisher
- Fire exit doors need new signs	- Staff, clients and visitors	- Inherited from previous tenant	- New exit and fire door signs purchased and placed
- One fire exit blocked by stock boxes	- Staff, clients and visitors	- Manager to have removed all stock items to designated stock room	- Manager cautioned

NOTES
- We have replaced one incorrect extinguisher, total present in salon is now 3 – all are suitable for electrical and chemical fires
- Managers Comments: Salon had been very busy at the time of a delivery and driver placed boxes in front of the fire exit

| NAME *Claudine Rowley* | SIGNED *CERowley* | DATE *10.01.02* |

Fire risk assessment form

Review all the information you have gathered on a regular basis. If any new substances or machinery are introduced then they should also be considered. It is also a good idea to check regularly that any precautionary measures remain in place and are still working properly.

Two styles of form which could be used when conducting a risk assessment are illustrated.

The Fire Regulations and the Fire Protection Act 1971

All workplaces should have or make arrangements for detecting a fire. If smoke alarms are used they must conform to British Standard 5446: part 1. Another option is smoke detectors, but you must make sure they are designed for the purpose, as those used for the domestic market are manufactured to a different standard than those for automatic detection in business premises. Smoke alarms tend to be more sensitive than smoke detectors, thus sometimes causing unwanted fire alerts. Ensure that what you use is suitable for the situation, for example a heat detector may perform better than a smoke detector in a fume-laden or dusty environment, but may not be appropriate for the rest of the premises.

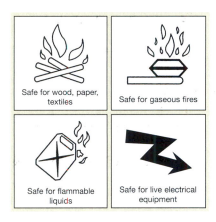

Fire extinguisher symbols

Flammable liquids can present a significant risk of fire. Vapours are usually heavier than air and can travel long distances, so are more likely to reach an ignition source. Fire extinguishers can be purchased from local DIY stores, but in order for insurance policies to be valid they must be annually serviced and maintained. Fire extinguishers can last for several years and some are guaranteed for up to ten years but the correct maintenance is essential.

Fire extinguishers are available for different types of fire. The type required for your business will depend on the risk classification and the kind of fire to which your business is vulnerable. Fire extinguishers should normally be located in conspicuous positions on escape routes, preferably near exit doors. If for any reason this is not possible, Health and Safety (Signs and Signals) Regulations 1996, require that their location must be indicated by signs and, where possible, directional arrows.

Fire drill training

The fire training given to your employees should be specific to your workplace. You must make provision to explain emergency procedures to all staff and personnel; information should be clear and understood by all your employees. Take into account the findings of the risk assessment and the work activities, duties and responsibilities of employees. Training should include practical fire drills, arrangements for calling the fire brigade and evacuation of the premises.

Fire precaution legislation deals with general fire precautions. These include:

- means of protection and how to give warning in case of fire
- the provision of means of escape
- ways of fighting fire
- the training of staff in fire safety
- how to raise the alarm

Fire regulations include a requirement to undertake an assessment of the fire risks on your premises. This is to include the risk of a fire occurring and the risk to people in the event of fire. Before starting your risk assessment, check if there are any existing arrangements. Your risk assessment could identify additional requirements that need to be addressed. If you have any doubts or queries about the regulations or how they apply to your business contact the local fire authority for advice.

A fire risk assessment can be carried out independently or as part of the general risk assessment process. Using the form shown earlier, draw a floor plan marking doors, windows, fire extinguishers and other exits. This will help you to identify any obstacles in the event of evacuation and allow you to pinpoint problem areas. After completing the floor plan the risk assessment can be conducted in the following way:

- identify all ignition sources and any fire hazards

This is the most vital step. Once complete you should next check:

Safety Tip

Fire fighting should only be undertaken if it represents no risk to the individual.

Activity

- Design a written test sheet.

- Identify a training programme for all appliances if none is in place.

- Identify a person to take responsibility for electrical appliances.

- Draw up a list of all electrical appliances in the salon.

- Design a chart to record:
  - the appliance serial number
  - the date when the appliance was last tested
  - whether the appliance is working or not working
  - the fault
  - the date the appliance was withdrawn
  - the date the appliance was repaired

- the location of people who are likely to be in danger in the event of a fire occurring
- that any existing fire precautions are adequate
- that all ignition sources are controlled
- that fire detection warnings are in place
- that the means of fighting fire are in place
- the maintenance and testing procedures of all existing fire precautions
- that the means of escape are unobstructed and clearly marked

Finally, put the following procedures in place:

- staff fire training for all employees
- record all comments from employees and the findings of the assessment; draw up a plan of action; inform, train, and give feedback to all those concerned
- revise your assessment and procedures if any changes occur; set a date for the next review

The Electricity at Work Regulations 1992

All the electrical equipment that is used in the salon should be tested once a year by a qualified electrician. This is sometimes called PAT (Portable Appliance Testing). Care should be taken when using all electrical equipment and staff must be fully trained. Although it is the responsibility of the owner or supervisor of the salon to ensure the equipment is safe to use and is maintained, it is also the duty of staff to check the equipment is safe to use.

The following precautions should be taken:

- keep written test sheets (the HSE can ask to see these)
- check electrical flexes for signs of wear or damage
- check the date of last PAT test
- all appliances must be switched off and unplugged at the end of the day
- all electrical appliances should be kept away from sources of water
- when not in use all appliances should be placed in a cupboard with the flex secured around the appliance
- if there is a problem with an appliance it should be removed from use and labelled
- electrical appliances should only be used by trained personnel
- all broken, loose or worn plugs or sockets should be replaced
- do not overload sockets with too many plugs

The main causes of hazards in the case of electrical appliances are:

- inadequate or non-existent earthing
- incorrect fuses being fitted
- inadequate maintenance of equipment
- incorrect or bad wiring of plugs or equipment

Overexposure

It is possible for an **allergic reaction** to occur with any of the professional treatments clients receive in the salon environment, for example, hair, beauty, nails and massage with aromatherapy oils. This can be a real problem for a sensitive client. Fortunately the majority of problems which are related to the fingernails can be avoided through good education as supplied by manufacturers on their beginner and foundation courses, and by practising safe techniques with an understanding of overexposure.

Overexposure

For every chemical there is a limit to the level of exposure which is safe. When the safe level is exceeded, the body reacts, so any early warning signs should not be ignored. If the same treatment or procedure is repeated in the same way on a regular basis under such conditions, it is very likely to lead to a major allergic reaction. Both clients and technicians are susceptible to reactions to certain substances.

When a person experiences an allergic reaction to a substance or chemical, it is necessary to remove the product or irritant from the body. Medical advice should then be sought. Many technicians wear thin rubber gloves to work in if they have an allergic reaction to a product. However, if the skin is broken the technician will often experience a further irritation and subsequently become allergic to the rubber or latex gloves. The only real solution is to withdraw from the substance or product and recover.

There will usually be clear warning signs that the nail technician, or client, is becoming sensitive to a product or substance. Watch out for:

- localised skin or **cuticles** that become sensitive to pressure or which itch
- redness or sores for a while after application

Although this discomfort may only be temporary and will usually subside after a few hours, it could be an early warning sign and must not be ignored.

Once a person develops an allergy to a product, or an ingredient of it, they will always be allergic to it in varying degrees. Each time they are exposed to it, the reaction becomes more violent and there is no alternative to the decision to stop using the product. In reality,

Safety Tip

Remember, an allergic reaction will not happen overnight. It is repeated or prolonged contact with chemicals over a period of time that causes this unpleasant experience – usually four to six months.

Safety Tip

Roughing up, over-filing or over-buffing the natural nail plate is not necessary with modern nail products. It is very destructive and causes the nail plate to become porous. Consequently, products can be absorbed through to the nail plate and into the **nail bed** much more easily.

this will mean a loss of income for the nail technician and a period of recuperation without nail extensions for the client.

With knowledge and understanding of how the body becomes sensitive to a product, or substance, most allergy problems can be avoided. A body can react to all nail product systems – UV acrylic, UV gel, acrylics and other **wrap** systems.

At the first indication of overexposure, you should check your application techniques around the cuticles and sidewalls. If you continue the application in the same way, an allergic reaction will result. The **nail plate** can become overexposed due to the acrylic having a consistency which is too wet. This can result in the nail plate becoming very white in colour.

If a client has become allergic to an acrylic system, even if their skin has returned to normal, they would not be a good candidate to wear a gel system. Gel is an **acrylate** that is also likely to cause an allergic reaction to a sensitised client, especially if the gel is not applied properly. The only real alternative system for this client is a **fibreglass** system.

We have a responsibility not to put ourselves, work colleagues and clients at risk through overexposure. It is possible to work safely with chemicals and products, but there are strict rules and guidelines to follow. It would be very foolish not to learn these rules as the practice of using safe techniques is paramount to a long career in the nail industry.

Routes of entry into the body

The three main ways that substances are taken into the body are:

1   **inhalation** – breathing fine dust particles or vapours
2   **absorption** – through the skin, or through cuts and abrasions
3   **ingestion** – by consuming chemicals accidentally

These are known as **routes of entry** to the body.

Inhalation

Nail technicians need to take great care to maintain the quality of the air in their salon or work area. **Vapours**, which are formed when a gas or liquid evaporates into the air, and dust resulting from filing are the two key dangers.

The lowest level that an ingredient or odour can be detected in the air is one ppm (part per million). When researching the safe limits for **ethyl methacrylate**, the latest recommendation by the Cosmetic Ingredient Review (CIR) Panel – an independent review panel comprising toxicologists, dermatologists and medical doctors from the United States of America – is that the conservative safe limit for continuous long-term occupational exposure is 100 ppm. In salons the average measured value is one-fifth this level.

In addition to overexposure, prolonged or repeated inhalation of products may cause other problems such as

- headaches
- sickness
- dizziness or fainting
- fatigue
- coughing or irritation to the respiratory system

If these problems occur, the person should be moved outside into the fresh air until he or she stabilises.

Preventing inhalation

A controlled approach to product application, good housekeeping, including the correct disposal of waste and proper **ventilation**, all contribute to good air quality and help to prevent overexposure through inhalation.

Controlled approach to application

- When using a liquid and powder system, it is good technique to pick up the correct **mix ratio** every time. This avoids the need to constantly wipe the excess **monomer** onto a paper towel, indirectly extending the surface area of product evaporating into the atmosphere. This also makes commercial sense – consider the amount of monomer that is absorbed onto a paper towel and disposed of each day by a careless nail technician.
- Use accelerator or setting sprays sparingly and at a downward angle to reduce the risk of inhalation. Again, this procedure is also more cost effective.

Dappen dishes

Good housekeeping

- Keep all products tightly capped until required. Recap as soon as possible. Limiting exposure just to the application time greatly reduces both evaporation and contamination.
- Decant monomer into small containers for use. Dappen dishes are ideal as they are stable and reduce the evaporation by limiting the exposed surface area of the product.
- Put all items away after use.
- Use metal containers for chemical and product storage.
- Use suitable waste bins. They need to be of metal construction with close-fitting metal lids. Plastic bins, or bags, are not suitable as they allow vapours to escape and contaminate the breathing zone. Remove waste before bins become full to prevent lids being wedged open and vapours escaping into your breathing zone.

Metal bin

Ventilation

Overexposure through inhalation is a real hazard. There is a 60 centimetre sphere around our heads from which all the air we inhale is drawn, known as the **breathing zone**, and this must be kept as free as possible from vapours and dust to prevent overexposure by inhalation.

Technical Tip

The rate of evaporation of products and chemicals used in nail treatments is affected by temperature so this must be monitored when handling volatile chemicals.

Ventilation unit

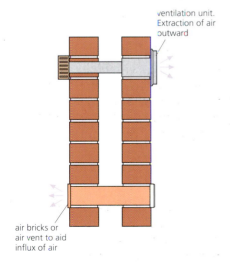

ventilation unit. Extraction of air outward

air bricks or air vent to aid influx of air

Airflow

Nail technicians working from home need to look at ventilation issues carefully and seek professional advice from their product supplier or local air extraction supplier. Problems with ventilation are less likely in the salon environment where there should be a greater awareness of ventilation and of the side effects of overexposure through continuity of product training.

Adequate ventilation is a necessity. Although a number of options exist, as the air needs to be changed regularly (this varies on the size of the salon and the number of technicians) the only real solution is an extraction unit.

Ventilation/extraction unit

A professional fitter of ventilation systems will measure your working area, note the number of nail stations and advise on a suitable extraction unit, and where it would be best fitted. This is usually to an outside wall or window.

Advice should also be sought on the airflow in the salon as the air cannot just be extracted without being replaced. There needs to be an air inlet so the new extraction unit can work efficiently. This is normally achieved by an additional vent lower in the wall or window.

You should also consider a control switch for the extraction unit, as it may not be required all of the time. To keep the cost down some companies suggest wiring this into the light switch so that if you always have the lights on when you are open the extractor is running. You may also need to update your heating system if the extraction unit is high on the wall or window and heat rises.

Local exhaust

Local **exhaust** methods of ventilation can work efficiently if some simple rules are followed. The hose must be placed to the side of the nail station so that the source of vapours are pulled away from the nail technician and client. If the hose or canopy is placed above the nail station, all the vapours are pulled up through the breathing zone, increasing the risk of overexposure through inhalation.

Charcoal filters

There are some desks available on the market with a filter and a fan fitted into the table top directly under the work area. There are also charcoal filters available which can either be set in a desk or free standing. The filters need to be changed each week, however, which can make them very expensive.

These units work by the activated charcoal absorbing the vapours like a sponge, but some of the filters are very light. This form of protection can prove ineffective for monomer vapours which are not easily absorbed by activated charcoal. The filters very quickly become saturated with vapour and dust rendering them ineffective.

Fans

Fans only serve to circulate air that is already contaminated by simply moving the vapours around. Opening a window would not

Control switch for extraction system

Safety Tip

Don't be fooled into thinking that 'odourless' products are free from vapours. They are still present, just harder to detect, and need the same precautions. The amount of vapour in the air is not determined by the **odour**, it is controlled by the evaporation rate.

Dust masks

Safety Tip

Air fresheners do not improve air quality. They only mask odours for a short period of time.

be sufficient to extract unclean air and may cause another set of problems such as the nail products not setting correctly. Some products crystallise at low temperatures and many products set too fast at high temperatures, sometimes before the application is complete, making the finishing very difficult. **Primer** freezes at approximately 11°C or 52°F. Some UV gels set if used in a warm, bright environment such as a conservatory or even by a south-facing window on a very bright day. Many nail technicians have unintentionally **cured** a pot of gel!

Personal protection

Inhalation

As a nail technician, you will be working all day with the substances discussed in this chapter. You should always take sensible precautions to prevent overexposure to yourself. However, you must also act to protect your client.

Dust masks are an option to prevent unnecessary inhalation when filing, especially if using drills. Drills create very fine airborne dust particles that are easily inhaled so dust masks and efficient extraction systems should be high on your priority list. Dust generated by hand filing produces much larger particles and the majority of these will fall to the table and can be collected on a paper towel for disposal.

Absorption

Absorption of chemicals is through the skin or nail plate. Prolonged or repeated contact is usually required to cause an allergic reaction, the symptoms of which include:

- redness
- swelling
- sores
- rashes
- itchiness
- blisters to the local area of contact

The corrective action is to refer your client to his or her GP for expert advice and treatment. Products can be absorbed through the skin by failing to take the correct precautions when applying or dispensing them, or through bad housekeeping.

Preventing absorption

Application

You can help prevent absorption by the correct and safe application of chemicals.

- Cover all cuts and abrasions on both the nail technician and client before commencing any nail treatment.

- Leave a tiny free margin (1 mm) around the cuticle line when applying any type of nail **overlays**. No product should touch the skin under any circumstances. Do not use your finger or thumb to clean around the client's cuticle area when too much product has been applied to the nail plate. Avoid touching the cuticle with either product or brush.

- Avoid back brushing the **smile line**. The monomer that is still in the brush can cause the nail plate to become wet with monomer which could affect the mix of the next bead that is applied, making the bead too wet.

- Any excess monomer that is on the natural nail can be absorbed by the nail plate, which could lead to a possible overexposure problem. Too wet a mix may also cause the overlay to pop in the centre of the stress area.

- Never apply monomer to the nail bed without the **polymer powder**. Some nail technicians wrongly believe that this procedure increases **adhesion**. In fact, the only result is that the client will have a reaction over a period of time as the nail plate will absorb the excess monomer.

- It is common practice in some salons to add more monomer to a too dry mix to make it easier to work with. This will not change the mix ratio of the product as **polymerisation** has already started to take place. All that will happen is that since it cannot be absorbed by the powder, the excess monomer will flood onto the surrounding skin or cuticle and lead to overexposure.

- Keep the nail plate clean and dry when applying a product.

- Spray accelerator at the manufacturer's recommended distance to avoid burning and thinning of the nail plate.

- Never intentionally touch the skin with any nail product during application regardless of the system being used.

- Good after care advice to clients is also a requirement, as a small minority of clients actually overexpose themselves by continually gluing nails back on after letting the maintenance appointments slide for a week or two.

- Avoid applying a 'wet mix' of liquid and powder to the nail plate.

- Use the appropriate size of brush when applying a liquid and powder. A large brush will hold more liquid or product in the belly of the brush, thus affecting the mix ratio.

- Apply gels in thin layers to aid curing of the product.

- Apply fibreglass **resin** in a thin controlled manner.

- UV gel can also cause overexposure problems. If the nail technician touches the skin with gel before the curing process has taken place this could cause a reaction to take place on the skin over a period of time. If the gel product is applied in thicker layers, the UV rays cannot penetrate the gel and will leave uncured gel on the natural nail. This is a very common reason why clients can become overexposed to UV gel systems. If the bulbs in the UV lamp are in continuous use, they should be changed every four to six months. The UV bulb can wear out, resulting in cold spots and inefficient curing. This will leave uncured gel on the nail plate and may result in overexposure. Also if the product is applied too thickly the client may complain of burning; the cause of this is that some gels shrink by up to 25 per cent during the curing process – it can feel like the natural nail plate is being pulled back with it. The remedy is to apply thin layers, then the gel will be fully cured.

Good practice

- Change towels after filing. If you don't, there is a danger that you will end up leaning in the dust which will cause a skin reaction over a period of time.
- Do not wipe your brush on a paper towel during application. There is a danger that you will end up resting your hand or arm on it during the filing and buffing stages.
- Clean your brush properly – even during application. Do not use your finger and thumb! If your brush handle gets dirty during application, stop and clean it. Monomer and gel can be very sticky substances and should be removed from the fingers and hands immediately.

Decanting chemicals

One of the main times when nail technicians can expose themselves to product absorption is while handling and decanting **chemicals**. Product suppliers usually discount bulk chemical supplies, but these then need to be decanted into more manageable containers. Always follow health and safety regulations and don't get lazy. Follow the correct procedures on the manufacturers' labels and use the correct equipment, for example:

- disposable gloves
- a dust or vapour mask
- safety glasses

Keep the area used for decanting well ventilated. Follow this process when decanting any chemical – even when using a pipette to decant small amounts of liquids into dappen dishes – or when cleaning up any spillage.

Ingestion

Although it goes without saying that you would never consciously ingest the chemicals you use as a nail technician, bad practice can lead to inadvertent ingestion, for example since vapours are attracted to hot drinks, a nail technician (and their client) could be drinking their products every time they have a hot drink which could add up to a large amount of ingested chemicals over time.

Preventing ingestion

- Wash your hands before consuming any food, from a casual sweet to lunch.

Safety Tip

Banging hands down onto a dirty towel will release dust into your breathing zone and the use of drills will cause finer dust particles that are more easily ingested.

- Do not store food in the same place as products.
- Use cups or containers with lids for drinks in the working area.
- Do not consume food at the nail station.
- Always use clean tissues and towels for clients.

As the nail technician, it is you who should be aware of the dangers and who has access to suppliers' information. Be aware that most clients – and possibly even other staff in your immediate working environment – may not have access to or completely understand this information. Consider the following people, for example:

- receptionist
- beauty staff
- members of your family, if working from home

Knowledge of chemicals is the best defence against overexposure and good practices are a necessity not a luxury!

Ways to protect the individual

There are rich rewards to be made from the nail industry today, especially if you are proficient and adaptable to the clients' needs. A good nail technician will always be in great demand and have a thriving clientele. Their earning capacity is vast and a nail technician's working career could span 20–30 years. To maintain this, an awareness and understanding of all the chemicals and their specific use in the salon is needed.

Many of the best nail technicians overexpose themselves in the early stages of their career when they are still learning their craft. This is the time when they start to sensitise themselves. An understanding of overexposure is of great importance. If you ignore the signs you could one day find you have lost your livelihood or business. Look for an alternative system that you are proficient in and prefer to use.

Prevention is the best course of action rather than the cure. Personal protection in the salon is really important for ourselves, our colleagues and our clients.

Eye protection

The wearing of safety glasses is a precaution and you should offer a pair to your client. If a client asks why, be honest with them and they will respect you for your honesty. Take the opportunity to explain proper precautions. Clients will probably enquire why some of the other salons do not offer them a pair.

A nail technician should not wear contact lenses in the salon environment for the following reasons:

- although safety glasses offer good protection against accidental splashing they offer no protection against vapours or airborne dust
- vapours can collect behind the contact lens and etch the eye, leading to permanent damage to the eyesight

Useful Tip

Ignorance is not a valid excuse for overexposure.

Activity

- Find out about the salon safety procedures that are in place regarding storage and transportation of products.
- Is the equipment used in the salon to the required standard?
- Does the safety equipment offer maximum protection?
- Are the procedures suitable and adequate for the task?
- Has a risk assessment been completed or updated?

Safety glasses

- soft lenses can absorb the vapours also causing etching of the eye
- if any solvent or chemical is accidentally splashed into the eye, cleaning can prove very difficult – consider how a solvent or chemical degrades a plastic surface or workstation

Good practice

To work safely, you need to understand:

- sanitation, disinfection and sterilisation (see next section)
- ventilation and extraction
- the advantages and disadvantages of your chosen system
- possible routes of entry and overexposure issues
- the consequences of ignoring dust control
- the effects of temperature on nail service
- storage and waste disposal
- odourless products
- the effects of fans and draughts on products

Good practice includes:

- reading all labels and seeking advice from your trainer or manufacturer if you are in any doubt
- taking personal protection seriously – use gloves, masks and eye protection. Remember, there are two types of face mask – one for vapours and one for dust – and don't forget to renew your mask every few days
- using a covered dappen dish for monomer

Cross infection and salon hygiene

Learning objectives

In this section you will learn about:

- **how to protect yourself and your clients**
- **pathogens – bacteria and viruses**
- **decontamination – sanitation, disinfection and sterilisation**
- **hygiene procedures**

When you work as a nail technician you will come into contact with members of the public and perform treatments on nails – on both hands and feet. There is always a risk to you of injury or infection when working on your clients. Every surface from our hands to desk tops, door handles, floors and tools can potentially carry microscopic **pathogens**, that is disease causing organisms. It is our duty as

professionals to be able to recognise these and control them. We do this by decontamination, which comes in three stages: **sanitation**, **disinfection** and **sterilisation**.

Pathogens

Disease can be spread through direct contact with the source of infection. This includes direct contact with bodily fluids, whether from coughing, sneezing, direct contact with contaminated blood, pus, sores, cuts or grazes. All cuts on the hands must be covered with sticking plaster or suitable dressing to prevent a secondary infection.

Bacteria

Bacteria are either pathogenic or non-pathogenic. Non-pathogenic bacteria are not harmful to human beings, in fact they are often beneficial, for example they aid the digestive system. However, pathogenic bacteria – which probably constitute less that 30 per cent of all bacteria – are undesirable in the salon environment. They are sometimes referred to as germs.

The growth pattern of bacteria

Bacteria multiply and thrive in warm, dark, unsanitary places and conditions. Each **cell** of bacteria has the ability to grow and, when mature, the cell divides. In turn, these two cells grow and divide, and so the pattern continues. You can therefore see how important it is to control pathogenic bacteria, as in a matter of hours millions of bacteria can be present on implements or surfaces.

Different types of bacteria

- *Spirilla* are spiral shaped. This type of bacteria causes syphilis.
- *Diplococci* grow in pairs. This type of bacteria is responsible for pneumonia.
- *Bacilli* grow in rod shapes. This type of bacteria is responsible for tetanus, typhoid, influenza, diphtheria and tuberculosis.
- *Cocci* can grow in groups or singularly. This type of bacteria produces pus.
- *Staphylococci* bacteria grow in clusters. Infections are usually inflamed, causing pustules, boils and abscesses.
- *Streptococci* is the form of bacteria responsible for strep throat infections, rheumatic fever and blood poisoning.

How bacteria spread

Bacteria can be transmitted through direct and indirect contact. They are airborne and can also spread in water. Spirilla and bacilli are capable of propelling themselves in liquid.

Different types of bacteria

SPHERICAL BACTERIA (COCCI)

Diplococcus
(pneumonia)

Staphylococcus
(pustules, boils, etc.)

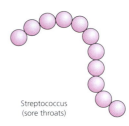

Streptococcus
(sore throats)

ROD-LIKE BACTERIA (BACILLI)

Bacillus tuberculosis
(tuberculosis)

Clostridium tetani
(tetanus)

Bacillus typhosus
(typhoid fever)

SPIRAL FORMS (SPIRILLA)

Spirillum

Treponema pallida
(syphilis)

Safety Tip

- Cover all cuts and abrasions with dressings or plasters.

- Wash hands in soapy water before and after each client.

- Do not use sharp or pointed instruments near any obvious infected areas of skin.

- If the nail technician is cut he or she must hold the cut under running water until the blood flow has stopped; then apply a dressing or plaster before resuming work.

- If you come into contact with another person's blood or bodily fluids the area must be washed with soap and hot water as soon as possible.

Viruses

Viruses are also pathogenic but are much smaller than bacteria. These often spread by coming into contact with an infected person. Viruses are responsible for chicken pox, measles, mumps, influenza, colds or coughs. The following precautions should be taken to prevent cross infection:

- change workstation and washroom towels regularly
- use paper towels where possible
- wash and sanitise hands before and after each client as this is very reassuring for the client to see

AIDS and Hepatitis B

AIDS (Acquired Immune Deficiency Syndrome) is the most serious result of infection by a virus known as HIV. People with this virus in their bloodstream are said to be HIV Positive. Not all HIV Positive people develop AIDS – some stay well with no indication at all that they are carrying HIV. HIV can disrupt the body's normal defences against disease and leave the body open to infections that would not normally occur. HIV is quite easily destroyed outside of the human body. Once any blood has dried – which can take a matter of seconds – the virus particles cannot survive. That is why HIV can only be spread by contact involving the direct transfer of blood or serum from one infected person to another. To date there are no reported cases of anyone catching the HIV virus through any nail or beauty treatments. If all sanitary procedures are followed it would be practically impossible for this to happen.

Hepatitis B causes inflammation of the liver leading to severe illness and usually jaundice. This disease can be fatal. It is transmitted by blood and serum from an infected person to another. Once a person has had this virus it can remain in his or her bloodstream for many years making the person in question a carrier of the disease. Adequate precautions should be taken in the salon to prevent the transmission of this disease. It is an employer's responsibility to advise their staff to have a vaccination against Hepatitis B and also to make sure they are correctly trained in the disposal of contaminated waste.

Decontamination

Decontamination by sanitation, disinfection and sterilisation minimises the risk of cross infection. All nail technicians should be aware of the guidelines laid down by the Local Government Miscellaneous Provisions Act. Guidelines on the following areas are available from your local authority:

- personal hygiene and working practices
- cleaning and sterilising of implements
- salon cleaning to a high standard

Sanitation

Sanitation will reduce the number of pathogenic bacteria on a surface. This is the lowest form of decontamination and should be carried out before disinfection and sterilisation. Simply washing hands and tools will remove most harmful bacteria and control the spread of disease. Washing in soapy water can remove dirt, oil and other product residues and is essential, for instance, before immersing tools in a steriliser to allow full decontamination to take place.

Your clients will appreciate cleanliness in all its forms and sanitation will prove how seriously you take their custom, welfare and health.

The following points should be taken into account when carrying out your sanitation procedures for the working area or salon environment:

- always try to provide hot and cold running water
- change towels in the washroom/kitchen regularly
- use and provide liquid soap, preferably with anti-bacterial ingredients
- both the client and technician should wash their hands before and after each treatment
- there should be a separate sink for clients to wash their hands – never have a bowl full of cups under the tap when washing hands as this contravenes Health and Safety regulations
- toilet tissue and paper towels must be provided at all times
- clean uniforms should be worn every day
- hair should be tied back
- wedding band and small earrings only to be worn when working

Safety Tip

Sanitation processes are vital and must not be ignored.

- avoid touching your face whilst working and warn the client of this too
- all consumables should be removed and put into the proper waste bin
- bins should be emptied regularly and not allowed to overflow
- remember to clean door handles when cleaning other surfaces
- no eating, drinking or smoking in the salon
- food should not be kept in the same storage facility as nail products – this includes the fridge as well as cupboards
- soiled and dusty towels and linen should be removed and kept in a lined bin
- all laundry should be washed at the correct temperature
- floors, walls and other surfaces must be constantly dusted and wiped clean
- children should not be allowed in the salon, but if this is unavoidable then it is the parent's responsibility to control them; make sure they are aware of this
- pets should not be allowed in the working environment under any circumstances, with the exception of guide dogs for the blind or disabled
- when cleaning the top of a desk make sure all the containers are wiped as well
- do not place any tools or implements in your pockets, behind your ears or in your mouth

There are many ways to ensure that your working environment is clean and as dust-free as possible. Make sure you make time for *good housekeeping*.

Sanitation sprays are normally available from your product manufacturer for use on files, buffers and workstations. Some manufacturers recommend hand sanitisers which are available in the form of soap, a spray, cream or a gel.

Disinfection

This is the second stage of decontamination and greatly reduces the pathogenic bacteria on a non-living surface. This method is not suitable for the hair, skin or nails. Disinfection is used for the following:

- floors
- walls
- workstations
- chairs
- pedicure and manicure bowls

Note: This process does not remove **bacterial spores**.

When using disinfectant it is important to follow the manufacturer's instructions and dilute to the correct level. If the concentration is too weak, the disinfectant may be inadequate to remove the pathogenic bacteria and may possibly act only as a sanitiser.

Disinfection is almost as thorough as sterilisation and can be used quite effectively in the salon. Disinfectants are designed to remove pathogens and some are very strong, so should be used with care. However, they can be an **irritant** to skin tissue and can be dangerous if the manufacturer's instructions are not followed properly. Always make sure you read all instructions and keep disinfectants out of the reach of children. All disinfectant manufacturers are legally bound to give you a list of ingredients and directions for safe use. They must also advise you which pathogens the product is able to control.

There are many disinfectant solutions on the market today and it is up to you which one you use. Before investing in a disinfection system look at what is available, what they are designed to do and your requirements for your work environment. It is a good idea to review your system every year, see if there are any new products on the market, if your salon requirements have changed and, lastly, whether what you are using is still performing properly.

All disinfectants should be able to kill a variety of pathogens and the following must all be covered by your disinfection system:

- bactericides
- fungicides
- viricides

There are two main methods of disinfection within the salon:

- heat treatment
- chemical treatment

Heat treatment could be applied, for example, by a steam cabinet. This is a dangerous item and the siting of such a machine needs careful consideration. The ideal would be to place it in a separate room or kitchen as it is not a suitable piece of equipment to have within the salon itself. When using any type of steam or boiling water the implements need to be washed first to eliminate any dust and **contamination**. This method can only be used on metal tools. All employees must be trained in the proper use of the equipment.

For chemical disinfectants to be effective tools need to be immersed for longer than 15 minutes and not just wiped over. Alcohol will erode and blunt, possibly even rust, metal tools and should be used carefully. Alcohol can also be used as an antiseptic on the skin.

There are many chemical solutions available as disinfectants. If using these make sure they have a rust inhibitor such as sodium nitrate, otherwise you may find your expensive nippers will be useless after a few weeks.

Sterilisation

Sterilisation is the total destruction of all living organisms on an object. The word sterilisation is often misused, for example living

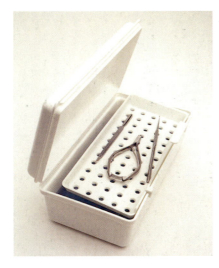

Sterilisation tray

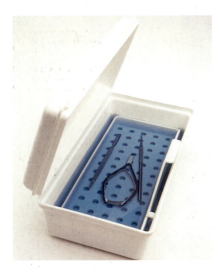

Sterilisation tray with liquid

tissue cannot be sterilised. You cannot sterilise a cuticle, nail plate, skin or hair. The salon's hard surfaces, for example floors, walls and nail stations, can be disinfected or sanitised – complete sterilisation would be impossible to achieve.

Items that can be sterilised are

- all metal tools and implements
- plastic tools

All tools must be washed in warm soapy water then rinsed and thoroughly dried before proceeding to one of the following methods of sterilisation.

Chemical sterilisation

Chemical sterilisation is the most popular and effective way of maintaining the hygiene of tools and implements. After washing tools in hot soapy water, they should be rinsed and then thoroughly dried. The tools should be completely immersed in a chemical solution for a period of 20 minutes. All chemical agents must be diluted according to the manufacturer's instructions. Diluted solutions must be changed on a regular basis, as recommended by the manufacturer. If the solution is diluted too much it acts only as a disinfectant or sanitiser and is ineffective as a sterilising agent.

Sterilisation should be carried out in a deep container with a close-fitting lid. It is advisable to have an inner perforated tray with handles which will allow the tools to be lowered into the solution. If the solution becomes cloudy change it immediately. In a busy salon you could consider having two sets of tools.

Some of the main sterilising agents on the market are:

- alcohol
- gluteraldehyde
- quaternary ammonium compound (QAUTS)

The autoclave

An autoclave is suitable for small metal implements. An autoclave is a metal container that is specifically designed to create and withstand heat and pressure. It uses high pressure steam at a temperature of 126°C. The only type of autoclave that can be used effectively and safely within the salon environment is an electrical one that has an automatic cycle. A measured amount of water is placed into the autoclave and pre-washed tools are put onto a rack above the water so that the steam can circulate freely around them, ensuring all surfaces are sterilised. The lid must be closed and locked before the machine is switched on. Pressure builds up inside the unit and causes the temperature to rise. After the programme is complete you must ensure that the pressure has returned to normal before trying to remove the lid.

Any equipment or tools that are removed will be sterile only until they come into contact with other items, fingers or the air which can hold pathogens. It is a good idea to have a sealed, clean container in which to keep sterilised implements until they are needed.

Autoclave

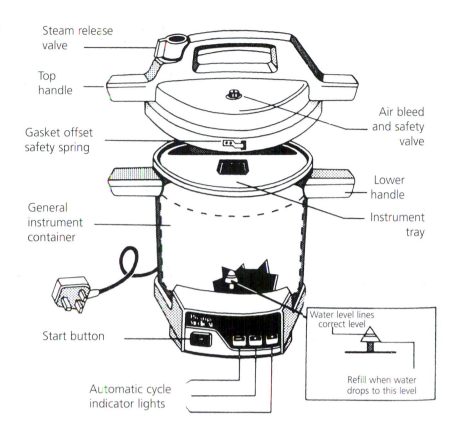

Steam release valve

Top handle

Gasket offset safety spring

General instrument container

Start button

Automatic cycle indicator lights

Air bleed and safety valve

Lower handle

Instrument tray

Water level lines correct level

Refill when water drops to this level

Glass bead steriliser

Glass bead sterilisers are not suitable for the salon environment due to the high temperature dry heat they use. There is a high risk of burns if used by untrained staff.

This type of steriliser is used for small regularly shaped objects which have little surface detail, as only the surface area that is in contact with the glass beads can be considered to have been sterilised. The irregular shape of a pair of nail clippers would not be deemed sterile because the entire surface area could not possibly be in contact with the glass beads. Also the high temperatures used may affect the metal and cause sharp edges to become blunt.

Ultra violet cabinet

Ultra violet light has limited use as a sterilisation method due to the fact that tools would have to be turned to expose all surfaces to the UV rays. However, if the tools are already sterilised a UV cabinet can provide a germ-free environment for storing implements.

Hygiene procedures

Good **hygiene** procedures prevent the spread of infection. Aim to make the following points part of everyone's working day in the salon:

- sterilise all metal tools
- disinfect all work surfaces
- make sure the technician and client wash their hands before commencing any consultation or treatment

- cover any cuts or abrasions
- sanitise hands and clients' hands
- sanitise all files and buffers in the presence of clients
- use clean towels and disposable paper towels
- use pump dispensers instead of open containers
- replace all lids and caps on containers immediately
- only have out on the nail station the items or products required to perform the treatment; they should then be put away

Dispensing creams and lotions

If possible choose pumps or sprays as containers for creams and lotions, as these are more hygienic. If your chosen hand cream is only available in a tub or a pot you should always use a disposable spatula. Never use your fingers, as you will add bacteria to the cream, and those bacteria will multiply and could infect your next client.

If a client with an obvious infection has been worked on with cuticle creams, polishes or other such products these should then be disposed of and not used on any other clients.

Washing towels

Towels should be laundered in hot soapy water at a minimum temperature of 60°C. The towels should be washed on their own and not with any other household laundry. Each client should have a clean towel for their treatment, to prevent the build-up of dust and reduce the risk of cross infection from the previous client. If you are faced with a high towel rotation rate in a busy salon, use thin towels. They are quicker and cheaper to dry.

Files and buffers

Cost often dictates that files and buffers are used for more than one client before disposal. This requires them to be sanitised before and after use. At the end of each day use a small nail brush to scrub the files and buffers that are not being disposed of with anti-bacterial soap. Should a client suffer a cut or abrasion to the skin during the treatment, then the file or buffer must be disposed of immediately on completing the service. This action is taken to avoid cross infection. An alternative is for the client to purchase their own. This should be sanitised before treatment, then washed after treatment and placed in a clean envelope and attached with a safety clip to the client's record card.

The nail desk

Do not use the workstation surface as a storage area as the nail desk must remain clear and uncluttered to enable thorough disinfection practices between client treatments. This will promote clean and tidy work habits. To give the client confidence in your hygiene standards, sanitise the work surface in the client's presence. Tools should, if possible, be removed from the sterilisation unit only as required or stored in a UV cabinet.

After care for your client

Learning objectives

In this section you will learn:

- **the importance of giving a client after care advice**
- **what advice to give**
- **the consequences of not giving sound advice**
- **homecare advice and retail**

In this section we will cover the importance of giving good **after care advice**. It is critical to your reputation that you ensure that every client has specific after care advice and the homecare items required. To ignore this subject when performing treatments could seriously affect your reputation and nail art business. The information in this section is general and in no way replaces any specific instructions you may have from your manufacturer or nail art supplier that applies to their products.

The importance of good after care advice for your client

Courtesy of Creative Nail Design

Solar range

Every client is entitled to sound advice on how to look after their nail art designs and for their hands or feet in general. The person giving that advice should be you if it is you who performed the treatment. The client needs to know what to do, what homecare products to use, when to come back and what to do in the event of any problems. It is your responsibility to know what advice to give to each client depending on the service that you have provided. Nail art services are now so diverse that, although there may be some general advice, you will find that some is specific to particular treatments. Make sure that your training school, educator or professional, if that is who taught you, gives you this knowledge. The same as for any other nail treatment, it is a good idea to have an after care leaflet to hand out to each client. This will ensure that the client cannot say you have not given the advice if anything does go wrong or if they are unhappy in any way after they have left you. Make sure that your client record cards are always up-to-date and that new information is recorded every time the client returns. Remember that the client record card is your insurance that both you and the client know what was done during the treatment and what homecare advice was given. In a salon, they may also be referred to by other professional staff should there be a query in your absence.

After care and homecare advice

Please remember that the following points are only guidelines and that there may be specific advice about products from the manufacturers that you must let your clients know about. In general the following points should be passed on to a client before they leave you; clients should:

Safety Tip

Your client record card is your insurance policy.

Treatments

- return to you for the removal of nail art design involving jewellery or charms
- return for maintenance on treatments involving acrylic, fibre or gel extensions
- use top coat at home to assist the longevity of the design
- use oils and creams to keep their skin and cuticles in good order
- return to the salon if any problems occur
- always use non-acetone polish remover
- be careful when opening doors and cupboards
- try to use the pads of their fingers especially if 3D designs are being worn as these may catch and cause damage to the natural nail
- have regular manicures or maintenance to keep their nails looking good
- use only manufacturers' recommended products for appropriate treatments
- wear rubber, cotton lined gloves for housework and gardening
- *treat their nails as jewels, not tools*

The consequences of not giving after care advice

Although we have stressed how important it is to give a client good, sound after care advice, we do need to point out how devastating it could be for a client who is not given any advice by their nail artist. Nail artists provide a luxury service and some treatments involve the use of expensive jewellery and decals and therefore need to be looked after. The client has a right to know how to maximise this investment. The consequences of poor or no advice could be:

- loss of jewellery, charms and decals
- loss of rhinestones, flat stones and polish-secured charms
- peeling of polish, foils, striping tape and transfers
- lifting of acrylic and gels
- loss of shine on jewellery through chemical abuse
- tearing of the natural nail due to accidents
- premature loss of polish or designs
- damage of the natural nail through incorrect removal

All of the above problems can be avoided, or at least your client can minimise the risk with the help of your sound advice. If you give good advice it makes it much less likely that a client will come back and blame you for bad work. Remember that each new nail art client is a walking advert for you, and you want their designs to stay looking good as long as possible. Your work is a statement that your client is wearing and when they use their hands they are going to attract the attention of other potential clients. Educate your clientele!

Technical Tip

It is important to make sure that your client has specific after care instructions for gold nails, jewellery and charms as the finish or gems in these can be seriously spoilt or tarnished by the misuse of detergents and chemicals. Always make sure you recommend clients wear protective gloves when working with the hands, or alternatively remove jewellery if possible or cover with tape.

Retail

Once you have given your client good after care advice, you need to recommend the professional products they should take home with them. If you do not hold a minimum stock of retail items your client will be forced to go and buy them elsewhere. You should aim to have the following retail items available for your clients to purchase:

- non-acetone polish remover
- cuticle oil or cream
- good quality top coat
- base coat
- polish
- hand cream
- soft file or buffer
- replacement rhinestones or gems
- various post and dangle charms
- polish secure charms
- flexi-wrap or similar to cover jewellery or gold nails

Technical Tip

Every client you service will be sitting with you for a reasonable amount of time – use that time effectively to sell the products that you know they need. This is money that you can earn as an add-on to the service, which costs you nothing in time. If you do not sell your clients the products they need, they will go to another outlet and buy items that may not be suitable or compatible for your products.

There may be other products that your manufacturer recommends you add to this list. You do not have to hold large stocks but you should at least have a few of each of the items listed above if you are providing nail art services.

It is important to remember that you cannot sell an item if you do not know what it is or believe in it. It is worth spending a few hours learning about the features and benefits of *all* the products you are using so that you can talk knowledgeably about them. It will not only give you confidence in yourself but your client will have respect for your professionalism and knowledge of your products. Your clients may possibly ask you the following sorts of questions:

- Why do I need to use this?
- What ingredients does it contain?
- What benefit is it to me?
- What will happen if I do not use it?
- How much is it?
- When do I use it and how often?
- What is the shelf life?
- Why is this product so different to others?

Polish bottles and treatments

Courtesy of Creative Nail Design

Girl Gone Bad collection

Technical Tip

Remember, it is logical to use complementary products from a range as recommended by your manufacturer as they are guaranteed to be compatible.

The authors experienced a situation many years ago where a client chose not to buy our polish remover even though we explained to her all the features and benefits and pointed out the consequences of using an acetone-based remover. The client did take our advice a week later and purchased an acetone-free remover from a leading supermarket, but with dire consequences. Her nails became very tacky and started to dissolve. When she came in to see us in a panic with the offending bottle we discovered that the acetone ingredient had been masked with a different name. The client took the bottle back to the supermarket and not only got a refund but also received sufficient compensation for a completely new set of nail enhancements. This client always took our advice after that!

There are a number of professional qualifications in nail art at the moment and further standards are due in 2004. With this in mind we have put together a variety of scenarios that you may come across in your work. These will hopefully help you to handle situations professionally and may also help you with the projects and assignments you have to complete to gain your qualifications.

After care advice

As a professional it is your duty to inform all of your clients, without exception, how they can maximise their investment and prolong the benefits of the treatment you carried out. After care advice should be general to the treatment, but should also be specific to the client's requirements.

Treatment plans

It is the nail technician's responsibility to point out any limitations to the treatment the client has requested. Sometimes this takes a great deal of tact and, as a professional, you might need to suggest an alternative treatment or plan of action to help the client achieve their goal – this is often called a treatment plan.

Case Scenario One

The client has very short, bitten nails and requests a nail art service for a special occasion.

Consultation

- Inspect the client's hands
- Conduct a complete and thorough client consultation
- Take the client's medical information
- Get the client's signature – this is a legal requirement

Treatment plan

- Listen to and record the client's request
- Point out all the limitations to the treatment

The nail design the client has chosen is an airbrush design with lots of colour. After completing the client consultation, it was clear that growing natural nails in time for the special occasion was not going to be an option.

- The recommendation is for a full set of nail enhancements, airbrushed with the required design. Airbrush designs on bitten nails and ragged cuticles are always unsatisfactory as the paint has an uneven look and the surface is not large enough for the design to be completed.
- Point out the added advantages of wearing nail enhancements
  - instant length so the design can be applied
  - all the nails will be even in shape and length
  - the airbrush design will last until it is removed or rebalanced/maintained
- Explain that the enhancements can be removed after the special occasion or worn for longer with the correct maintenance

Technical Tip

Remember, rebalance/ maintenance is designed to prevent problems occurring, not to correct problems after damage has been done. If insufficient or no after care advice is given, the client will not understand how important it is to return to the salon and will often try to stretch out the time between appointments.

After care advice

- Book an appointment for a removal or rebalance/ maintenance appointment after one week for a nail biter then every two weeks thereafter. It is worth informing the client that bitten nails grow faster when the finger tip is covered.
  - follow the manufacturer's recommendations for the use of professional oils and creams
  - return to the salon if any problems arise
  - return to the salon for professional removal
  - do not attempt to remove nail enhancements – this could result in damage to the natural nail plate

Homecare advice

- Wear rubber gloves for housework
- Use the pads of the fingers when typing or using the phone
- Treat nails as jewels, not tools
- Take care with car doors, ring pulls on cans of drink, etc.
- Do not pick at nails or attempt home maintenance; if problems are experienced contact nail technician

Retail advice

Most manufacturers supply a range of products designed to complement salon treatments and to extend the longevity of the service

- The nail artist should know and understand the features and benefits of products in order to be confident when client asks questions such as:

- Why should I use this brand?
- What will it do for my nails?
- What does the product contain?
- How and when should I apply it?
- It is the nail artist's responsibility to recommend the products required and advise the client how to obtain the best results eg:
  - a cuticle oil for all clients – this is not an option
  - for clients with rough cuticles – cuticle cream or eraser
  - for clients with dry hands – hand cream
  - for all clients – base coats, top coats, acetone-free polish remover

Case Scenario Two

The client has wide flat nails and requests a nail art service for a special occasion.

Consultation

- Inspect the client's hands
- Conduct a complete and thorough client consultation
- Take the client's medical information
- Get the client's signature – this is a legal requirement

Treatment plan

- Listen to and record the client's request
- Point out all the limitations to the treatment

The nail design the client has chosen is dark red enamel to match an outfit. After completing the client consultation, it was clear that the client was unhappy with the width of her natural nails.

- The recommendation is for an airbrushed contour. The colour selected by the client matched her outfit and a second, darker colour was airbrushed evenly down each side of the nail wall
- Point out the added advantages of wearing airbrushed colour
  - it gives the illusion of thinner or longer looking nails
  - paints can be mixed to match any colour
  - an airbrush design will last longer than enamel
- Explain that an airbrush design can be removed in the same way as normal enamel, using non-acetone polish remover, which is less drying on the skin and nail plate

After care advice

- Recommend regular appointments for manicure and airbrush treatments every two weeks

Technical Tip

If the client requires an illusion of length, a colour fade may be used, starting with a lighter shade at the cuticle, grading diagonally to a darker shade towards the free edge. You could also shade to black right on the corner of the tip – the black should only appear as a shadow, not a definite colour.

- follow the manufacturer's recommendations for the use of professional oils and creams
- return to the salon if any problems arise

Homecare advice

- Apply top coat every two days to prolong the airbrush design
- Wear rubber gloves for housework
- Use the pads of the fingers when typing or using the phone
- Treat nails as jewels, not tools
- Take care with car doors, ring pulls on cans of drink, etc.

Retail advice

Retail advice will be the same as for Scenario one.

Case Scenario Three

The client has very dry and red cuticles. The nails are a good length but different shapes. The request is for a bright red nail art design for a special occasion.

Consultation

- Inspect the client's hands
- Conduct a complete and thorough client consultation
- Take the client's medical information
- Get the client's signature – this is a legal requirement

Treatment plan

- Listen to and record the client's request
- Point out all the limitations to the treatment

The nail design the client has chosen is a bright red nail art design with lots of rhinestones. After completing the client consultation, it was clear that the client has a job in a restaurant that is quite hard on the hands. The client does not usually wear enamel or nail art because of this work, but was attending her engagement party and wanted to show off the ruby engagement ring.

- The recommendation is for a hot oil manicure with more time allowed in order to perform the meticulous cuticle work required
- Point out the advantage of choosing a red colour that is blue based as opposed to orange based, because it will pull out all the red in the cuticles
- An alternative would be to choose a French manicure finish with a small flower design and ruby-coloured rhinestones to match the ring
- Explain that the skin should be cared for and moisturised. The cuticles also need moisture after being immersed in water

- The client should think about a weekly manicure or a two-weekly manicure if the after care advice is followed

Aftercare advice

- Do not attempt to remove nail art yourself as this could result in damage to the natural nail plate – make an appointment for removal
- Have regular manicures to keep the hands and nails healthy
- Follow the manufacturer's recommendations for using professional oils and creams
- Return to the salon if any problems arise

Homecare advice

- Wear rubber gloves for housework
- Use the pads of the fingers when typing or using the phone
- Treat nails as jewels, not tools

Retail advice

Retail advice will be the same as for Scenario one.

Case Scenario Four

The client is visiting the salon for the first time – normally she goes to another salon – and requests a maintenance treatment and application of an airbrush design.

Consultation

- Inspect the client's hands
- Conduct a complete and thorough client consultation
- Take the client's medical information
- Get the client's signature – this is a legal requirement

Treatment plan

- Listen to and record the client's request
- Point out all the limitations to the treatment

The client has evidence of water blisters around the cuticles and down the side of three fingers, high skin colour and small cracks in the skin at some of the first knuckles on the fingers that are open but not bleeding. The skin is very dehydrated and sensitive to light touch and pressure. After completing the client consultation it was clear that the skin reaction had for some time been getting worse and the client thought she may be allergic to a hand cream or soap powder.

- The main recommendation is that no treatment should be carried out today and the client should be referred to a doctor

Technical Tip

The following information is for those who are nail artists only, so that they have an understanding of the situation:

- After an allergic reaction the skin is very dehydrated. Tip remover and acetone greatly dehydrate healthy skin – this effect will be heightened on sensitised skin – so, as a professional, we would not place the finger tips in this solution for any length of time, especially the time it takes to remove a set of nails.

- Once the product has been totally cured – 24–48 hours – taking it off would cause further dehydration and trauma to the skin. After an allergic reaction, there is no advantage to removing the product – it would only worsen the situation. Direction should be taken from a GP on the removal of the product.

- Explain that the skin is very sensitive and if treatment is performed it could make the skin condition worse
- Explain that nail treatment can only take place when the skin has returned to normal
- Remember that, although as a nail artist we may recognise a disorder, we should not alarm our client and attempt to diagnose a problem. Nail artists have no medical training and clients should be referred to a professional

After care advice

- You should not, under any circumstances, attempt to remove nail enhancements if the skin is open, cracked, swollen or shows water blisters
- Only attend the salon for further treatments when the problem has subsided
- Look at possible alternative treatments that may be more suitable

Case Scenario Five

The client has decided to have a new image as she has recently separated from her partner and embarked on a new career. Her new image involves a makeover of which nail care is just a part – it includes her hair, make up, clothes and a belly button piercing!

Consultation

- Inspect the client's hands
- Conduct a complete and thorough client consultation
- Take the client's medical information
- Get the client's signature – this is a legal requirement

Treatment plan

- Listen to and record the client's request
- Point out all the limitations to the treatment

The client is middle aged and has 'hard working' hands with age spots. Her nails are a decent length but they need shaping and a manicure. She has asked if she can purchase a cubic zirconium stud that she has seen on the shelf for her ring finger.

- The recommendations are for a specialist manicure, including a paraffin wax treatment, and then a nail enhancement overlay on the ring finger with the stud
- Point out the added advantages of a specialist manicure
  - all the nails will be even in shape and length
  - the skin will be in a much better condition
  - a manicure will give the client instant confidence in her hands

Technical Tip

When applying any posted or dangly charms you must ensure that the natural nail is coated with an overlay of one of the systems to give extra strength and protection against damage to the natural nail.

- The overlay needs to be maintained or removed after 2–3 weeks
- The stud needs to be taken out or covered when doing any heavy work; show the client how to do this

After care advice

- Use hand cream – especially after washing up, etc.
- Apply cuticle oil – two or three times a day
- Have paraffin wax manicures to help re-hydrate the hands
- Book an appointment for maintenance of the overlay every 2–3 weeks
- Follow the manufacturer's recommendations for the use of professional oils and creams
- Return to the salon if any problems arise
- Return to the salon for professional removal
- Do not attempt to remove nail enhancements yourself as this could result in damage to the natural nail plate

Homecare advice

- Wear rubber gloves for housework
- Use the pads of the fingers when typing or using the phone
- Treat nails as jewels, not tools
- Take care with car doors, ring pulls on cans of drink, etc.
- Do not pick at or attempt home maintenance; if problems are experienced contact a nail technician
- In case of any contra-actions, e.g. lifting, cracking or loss of overlay, return to salon

Retail advice

Retail advice will be the same as for Scenario one.

Chapter summary

Setting up a nail art business can be an exciting time, and the potential rewards are very good. However, as with any new business, there can also be problems and pitfalls. You can avoid many of these if you make sure you obtain good training and qualifications, that you research your market and target your advertising carefully and that when you have attracted your clients, you give them excellent treatments at a sensible price and impress them with your professional, knowledgeable approach.

We owe it to ourselves and our clients to work in a safe and hygienic way, using all the rules laid down by our product companies, local councils and the Health and Safety Executive. The current situation has been covered in this chapter, but we do advise you to check on all issues at least every 6–12 months. The modern professional nail technician has no reason not to follow the rules and regulations that have been identified within this chapter.

Remember that health and safety regulations address potential hazards and have all been laid down for the benefit of yourselves, your colleagues and your clients.

Never forget the importance of after care advice. Every client is entitled to good and appropriate after care advice as part of their nail art treatment. Obviously, this is to their benefit, improving the service you have given, but it is also important for you as protection against complaints, thereby serving to build and protect your reputation as a professional.

Knowledge review

1   What course would you take when starting out your nail art career?

2   Where would you look for possible nail art courses?

3   List five ways you could market your services.

4   How could you incorporate nail art services into your existing nail business?

5   How would you price your services?

6   Who wears nail art?

7   Why is it so advantageous to gain a professional qualification in nail art?

8   Why are Health and Safety Regulations so important to a nail artist?

9   What other key pieces of legislation do you need to be aware of?

10   List five possible hazards in the salon environment.

11   What is a risk assessment?

12   What does COSHH mean to you?

13   What is cross infection?

14   List five ways that you can protect yourself and your client.

15   What is the correct procedure for disposing of salon waste?

16   Give six contra indications to a nail art service.

17   Why is it so important for a client to be given sound after care advice?

18   Give six points that you would include on your after care leaflet.

19 What could be the consequence of not giving any after care advice?

20 Why should a client buy retail from a professional nail artist?

21 What treatment would you recommend to a nail biter who wants nail art?

22 Why is it so important for you to know the features and benefits of all of your products?

23 Why is it so important for your client to sign their client record of treatment?

Anatomy and physiology of the skin and nails

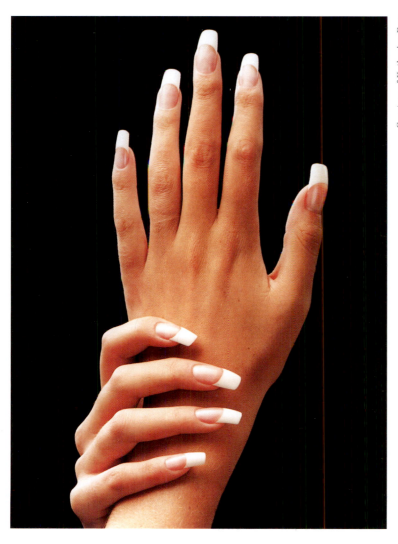

2

Courtesy of Katherine Ray

Learning objectives

In this chapter we will consider the following aspects:

- **the anatomy of the skin and natural nail**
- **diseases and disorders of the nails and surrounding tissue**
- **contra actions to nail art treatments**

It is important to understand how the body works and how we can affect the working of the body with our treatments and products. In this chapter the structure of the skin and nails is considered in some detail and we will look at how we, as nail technicians, can enhance the appearance of both. In this book, we do not discuss the other major systems of the body, but further information can be found in Jefford and Swain, *The Encyclopedia of Nails*.

It is impossible for us to do a good job without a thorough knowledge of the natural nail, its structure and growth pattern. Whatever treatment we perform – whether it is a natural nail manicure, nail enhancements or nail art – we are working on a living area and this should be treated with care and respect. It is possible to cause damage to the structures we work on through lack of knowledge or improper techniques and it is important that we learn how to prevent this happening. Nail disorders and diseases are identified and explained in this chapter – every nail technician must be able to recognise any contra actions for a particular treatment and know when to refer a client to a GP. Never be tempted to make a diagnosis.

The anatomy of the skin and natural nail

As a professional nail artist you need to have a clear understanding of the anatomy of your clients' hands, feet, skin and nails to be able to carry out your treatments and advise your clients on after care, maintenance and any problems that your clients may come across.

Learning objectives

In this section you will learn about:

- **the structure of the skin**
- **the structure of the natural nail**
- **the growth pattern of the natural nail**
- **possible contra indications to nail art treatments**
- **contra actions arising because of treatments**

The structure of the skin

The skin is the largest organ of the body and covers a total area of between 1.3 and 2 square metres depending on the size of the person. The skin has to be tough enough to be able to withstand the damage it sustains in daily life and also sensitive enough to be able to send signals when we are in danger or are facing environmental changes such as heat and cold. The skin is constantly working even when we are asleep or relaxing on a beach. It helps to regulate other body processes and protects us from the following:

Hands and feet

- allergens
- chemicals

Structure of the skin

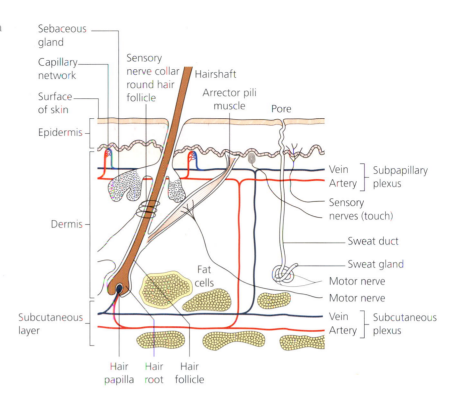

- UV rays
- micro-organisms

The skin needs to be kept in good condition at all times if it is to protect our bodies from harm. A closer look at the structure and functions of the skin will help you understand how we can help to keep our clients' skin in good condition.

The skin is divided into two layers:

1   The **epidermis** – topmost layer
2   The **dermis** – basal layer

Below the dermis is subcutaneous tissue which serves to anchor the dermis.

The epidermis

The epidermis is made up of five layers of tissue that contain no blood vessels and very few nerves. It is pierced by hair follicles and the ducts of sweat and sebaceous glands.

The five layers of the epidermal layer are:

1   **Stratum germinativum** (basal layer). These cells, packed tightly together and constantly being reproduced, form the deepest stratum of the epidermal layer that rests on top of the dermis. As these cells are pushed towards the surface they become components of other layers. This cellullar regeneration can be increased or decreased by a number of factors including ill health or age. The colour of the skin is also determined by this layer as it contains pigment-bearing cells known as melanocytes which produce melanin.

Layers of the epidermis

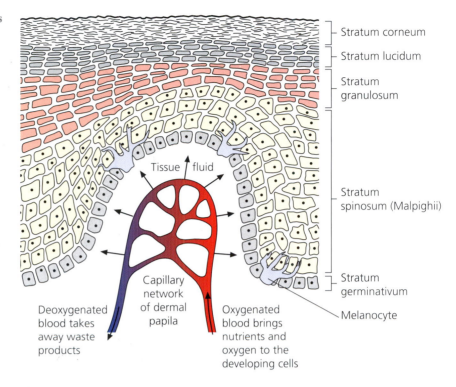

Stratum corneum

Stratum lucidum

Stratum granulosum

Tissue fluid

Stratum spinosum (Malpighii)

Capillary network of dermal papila

Stratum germinativum

Deoxygenated blood takes away waste products

Oxygenated blood brings nutrients and oxygen to the developing cells

Melanocyte

2   **Stratum spinosum**. This layer is composed of several layers of cells that vary in size and shape. The upper portion of this layer is known as the prickle cell layer. The cells are linked by very fine threads which give them a spiky appearance.

3   **Stratum granulosum** (granular layer). As the cells from this layer rise to the surface they flatten and become progressively larger and accumulate granules containing keratohyalin which helps in the production of epidermal keratin. It has between one and four layers.

4   **Stratum lucidum**. This layer has cells with no nuclei, which are narrow, transparent and have little outline. The cells at this stage are nearly at the end of their life cycle and are becoming dehydrated. The keratohyalin granules that are present in the stratum granulosum are now being turned into keratin.

5   **Stratum corneum** (horny layer). This is the outermost layer of skin and is composed of several layers of flattened irregularly shaped cells. They assume this flattened form from the evaporation of their fluid content. This layer consists almost entirely of keratin.

As the cells near the surface they are shed or rubbed off during normal daily routines. This layer protects the skin, preventing dehydration of the skin tissues. It can take 3–4 weeks for cells to activate in the stratum germinativum and rise through to the surface stratum corneum.

The dermis

This is called the 'true skin' and it lies immediately beneath the epidermis. This layer contains blood vessels, lymph vessels, nerves, sweat and sebaceous glands, hair follicles, arrector pili muscles and papillae. The dermis is comprised of two separate layers:

1 The papillary layer (pa-pil-ah-ry)
2 The reticular layer (re-tik-u-lar)

The papillary layer lies directly under the epidermis and contains the small cone-like projections that extend upwards into the epidermis, called *papillae*. Papillae contain small blood vessels or nerve endings. This layer can also contain some melanin.

The reticular layer is the lower area of the dermis where the blood and lymph vessels, sweat glands and sebaceous glands, hair follicles and the arrector pili muscles are situated. It also has a dense network of collagen fibres which run parallel to the surface. These fibres give the skin its elasticity and can be damaged by ultra violet light.

The subcutaneous tissue

The subcutaneous (sub-koo-tay-nee-us) layer is made up of fatty tissue more commonly known as adipose tissue. It is not technically skin, but anchors the skin and acts as a protective cushion for the body. It also stores fat to be burned for energy. It can vary greatly in thickness according to the age, sex and health of the body. Sitting beneath the dermis layer, it contains the following:

● **Blood** supply. There is a network of arteries that run parallel to the surface of the skin contained in the subcutaneous layer. These branch into smaller capillary networks around hair follicles, sebaceous and sweat glands. The capillary network is responsible for transporting vital food and oxygen to the living cells. The amount of blood flow to the surface is controlled by the nerve endings in the capillary walls.
● **Lymph**. The lymphatic capillaries drain away tissue fluid which contains waste products from cell activity and foreign bodies such as bacteria. There is a network of fine lymph vessels throughout the dermis.

The nerves

A nerve is a collection of fibres that send messages from the organs of the body to the central nervous system. The skin is one of the major organs of the body and therefore contains many nerve fibres. There are two types of nerves within the skin's structure:

1 motor nerves
2 sensory nerves

Four sensations can be experienced through the skin:

1 pressure
2 touch
3 pain
4 temperature

All sensations are due to the network of sensory nerves and receptors within the skin. The majority of receptors lie deep within the dermis but those that register pain are to be found in the lower epidermis. All sensations are stimulated by influences external to the body, such as extreme heat or cold. This message is then taken along the central nervous system and the brain decides how to act on this information. If the brain decides that action is required, it will send a message along the motor nerves to the necessary organ or muscle. If the original message was, for example, that the skin was cold, the brain instructs the arrector pili muscle to contract and trap air next to the body for warmth; this is what we call 'goose-bumps'.

Other components of the skin

Hair follicle

A hair follicle is a depression of epidermal cells pushed deep into the dermis responsible for the production of the keratinised structure called hair. The blood vessels in the dermal papillae supply the food and oxygen necessary for hair growth. The arrector pili muscle is responsible for causing 'goose-bumps' as it is attached to the hair follicle and pulls it into an upright position when the muscle is contracted.

Sebaceous glands

With the exception of the soles of the feet and the palms of the hands, these glands are found all over the body. There are more in areas such as the chest, face, back and the scalp, and less on the knees and elbows. They usually open out into a hair follicle, although some may be found on the skin's surface, keeping the skin soft and supple by preventing moisture loss from the dermis. An invisible layer called the acid mantle is formed by sweat and sebum and protects the skin from harmful bacteria. Another function is to keep the skin waterproof and healthy. When the sebaceous glands increase activity, seborrhoea or oily skin occurs, which can lead to blocked pores and other skin conditions. The reverse will cause dry skin, which can lead to flaking and dehydrated conditions.

Sweat glands

There are two types of sweat glands within the skin. Both types are deep in the dermis and consist of long narrow tubes or ducts that pass up through the epidermis to the surface, where the sweat is excreted through an opening in the skin called a pore. These glands are of two types:

1   eccrine
2   apocrine

Eccrine glands are found all over the body and only secrete water and salts. Their only function is to regulate body temperature.

Apocrine glands are found in the armpits and genital areas and open into the hair follicles instead of the surface of the skin. These glands secrete water, urea and fats. It is the breakdown of this type of sweat that causes body odour.

To become a nail technician, you must learn about **dermatology**, the study of human skin, and this should cover skin disorders and skin diseases. The skin on the human body is thinnest on the eyelids and thickest on the palms of the hands and the soles of the feet. It is part of our work as nail technicians to educate our clients on the processes they can use to maintain healthy skin on their hands and feet.

The structure of the natural nail

Professional nail artists must know when and when not to perform treatments, recognise – but not diagnose – conditions and be able to advise clients in the event of any contra actions occurring. You can only do this if you have the right knowledge. It may seem boring or irrelevant to have to study anatomy and physiology, but it is an integral part of our job as nail artists and it will help to protect us and our clients from bad practices.

Even in the early stages of a foetus growing in the womb, human nails begin to form. At 14 weeks the foetus has developed the area where the nail plate will grow and the nail plate can be seen growing out from the proximal nail fold. The speed at which the nail will grow will depend on many factors, for example nutritional levels. Around week 21 the nail plate will be completely formed and tiny fragile free edges can be seen. As always, throughout our lives, our toenails grow much more slowly than our fingernails.

Histology of the nail

The cells of the nail are flattened and filled with **keratin**. They have no nuclei and are thought to be similar to the cornified or uppermost layer found in the epidermis. They begin their life in the germinal **matrix** which extends to include the deep layers of the underside of the **proximal** nail fold. This area is where the cells divide and produce *keratinocytes*, capable of rapid terminal keratinisation. Keratin, made in the body, is a tough fibrous protein polymer made up of amino acids. On average it is believed that the fingernail plate is approximately 100 cells thick. As the cells leave the matrix most are already bonded. Inside the cells are long fibrous keratin tissues that bond into the next cell. Most cells have between three and six sides which interconnect and bond as the cells leave the matrix.

Unlike the cell structure of the skin, there is very little lipid or fat between the keratinised cells of the nail plate. This may account for the fact that nails are ten times more permeable to water than skin. Usually the nail plate will have a low water content but under certain physical or medical conditions this can change. The base of the nail is developed from the germinal matrix and these cells have the furthest to travel, whilst at the same time the thin surface layer is formed by the deeper layers of the proximal nail fold and the proximal portion of the germinal matrix. If the matrix is short, the nail plate will be thinner, whereas a long matrix will produce a thicker nail plate. It is also a fact that the wider the matrix the wider the natural nail plate.

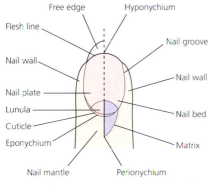

Free edge
Hyponychium
Flesh line
Nail groove
Nail wall
Nail wall
Nail plate
Nail bed
Lunula
Cuticle
Eponychium
Matrix
Nail mantle
Perionychium

**Cross section of the nail
(front view)**

As nail technicians our work is mainly on the natural nail itself, but we do need to be aware of all the other structures that support the nail unit to be able to perform our job effectively. This nail unit consists of the following:

- nail bed
- hyponychium
- eponychium
- perionychium
- nail grooves
- mantle or proximal nail fold
- matrix
- lunula
- cuticle
- nail plate
- free edge

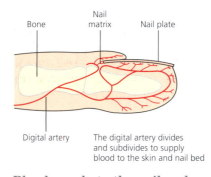

Blood supply to the nail and the nail bed

The nail bed

The **nail bed** is positioned directly under the **nail plate**. It starts at the front edge of the matrix (near the **lunula**) and continues through to the **hyponychium** just before the **free edge**. It is made up of two types of tissue:

1 dermis
2 epidermis

The epidermis is the upper layer of skin and is attached to the underside of the nail plate. Although it has the same name as that of the upper layers of skin on the fingers and hands its structure is slightly different and more closely resembles the skin on the inside of the mouth. This is more commonly referred to as the *bed epithelium*.

The dermis is the lower part of the skin and is attached to the bone underneath. It contains many thousands of tiny blood vessels that carry food, oxygen and nutrients to the nail unit whilst also taking away any waste and toxins.

The following elements are all seals that totally encompass the nail plate and the health of these structures is important to the health of the natural nail.

The hyponychium

The hyponychium is at the distal edge of the nail unit and is found directly under the free edge. It is composed of epidermal tissue and forms a watertight seal that prevents bacteria and viruses from attacking the nail bed. It is a thin strip of skin tissue that attaches the two lateral nail folds. If this seal is broken or damaged there is the possibility of infection.

The eponychium

The **eponychium** is the visible part of the skin fold that appears to end at the base of the nail plate. Sometimes this tissue is incorrectly referred to as cuticle. It has the same function as the hyponychium but is at the opposite end of the nail. When performing treatments on the nail, the cuticle should never be pushed back further than the eponychium. This area should be treated with care and not pushed aggressively. If the matrix seal is broken infections can occur.

The perionychium

The sides of the body of the nail are bordered by a curved fold of skin known as the **lateral nail folds** or walls. The cornified layer of the lateral nail folds extends fractionally onto the nail plate, forming a seal against the environment. This seal is similar to the hyponychium and eponychium and is sometimes known as the **perionychium**. The grooves at the sides of the nail move along next to the lateral nail folds, and are known as the lateral nail grooves.

The nail grooves

The grooves at the lateral sidewall guide the nail plate down the finger.

The mantle or proximal nail fold

The **mantle** or proximal nail fold is a deep fold of skin at the base of the nail where the root is embedded. This area is usually worked on when performing a manicure treatment to keep the skin soft, supple and in good condition. If it is neglected and becomes dehydrated the skin may split or tear and infection can occur.

The matrix

The matrix is a small area of living tissue directly under the proximal nail fold. All the nail cells grow in the matrix and if this is damaged in any way, the effects of the damage can be seen on the nail plate. In severe cases damage to the matrix can cause permanent deformities in nail growth. The developing nail within the matrix is very soft and care should always be taken when working on this area. As mentioned earlier, the length and width of the matrix determines the shape and thickness of the nail plate and this can only be changed by external factors such as physical or chemical damage. The matrix itself is white and it ends where the nail bed begins.

The lunula

The lunula is the visible part of the matrix, often referred to as the 'half moon', and is white in colour and opaque. The cells in this area become transparent and are not yet fully keratinised. The lunula lies directly under the thinnest part of the nail plate and is not fully

Fan   Trapezoid   Narrow   Square   Oval   Ski jump spoon concave   Hook claw convex   Pointed

Natural nail and cuticle shapes

compressed, so it is much softer. This part of the matrix can be destroyed if damage occurs, for example from heavy filing or accidentally by shutting a finger in a door.

The cuticle

The cuticle lies just above the eponychium and acts as a watertight seal that prevents bacteria and other harmful pathogens from invading the soft tissue. The cuticle is the primary matrix seal and serves the same purpose as the hyponychium. It is essential to keep cuticles healthy to support the other structures of the nail, such as the eponychium, and if this seal is broken infection can occur. The true cuticle on the underside of the proximal nail fold constantly sheds a layer of colourless skin. This shed skin attaches to the topside of the emerging nail plate and rides on the nail plate, seeming to grow from under the nail fold. It is one of the main areas of the nail unit where we perform treatments and on which we give our clients homecare advice.

The growth pattern of the natural nail

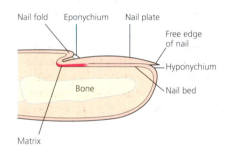

Nail fold Eponychium Nail plate

Free edge of nail

Hyponychium

Bone

Nail bed

Matrix

Cross section of the nail (side view)

Keratin cells are born in the matrix and are initially white and round. As they are pushed forward on their path from the matrix they remain soft and translucent. They harden and become more compact as they move along the germinal matrix and onto the nail bed. They grow in a horizontal, lengthways direction. The dermis and the epidermis of the nail bed lock into channels, like train tracks, under the nail plate. As new cells are pushed from the proximal nail fold the nail plate is guided along these tracks. The plate is attached to the nail bed until it grows past the fingertip. The **distal** edge of the nail is the hyponychium found under the free edge. The nail plate becomes the free edge and old dead cells are pushed beyond this point and grow forwards past the end of the finger.

Factors that can affect the growth and health of the natural nail

There are many factors that can affect the growth pattern and health of the natural nail. Some cannot be avoided and are due to *internal factors*, whilst others are caused by ourselves and our environment and are known as *external factors*.

Aspects of internal factors

- A doctor can sometimes tell from a patient's natural nails whether they are unwell and suffering from certain illnesses.

- Diet and nutrition play an important part in the health of the nails. Malnutrition or poor diet can affect nail growth through lack of vitamins and nutrients. However, there are no foods that can make the nails stronger than they naturally are – this is hereditary.

- Medication can affect the nails by making them grow more quickly or by slowing down growth and affecting the health of the nail plate.

- Pregnancy can cause an increase in the growth rate of the natural nail between the fourth and eighth months and there can be up to a 20 per cent increase in growth during the months either side of the birth.

- Bad or poor circulation can affect the blood supply to the matrix and the nail bed and therefore affect nail growth. Disorders such as Raynaud's or diabetes will sometimes induce fingernail and toenail problems.

Aspects of external factors

- Heat and climate can affect growth, as nails tend to grow more quickly in summer than in winter.

- Trauma or impact can be either deliberate or accidental and, depending on its severity, can affect the nail in many ways. If the matrix of the nail is damaged it can cause permanent deformity or affect the growth pattern of the nail. Injury to the nail seals, eponychium, hyponychium and perionychium, can result in an infection around the soft tissue and can also affect nail growth.

- Chemical damage ranges from not protecting the nails when using hazardous chemicals to the overuse of substances such as nail hardeners containing **formaldehyde** which can cause brittleness and, in the worst case, allergies. Water is also a chemical which can damage the natural nail if hands are constantly exposed to it without protection. There are some professionals who need to take care to use protective measures at all times when working to prevent overexposure to water or chemicals.

Good grooming is essential to keep the hands and feet in healthy and in good working order. We use our hands and feet more than any other part of our body and they are subjected to considerable wear and tear. There are straightforward ways to care for both:

- keep hands clean and moisturised
- keep fingernails and toenails to a sensible length
- use gloves for housework and gardening
- have regular manicures and pedicures
- change shoes often, do not wear the same pair all day, every day
- do not use nails as tools

The natural nail needs a constant balance of oil and moisture to protect its health and it is a daily battle for most people to maintain this balance. The nail plate will absorb water easily and can lose it quite rapidly, so care must be taken to avoid these extremes. Always ensure, as a professional, that you give your clientele good advice on homecare and the retail items they will need to maintain the health of their hands, feet and nails. You should be a good example of your profession with beautiful, healthy, well-groomed hands and feet at all times!

Diseases and disorders of the nails and surrounding tissue

Learning objectives

In this section you will learn about:

- **diseases and disorders of the nails**
- **diseases and disorders of the skin**

Checklist of nail diseases and disorders

A comprehensive list of nail diseases and disorders is given in the following table.

Checklist of nail diseases and disorders

ACAULOSIS UNGUIS	Infection of the nail with scopulariopsis brevicaulis
ANONYCHIA	Absence of the nail
BEAU'S LINES	Ridged nails, due to illness
DEFLUVIUM UNGUINUM	Brittle nails
DERMATITIS AND ECZEMA	Inflamed, irritated skin
EGG SHELL NAILS	Thin, white nails
HAPALONYCHIA	Soft nails
KOILONYCHIA	Spoon-shaped nails
LEUKONYCHIA	White, colourless nails or white spots
MACRONYCHIA	Large, but otherwise normal nails
MICRONYCHIA	Small, but otherwise normal nails
ONYCHALGIA NERVOSA	Intensely sensitive nails
ONYCHAUXIS	Thickened nails (old age, psoriasis, trauma, etc.)
ONYCHIA	Inflammation of the nail either post-traumatic or with paronychia
ONYCHODYSPLASIA	Abormal development of nail growth
ONYCHOGRYPHOSIS	Long, thick and curved nails
ONYCHOHETEROTROPHIA	Misplaced nails
ONYCHOLYSIS	Lifting away or separation of nail from bed
ONYCHOMADESIS	Splitting of nails into layers
ONYCHOMYCOSIS	Fungal infection, commonly known as ringworm
ONYCHOPHAGY	Nail biting
ONYCHORRHEXIS	Dry, brittle nails
ONYCHOTILLOMANIA	Picking at a nail from habit
PANARITIUM	Abscess at side of nail (whitlow)

PARONYCHIA	Inflammation of soft tissue
PLATONYCHIA	Increased curvature in long axis
POLYONYCHIA	Two or more separated nails on one digit
PSORIASIS	Abnormal thickening of the skin
PTERYGIUM	Excessive forward growth of the cuticle
TRACHYONYCHIA	Rough nails
USURE DES ONGLES	Wearing away of nails due to scratching
VERRUCA VULGARIS	Warts caused by viral infections

Bacterial infection

Bacterial infections of the nail usually take the form of **paronychias** (see below). However there is another type of non-invasive bacterial infection which can be encountered by nail technicians. This can occur as a green to black discoloration on the surface of the natural nail plate, but underneath a lifted section of the product overlay. There is a general misconception that this discoloration is either a 'mould' or 'fungal' infection. The correct term is *pseudomonas bacteria* and, in fact, most dark discolorations are formed by bacteria and not fungi.

A bacterial infection can also occur between the natural nail plate and the overlay. This can occur no matter which system is used, and for many reasons. The bacterial infection can be yellow or green in colour, the longer it goes undetected the darker green the colour becomes. The green discoloration is a by-product of the bacteria and not the bacteria themselves. Therefore, the green discoloration is where the bacteria have already been. A point to remember is that bacteria will only thrive in a warm, moist environment with a good source of food.

The *warmth* is supplied by heat from the rich blood supply to the nail bed directly under the natural nail plate, and the overlay will help to increase the temperature slightly. The *food source* can be moisture or non-living tissue that has not been correctly removed during preparation of the natural nail or application of the overlay.

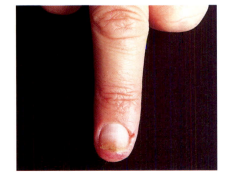

Bacterial infection

Brittle nails

Brittle nails may be divided into four groups:

1 isolated splits at the free edge which can sometimes extend proximally
2 multiple splitting which resembles the battlements of a castle
3 lamellar splitting of the free edge of the nail into fine layers
4 transverse splitting and breaking of the lateral edge close to the distal margin

Bruised nails

Bruised nail

Bruised nails are due to a clot of blood which forms under the nail plate after impact or trauma. They vary in colour from red through to maroon and sometimes black. The client may lose the nail but a new nail will usually grow underneath. Sometimes the nail plate may need to be pierced to release the pressure, but this should be done by a qualified medical practitioner.

Beau's lines

Beau's lines are horizontal, traversing ridges which can be shallow or deep and often slightly elevated. This condition may affect the surface of all ten nails or just the thumbs – and sometimes even just the big toes. Often the grooves are superficial or are more marked in the middle of the nail. Grooves are often the result of an illness, but they appear a few weeks after the onset of the illness.

Fragile or egg shell nails

Nails affected by this condition are normally thin and very curved on the free edge. They almost dip in the centre and have a white free edge. A client with this condition is not a good candidate for nail extensions, but will benefit from regular manicures.

Wet manicures should be avoided, as the nail plate will absorb the water and change shape by straightening when the fingers are soaked. After the polish is applied and the nail has dried, the shape will return to normal and the new polish will flake off. This is obviously disappointing for the client.

Furrows, ridges or corrugations

Furrows can run either horizontally or vertically (lengthways) across the nail plate. Ridges that run lengthways are normal and can increase with age. Ridges that run across the nail plate could be caused by illness, trauma or poor circulation.

Hang nail or agnails

Hang nail is a very common problem caused by dry cuticles or resulting from the cuticles being cut. This procedure is not advised, as clipping excess cuticle on a regular basis just serves to perpetuate the condition. A client with this problem would benefit from the use of oils, and regular manicures would also improve the condition.

Leukonychia or white spots

Leukonychia is simply bruising or trauma to the nail plate. This condition can be the result of the cuticles being pushed back too harshly. Remember that the newest cells are the softest, that is

Courtesy of Blackwell Science Ltd

Furrows, ridges or corrugations

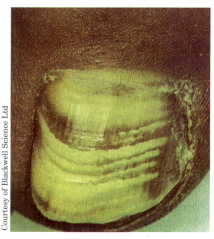

Courtesy of Blackwell Science Ltd

Trauma/leukonychia

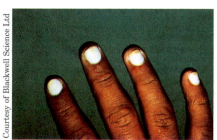

Courtesy of Blackwell Science Ltd

True/leukonychia

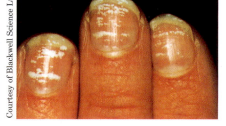

Courtesy of Blackwell Science Ltd

Spotting by trauma

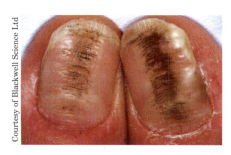

Habit tic

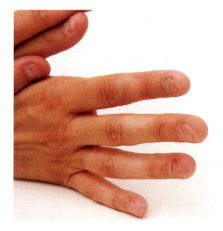

Onychopagy – bitten nails

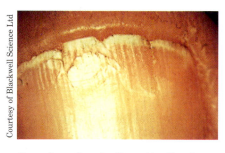

Onychorrhexis (longitudinal splitting/brittle nails)

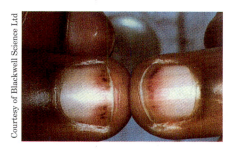

Splinter haemorrhage

those at the cuticle, and they harden as they are pushed up towards the free edge. Sometimes the cause is accidental or can be the result of various types of manual work.

Habit tic

A **habit tic** is caused by the client constantly picking or rubbing at the surface of the nail plate, usually at the proximal nail fold where the nail plate is softest. This is most often seen on the thumb. The condition is sometimes the result of a nervous habit – some clients are not even aware that they are doing the damage. After years of abuse, the damage can be permanent.

Onychophagy or bitten nails

Onychophagy or bitten nails is a condition that can sometimes be severe. Some nail biters just bite the free edge whilst others tear the nail below the hyponychium. Another sign of nail biting is broken and bitten skin around the cuticle or sidewalls. If the skin is broken or infected nail extensions should not be performed. Nail extensions can sometimes be the only form of help for a nail biter as they give instant beauty and length. It is very difficult for nail biters to grow their nails and most do not even realise they are biting them. Any little glitch or catch will send their nails straight back into their mouths. Nail extensions create instant order if they are maintained properly by the nail technician and cared for between appointments by the client. Sufferers should be able to grow their natural nails to a sensible length if they wear nail extensions for a few months.

Onychoclasis

Onychoclasis refers to a broken nail, normally occurring at the free edge. If the nail is broken below the free edge and has become infected do not treat the client. The cause is almost always due to mechanical trauma.

Onychorrhexis

Onychorrhexis refers to split or brittle nails. A split can be lengthways and is normally caused by mechanical trauma, excessive filing or the overuse of cuticle solvents. All nail services can be performed, providing the split is not below the free edge.

Splinter haemorrhage

A **splinter haemorrhage** is the name given to a nail showing tiny streaks of blood that run lengthways up the nail plate and are sometimes mistaken for tiny hairs. They are caused by minor trauma.

Onychia

Onychia is an infection in or on the nail plate. This can manifest itself as swollen tissue at the base. Redness, soreness or pus may also be present. It is sometimes caused by insanitary tools or implements. Sufferers should be referred to their GP.

Onycholysis

Nail separation from the nail bed, or **onycholysis**, is seen as an increased white area from the free edge. Common causes are trauma to the free edge, sometimes due to length, **psoriasis** or an allergic reaction to nail products or drugs. Nail extensions should not be applied to a client who has any separation, as extra length will only increase the problem. Nails should be kept short to avoid repeatedly catching them and to aid recovery. Onycholysis creates a **subungual** space that gathers dirt and keratin debris. The greyish-white colour is due to the presence of air under the nail, with the colour varying from yellow to brown.

Onycholysis

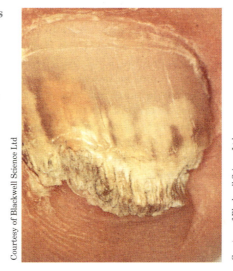 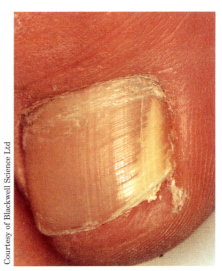

Courtesy of Blackwell Science Ltd

Courtesy of Blackwell Science Ltd

Onychomycosis or tinea unguium

Onychomycosis is an extremely contagious fungal infection. The client should be referred to his or her GP and not treated under any circumstances. The problem could be the result of infection setting in after onycholysis or a break in the tissue at the side or under the free edge. The condition can be manifested as yellow or white patches or even large areas of white that start at the free edge and invade and grow towards the root. There can sometimes be an unpleasant smell and the white areas look as if they could be scraped off. In advanced stages, the disease could penetrate the nail plate and cause superficial thinning, sometimes peeling off and exposing a diseased nail bed. Some occupations are more prone to this type of condition, for example those where the hands are constantly wet or are exposed to detergents and cleaning chemicals.

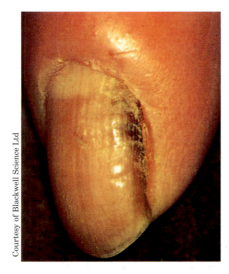

Courtesy of Blackwell Science Ltd

Paronychia

Paronychia

Paronychia is an infectious inflammatory condition of the tissue surrounding the nails. It is a common condition that appears as a red and swollen area around the cuticle and sidewall area of the nail. Pus formation may also be present and the condition is usually quite painful. The cause could be a cut or a break in the skin that has subsequently become infected. Nail biters and pickers are prone to hang nails which could lead to paronychia when the skin is bitten or torn off. You may find that some older clients cut their cuticles away which could be another route for infection. Try and educate clients into stopping this bad habit. The condition is contagious and in some cases may need treatment by a doctor. It is not wise to carry out any treatments until the condition has cleared.

Psoriasis

Psoriasis is an inherited skin disorder characterised by excessive cell proliferation. Histological changes in the nails are similar to those seen in the skin. It can manifest itself in several ways:

- discoloration of the nail
- pitting of the nail
- splinter haemorrhage
- extreme pitting of the nail plate

Psoriasis

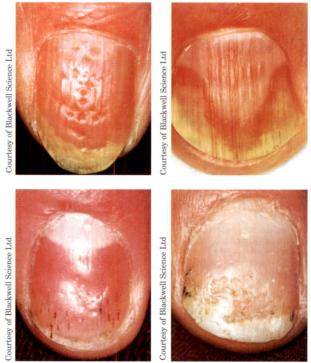

Courtesy of Blackwell Science Ltd

Discoloration of the natural nail can also involve onycholysis and it is not advisable to work on a client with this condition. You must always seek the approval of the client's doctor before attempting any treatment on a client with severe psoriasis, as there may be other conditions involved which you do not know of and cannot see. Psoriasis is not contagious and in around 36 per cent of cases is purely hereditary, although the condition can be brought on by stress. People who suffer from psoriasis of the nails should keep the length short and neat to prevent further damage. The nails will grow much more quickly on a person with this condition.

Pterygium

Forward growth of the cuticle is known as **pterygium**. This condition can and should be treated by the nail technician. If ignored, the skin can move up the nail plate towards the free edge.

Onychomadesis or nail shedding

Onychomadesis occurs most often after mechanical trauma to the natural nail. The nail may loosen at the base and subsequently the new nail may push the old nail off.

Koilonychia or spoon-nails

A client with **koilonychia** has a nail plate which is flat or concave, giving the appearance of spoon-shaped nails. This nail shape can be hereditary and, if so, will never change. Other customers may develop koilonychia due to anaemia, which is more commonly known as iron deficiency. In such cases, the shape will return to normal after the condition has been treated. Koilonychia may also develop due to working conditions where the hands are constantly in oils or soaps. These soften the nail plate and cause it to turn upwards. The only way to cure the condition is to stop using the chemicals or detergents and allow the nail plate to return to normal. A new-born baby's nails are often spoon-shaped, but this will correct itself during the first year.

Hapalonychia or soft nails

A soft nail condition, known as **hapalonychia**, is usually due to the client's nails naturally retaining a lot of water, or it could just be the way their nails naturally grow. However, it could also be linked to conditions such as dermatitis or eczema due to an inflammation of the skin caused by an allergy or chronic irritation. It usually starts at the base of the nail next to the cuticle and works its way up the nail.

Onychogryphosis or claw nails

In clients with **onychogryphosis** the nail plate usually has a lot of grainy fibrous tissue coming from the hyponychium, which makes the nail plate very thick and curved. If the nail is not kept short the curvature can make the nail look like a ram's horn. Care must be taken when cutting the nail as this could cause bleeding. This

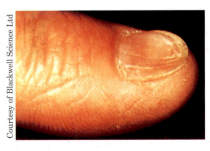

Koilonychia – spoon nails

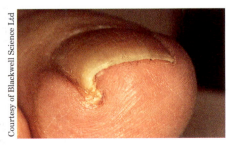

Onychocryptosis – ingrowing nail

condition is more common in toe nails than finger nails and can be caused by wearing badly fitting shoes. In the finger nails it could be caused by an injury. If the curvature is extreme or very thick then the client should be sent to his or her doctor or a chiropodist to be treated. This condition can be hereditary, or the result of psoriasis or trauma.

Onychocryptosis or ingrown nails

Also known as unguis incarnatus, **onychocryptosis** can be found on fingernails and toenails. It is more commonly found in toenails as people tend to cut them incorrectly. This condition can become infected and quite painful and should not be worked on if that stage has been reached. Onychocryptosis can be due to clients wearing socks or footwear that is too tight or may be the result of a congenital defect from birth. An ingrown toenail occurs when the edges of the nails grow forward and are pushed into the lateral sidewalls causing inflammation, pain and in some cases a bacterial infection. In severe cases this condition may need surgery but, if caught early enough, can be treated by a chiropodist. When performing nail treatments on clients it is imperative that the nail technician takes care to remove any sharp edges on the natural nail and uses proper cutting and filing techniques.

Diseases of the skin

Contact dermatitis (eczema)

The skin is capable of withstanding a significant degree of chemical insult but if this is prolonged the body will react, particularly if the chemicals are harsh, and irritant **dermatitis** may develop. This condition appears as an inflamed or broken rash. Often the irritant will cause the initial rash and broken skin, and water will then deteriorate the skin further.

Impetigo

Impetigo is extremely contagious. The bacterial organism which causes it remains within the outer layers of the epidermis. It is found most often on the face and manifests itself as inflammation, blisters, pustules and yellow crusts. The client must be referred to a GP for antibiotic treatment, which is normally in the form of creams to be applied daily. This condition is contra indicated for all treatments.

Impetigo is more common in children and can be caused by a cut or wound becoming infected by scratching or the knocking off of scabs. Staphylococci bacteria can then invade the skin and cause infection.

Allergic reaction

A swelling, rash, soreness or open sores may indicate an allergy to a particular product or chemical. The nail may also be white in colour or have white patches. The majority of products on the market today have a 48 hour cure time. After this time period, it is considered by

Important Note

It is very important for nail technicians to understand how an allergy can take place and the safety measures they need to take to prevent this.

experts within the nail industry that more damage will be done to the skin and surrounding tissue by attempting to remove the product by soaking in remover or acetone. Medical advice should be sought by the client before any attempt at removal is made.

Herpes simplex

Herpes simplex is a contagious viral infection, more commonly known as a cold sore. It is a skin infection caused by the Herpes virus and usually occurs periodically in people prone to the condition. It is normally seen around the mouth area and, if you suffer with this condition, care must be taken when dealing with clients to avoid cross infection.

Psoriasis

Psoriasis manifests itself as raised patches of red skin covered with very dry scales. This condition is not contagious, but the client should not be treated if the skin is broken in the treatment area. Stress, nerves, poor diet and also a genetic link can aggravate this condition. Psoriasis responds to sun beds, sunlight, steroids and sometimes coal tar treatments. Its implications for the nails in particular are discussed in the section on nail disorders above.

Scabies

Scabies appears as a raised itchy rash. It is caused by a mite and is highly contagious. It contra indicates for all treatments. It is almost exclusively passed by direct contact, so care must be taken if you see any unusual marks on your client's skin. Always refer a client to a doctor if you are in any doubt.

Tinea pedis (ringworm on the feet)

Also known as athlete's foot, tinea pedis is usually found between the toes but can spread all over the foot. It can dry up and reappear later. This condition is caused by a fungal infection (mycelium). Ringworm is contra indicated to all treatments.

Tinea unguium (ringworm of the nails)

This condition is rare, but when it does occur it usually affects more than one nail. The infected area will turn a yellow or grey colour and the nails will become very brittle. In severe cases the nail plate may separate from the nail bed. If the ringworm has infected the hands the main symptoms can be recognised as red lesions occurring in patches or rings; itching can be slight or severe. Treatment is the same for both the hands and the feet and a doctor's help should always be sought. This condition is highly contagious and contra indicates to all treatments.

As a nail technician it is important to learn about and have a good understanding of the skin in order to be able to recognise when something is wrong – however do not ever attempt to diagnose. If we have a sound knowledge of the skin and its problems it will enable us to make informed judgements on when to treat clients and when they need medical attention. The *golden rule* is that if skin is inflamed, infected, sore or swollen *do not perform* the treatment but *refer the client* to a doctor for diagnosis and treatment. A letter giving permission for treatment to commence should be obtained and filed with the client's consultation card and a note made on the record card for insurance purposes.

Contra actions to nail art treatments

Learning objectives

In this section you will learn about:

- **the recognition of conditions that have been caused by nail art treatments**
- **how to advise your client accordingly**

All nail artists should be aware of all contra actions that could possibly occur during or after a nail art treatment. Some conditions can happen while the client is still having the treatment, such as a reaction to a product, others could be caused by improper application of products or the use of tools either by you or by the client at home. In this section we will cover the main contra actions that you may come across, but if ever a contra action occurs and you do not recognise the condition then you must refer your client to a GP.

Being honest and open with your clients will gain their respect. Never pretend that nothing is wrong if you know that there is a problem. You should only ever give facts and not your opinions. Remember that prevention is better than cure!

Contra actions to nail art

Discolouration of the nail plate

Cause	Solution
Not using a base coat under polish	Always use a good base coat even under clear polish.
Using products with formaldehyde	Always check with manufacturer or supplier for product ingredients.

Thinning of natural nail plate

Cause	Solution
Over-buffing of nail plate by technician or client	*Technician* – Use correct amount of strokes with natural nail buffer. *Client* – Should be educated on buffing techniques and how often this should be done. Buffing paste should be used in moderation.

Cutting of skin around cuticles

Cause	Solution
Improper use of cuticle knife	Follow correct procedure – Use cuticle knife with water or oil, at correct angle and from side to middle, turn over and side to middle again.
Pushing cuticles back too harshly	Use oil or cream to soften skin before pushing back.
Pulling at hang nails rather than cutting	Use nippers correctly. Place under hang nail and then cut and release, do not tear.
Using nippers to cut cuticle away rather than just nip excess	Never cut away excessive cuticle as this will cause scar tissue and the skin to thicken. Use creams or oils daily to remove excess.
Using new sharp abrasives near sidewalls or cuticle	Use the correct grit file for a natural nail – 240 or higher. Always use the file at a 45° angle and pull the skin at the sidewall away with your thumb and forefinger when filing. File from side to middle and then repeat on the other side to stop splitting or flaking of the free edge of the natural nail.

Contra actions specific to nail extensions

The following tables list the causes and solutions of the main contra actions associated with nail extensions.

Softening of the natural nail

Cause	Solution
Natural nail has been thinned by constant filing	Ensure you use correct grit files when prepping and use in direction of nail growth only. Use a light touch when blending in tips. Do not use a heavy hand when filing nails in the cuticle area during a maintenance.
Natural nail has been thinned by over-priming	Follow manufacturers' instructions for application of primer and always ensure nail plate is dry before applying product.

Natural nail not dehydrated before product application	Always carry out your prep steps before tip application and again before application of product to ensure all oil and moisture is removed.
Product has lifted and moisture is trapped between layers	Ensure product application has been carried out properly including proper preparation and tip application. Do not carry out a maintenance if there is any lifted area of product showing. If lifting is too severe then remove nail extension, cleanse and reapply.
Nail plate is wet before product applied	Do not carry out a water manicure just before applying nail extensions. Make sure that all preparation has left the nails totally dehydrated.

Splitting, thinning and flaking of the natural nail

Cause	*Solution*
Over-blending of tips	Light touch with correct abrasive.
Over-buffing of natural nail	Use pre-tailoring and pre-blending techniques for tip application (see Chapter 6).
Nail extensions too long, too thin or too thick	The length rule applies – the free edge should never be longer than the length of the natural nail bed. When applying product ensure that the stress area or apex is the thickest part of the nail and that all other areas are thin and natural looking.
Client picking or biting extensions off	Educate your clients about correct removal techniques and timings of maintenance and the importance of keeping up with these. If you have a client who will not stop biting his or her nails or who has them repeatedly too long, then refuse to do nails for this client.
Maintenance overdue and extensions unbalanced	A client needs to be educated about when to come back for maintenance and the consequences of not returning for appointments.

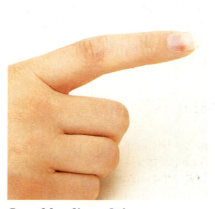

Over-blending of tips

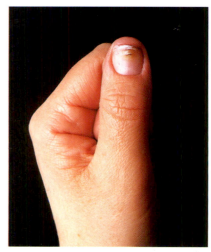

Thinning and splitting of the natural nail

Premature loss of nail extensions

Cause	Solution
Improper preparation of natural nail	Ensure the correct preparation techniques have been carried out.
Nail extensions too long	Carry out an in-depth consultation into client's lifestyle and hobbies, looking at areas such as whether they have children, are they sporty, what type of career they have. Look at their natural nail shape and condition to evaluate what system, products and length they can take.
Changes in client's lifestyle	Look at a client's stress levels, diet and any medication that they are currently taking. Adjust treatments, products and length of nails to suit individual requirements.
Improper use of or inappropriate products	Always follow specific manufacturers' instructions for product use, as these may vary greatly. Never mix products from one company with those of another.

Lifting of product

Cause	Solution
Improper prep of the natural nail	Ensure correct preparation to remove all oil and moisture from the natural nail plate before application of products. This will ensure proper bonding and adhesion.
Medication and stress levels of clients	Carry out an in-depth client consultation.
Nail extensions too long	Carry out an in-depth client consultation.
Contamination of products, tools and equipment	Use your housekeeping rules and always work in a clean, safe environment.
Incorrect mix ratio	Make sure you have had good training in the application of your chosen system and follow your manufacturer's instructions for application of products.
Improper application of products	If products are not applied to manufacturers' instructions there could be adverse chemical reactions that will occur on your clients' nails, causing many problems. Never mix chemicals that are not compatible.
Clients not returning for maintenance on time	If clients are not informed of the importance of returning on a regular basis for maintenance treatments it will cause problems for you and take extra time you may not have allowed for. If the client does not return for maintenance they are putting the integrity of their natural nails at risk and they should be made aware of this, otherwise they will blame you.

Discolouration of the natural nail plate

Cause	Solution
Improper prep of the natural nail	Make sure thorough preparation is carried out on the natural nail ensuring nail is completely dry and dehydrated.
Lifting or cracks in the nail extension	Cracks or lifting will allow contamination to enter. Diagnose why nails have problems, for example: • nails too long • improper prep • maintenance appointments not kept • nail extension out of balance • no homecare carried out
Overuse of primer	Ensure nails are clean and dry after application of primer and that manufacturer's instructions are followed.
Bacterial infection which may occur for any of the following reasons: • improper prep • maintenance appointment not kept • cracking of natural nail or nail extension • client picking, biting, tearing or ripping off • nail technician nipping off lifted product • lifting of product at free edge, sidewall or cuticle allowing moisture to be trapped between layers	Remove nail and do not buff or reapply until condition has cleared.

Bacterial infection under nail extension

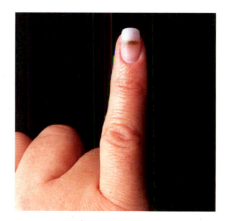

For more information refer to Jefford and Swain, *The Encyclopedia of Nails*.

Chapter summary

Once you have worked your way through this chapter you will realise just how much information we need to have on the structure of the natural nail and the skin surrounding it to be able to do our work effectively and safely, not just for the sake of our clients but also to protect ourselves from stress, injuries and infections. The guidelines outlined here will protect you from possible contra actions occurring to your clients and ensure that you have the knowledge to work safely and within legal requirements. Every client has a different lifestyle, health level and treatment needs, and this chapter should help you to identify whether a treatment can take place and any measures you might need to take to make it as effective and safe as possible for all concerned.

Knowledge review

1 Give three nail disorders where you could adapt and still give your client a nail art treatment.

2 List the major parts of the natural nail.

3 Explain how the natural nail grows.

4 What factors could affect natural nail growth?

5 What are the five layers of the epidermis?

6 What structures does the dermis contain?

7 What are the main functions of the skin?

8 What are the characteristics of a healthy nail?

9 What skin disorders would contra indicate a nail treatment?

10 Name five common skin disorders where you could still perform nail art treatments but would need to adapt your service.

Basic nail art techniques

3

Learning objectives

In this chapter we will look in detail at the following:

- **colour theory**
- **products, tools and equipment**
- **polishing techniques**
- **basic hand painting and freehand nail art designs**

This chapter covers the basics of nail art. It begins by discussing colour and how important the choice of the right colour is for your client and the end of result of the nail art treatment. It then goes on to look in some detail at the products required and the tools and equipment needed to put together a nail art kit and allow you to produce some stunning designs. As well as polishes and paints, it looks at the huge range of rhinestones, studs, glitter dusts, transfers and charms that are coming onto the market for nail artists. This is a rapidly expanding area, and this book could not hope to cover every available item. We have also included a large number of designs with step-by-step instructions for you to practice on and hopefully inspire you to create your own nail art. Be adventurous!

Colour theory

Learning objectives

In this section you will learn about:

- **understanding the use of colour**
- **the different types of colour**
- **how to mix and match colours effectively**
- **how to use the colour wheel effectively**

If you want to design and perform beautiful nail art designs you will need to have a good understanding of colour theory. Before we look at the products and equipment required to create beautiful nail art designs, this section will take you through the basics of colour theory and how to apply it successfully to your work.

Understanding the use of colour

If you look at the work of some of the most successful nail artists you will find that they have developed their own methods of using colours effectively without even realising what they are doing, they have an instinctive gift for selecting and the use of colour. Many people do not understand how the use of colour affects various parts of our life, that even our choice of colour for our clothes affects how we feel and how other people perceive us. Colour choices can be the making of a nail design or they can ruin it and a client will either love the finished design or hate it. What looks good on one person may not look good on the next because of their skin tone.

Splash of paint

There are whole books on the subject of colour theory and we cannot possibly cover in this section all that we would like to. We recommend that if you are interested in studying this subject further then you go to your local library and find some books on the topic. Once you have read this section, look again at a selection of trade magazines and see which designs work for you, which do not, and analyse the colours involved. Each colour has its own radiance, which is consciously or unconsciously interpreted in a certain fashion by whoever perceives it. This interpretation will vary from person to person but we can make general interpretations such as *pure white*, *ice blue*, *hot red*, *sunny yellow* and so on. Colour expression is important in the creation and emphasis of the design you are going to create, not only the hues of the separate colours, but how they work together.

When your clients select a colour they normally pick ones that they are attracted to rather than those that complement their skin tone. It is really important to have some knowledge of colour theory when working in the nail industry, as we are decorators as well as manicurists and nail technicians. Every good decorator should be able to use their knowledge to get maximum results. Ask your client whether they are going somewhere special and would like to match a look. Take into consideration the condition of the nails and surrounding soft tissue. All of your clients will have experienced trying on clothes and immediately knowing that they are not right for them – whether it is the cut, or more often, the colour that does not flatter them. The wrong colour against some skin tones can make people look sallow, ruddy or even ill. Other colours can make the skin radiate with health and camouflage skin imperfections. The same applies to colour on the nails. If your client's natural nails are short or bitten, then applying a bright red polish will draw attention to their short length. You might want to suggest a paler colour that will give the illusion of length whilst camouflaging any inconsistencies.

Some of your clients may have already visited a colour specialist and been colour coded. This is a process whereby a specialist, with the help of many colour swatches, matches colours to the client's skin tone, and then puts the client into a colour season:

- Spring
- Summer
- Autumn
- Winter

Different types of colour

Everything we see is light. In the seventeenth century Sir Isaac Newton allowed sunlight to shine through a glass prism. The light went through the glass prism and shone onto the wall beyond as a rainbow. If you would like to recreate this effect, try it with a piece of crystal or some rhinestones. Place the stone in the sunlight and you will see the colours reflecting onto the wall. Isaac Newton discovered that light contains colour and that visible light contains the full spectrum of colour represented by the true colours on the outside of the colour wheel. When something appears as a colour we are actually seeing light bounce off a surface and the colour we see is the only colour being reflected. When we see white we are seeing all visible light rays being reflected from a surface whereas black absorbs all the light waves. An application of this idea that we are all familiar with is being told to wear white in a hot country, as it reflects the light and heat, while wearing black will absorb the light and heat and make us feel hotter.

Technical Tip

It is important to remember that the light you choose to work with will affect your perception of colour. Incandescent lighting will have a warm influence, red through to yellow on the colour wheel, on your nail colours. Fluorescent lighting will have a cooling effect, green to blue-violet on the colour wheel, on your nail colours. It might be a good idea to invest in a good lamp with a daylight or natural light bulb to help you with your colour choices.

Primary colours

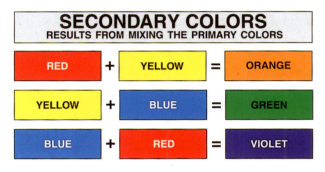

Secondary colours

There are three *primary* colours:

- red
- yellow
- blue

It is impossible to mix these colours using any others on the colour wheel and they are often referred to as the basic colours. All the other colours on the colour wheel are mixed from these three primary colours.

Secondary colours are:

- green
- violet
- orange

A secondary colour is the result of mixing two primary colours together: blue and yellow make green, red and yellow make orange, red and blue create violet.

Tertiary or *intermediate* colours are a combination of equal parts of one primary and one secondary colour. The primary colour name is always placed before the secondary colour name, for example yellow-orange (golden yellow).

Interesting fact

In early 2003 scientists in West London developed a paint that is called 'Super black'. This new black is blacker than any existing black, being up to 25 times darker. It is the least reflective surface on Earth, but it will probably never be used as a polish colour as it would cost over £1 million to make a coat from this colour. Ouch!

Mixing and matching using the colour wheel

When is black, black and white, white! Have you ever noticed how many different shades of black and white there are?

White is located on the outside of the wheel and will determine the true or base colour and influence it, and black is in the centre. Where the black is closest to the red section of the colour wheel you will see a red undertone in the black. *Value* is the lightness or darkness of a colour. Each section of the colour wheel represents a true colour. The lighter the true colour becomes, the more it travels towards the edge of the wheel, that is towards the white.

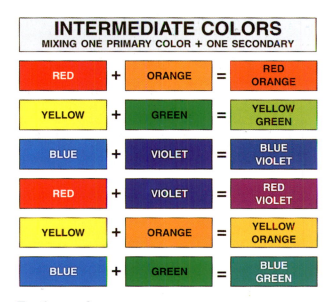

INTERMEDIATE COLORS
MIXING ONE PRIMARY COLOR + ONE SECONDARY

RED	+	ORANGE	=	RED ORANGE
YELLOW	+	GREEN	=	YELLOW GREEN
BLUE	+	VIOLET	=	BLUE VIOLET
RED	+	VIOLET	=	RED VIOLET
YELLOW	+	ORANGE	=	YELLOW ORANGE
BLUE	+	GREEN	=	BLUE GREEN

Tertiary colours

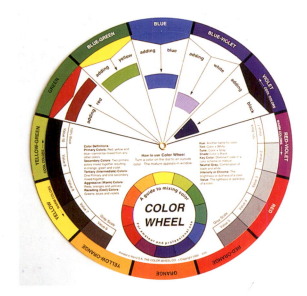

Colour wheel

Technical Tip

Remember that you have light and dark values of each colour so that you have a varied choice of colours to choose from in just one section of the colour wheel.

Note

We would recommend that you purchase a colour wheel from your local nail art distributor, art or hobby shop. This way your clients can understand when you are trying to explain colour theory and mixing.

As well as running the length of the colour section on the wheel, you may choose colours that are changing as they travel towards a neighbouring sections or the width of the section. For example, blue is true blue when centred in its section of the wheel. When you start to travel sideways towards its neighbouring colour, blue-green, the true colour blue begins to be influenced by blue-green, until it comes to the blue-green section.

Colour selection

Now we have established the various types of colour let us look at colour schemes and how we can use them to their best advantage in our nail art designs:

- *Monochromatic* – single colour
- *Triad of colour* – true colour and the colour on either side of it on the colour wheel
- *Complementary contrast* – the combination of a colour and the one opposite it on the colour wheel

It is usually the most conservative clients who choose monochromatic colour. The triad of colour utilises three sections from the colour wheel, all with a common denominator. Most clients would be comfortable choosing from within one colour's triad on the colour wheel. For example if you have a client who loves to wear a true blue, the triad would include blue-green and blue-violet. You could use the true colour for a more vivid look or a tint of the true blue for a subtle look. Using complementary contrast can show a high intensity of colour and be quite bold. The complementary contrast of the colour can be at the opposite side of the wheel. This is the scheme for your clients who want to be noticed. You will find that this combination of colours will mainly be used by airbrush nail artists. One example of complementary contrast is red and green.

Technical Tip

Before starting work on your clients spend a few hours mixing your colours in spare bottles and preparing a tray of various colour contrasts. You will not know what works and what doesn't until you have experimented on tips. Keep the ones that you like for your clients to choose from.

For a client who wants bold red nails with extra colour, that are going to be noticed by everyone, add a small amount of green to the tips and see how the colours contrast with one another. This is a good choice for Christmas nails. Other possible complementary contrast combinations are pale blue to pale yellow, pale pink to mint green.

Here are a few interesting points about colour:

- colour affects our mood
- man is the only animal that sees colour
- newborn babies only see black and white at first
- as we get older our colour taste changes
- reds and oranges are stimulating
- yellow is an intellectual colour
- pastel colours are used in hospitals to induce rest
- green is the colour chosen by well-balanced people
- blues symbolise cleanliness

There are many more interesting facts on colour and if you think about the way colour affects your life you will see how important it is to have an understanding of colour theory. If colour affects you, it will affect your clients as well. Take colour into account when choosing your uniform, your salon decor, your business cards, your polish range and your nail art designs.

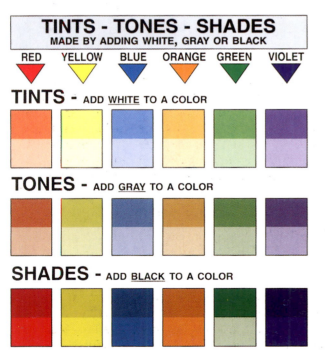

Tints and tones

Warm and cool colours

Products, tools and equipment

Learning objectives:

In this section you will learn about:

- **the tools required to create specific designs**
- **the equipment needed for your nail art kit**
- **the range of products needed to perform basic nail art treatments**
- **complementary products for your nail art kit**

This section covers the tools, products and equipment needed to set up a nail art service. Although we have made it as comprehensive as possible it makes no attempt to cover all the items available on the market. We recommend that you look at internet sites, trade magazines and visit hobby and craft shops to find others items that we may not have discussed here.

When we were given the go-ahead for this, Anne and Jacqui went to a very large hobby craft shop to source any items that could be included in the book. After spending over £700 – and shocking the girl on the till by telling her they were all for a nail art book – we proceeded to sift through our purchases. These included obscure items such as a range of ribbons and materials, glue guns, a drill and drill bits, crackle paints and many more. Some items have fitted into our nail art kits very nicely and some we have had to put on the shelf for our husbands to use!

Note

We would like to point out that the glue gun and drill were for the artistic sections of this book and were not intended for use on clients.

The tools required to create specific designs

Marbling and dotting tools

Marbling and dotting tools

The marbling tool comes in many different sizes; the most popular for nail art is the double ended one, which features two metallic balls at either end of a piece of wooden dowel. One ball is small the other is slightly larger. Many nail artists use this tool for creating a marbling design, blending colours, creating swirls and textured finishes. It can also be used for creating dots – of an even or decreasing size – and to pull dots into petal shapes when doing finely detailed flowers.

Nail art suppliers and art shops stock marbling tools of various sizes, from the very small to large.

Nail art brushes

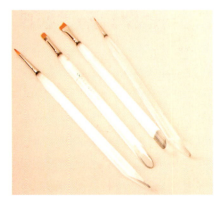

Nail art brushes

It is impossible to create all shapes, sizes and effects with only one brush, therefore a nail artist should have a good selection of different brushes in order to create a wide range of tailored designs. Your nail art brushes should range from the very smallest, as we work on very small areas, to a medium size for bolder designs.

Technical Tip

It is best to buy good quality brushes, take care of them as recommended by the manufacturer and use the appropriate solvent to clean them.

Remember some brushes are suitable for one purpose only, e.g. acrylic paint, glitter dust, water based paints, etc.

Fine nail art brush

Flexi brushes

Another point to remember is that there are various types of hair used in brush construction, designed for use with different types of paint or other mediums. For example, the bristles could be made of nylon, sable or synthetic hair, all of which will work differently with various types of paint. You will also find that the bristles differ in texture, being stiff or flexible, and can work differently depending on the medium you are using or the look you want to create.

Fine detail brush

This brush has short bristles that taper to a very fine point; it is an ideal choice for fine, intricate designs and as a finishing tool. Adding extra fine points with this brush can add dimension to a flat picture, for example by adding a different shade of green to a leaf or to the centre of a flower.

Shading brush

This brush consists of a flat, square head of bristles. It enables you to shade, fill in and float colour as well as to use a mixture of colours on either side of the bristles to create swirl effects. Using this brush can take a little time to master, so practise on old tips or even on shiny paper first.

Striping brush

This is a very thin, narrow bristled brush which is terrific for creating long straight lines. This brush can come in various lengths and thickness. It will be one of the most versatile tools in your nail art kit and is an absolute essential. With practice you can not only perform straight lines but also use it to flick or drag into a curved design.

Technical Tip

Remember to lay the brush on the nail and pull across the nail rather than paint with the tip of the brush for a straight even line. With a bit of practice you will be creating fantastic designs with the striping brush or incorporating it with other tools.

Glitter dust brush

It is advisable to use only a quality sable brush with short bristles that end in a fine point for glitter dust, as this will have to be cleaned in nail polish remover each time the glitter is picked up. After each application of glitter make sure you clean any excess product from your brush otherwise you will add glitter to your mixer and possibly spoil further designs.

Liner brush

A liner brush is similar to a striping brush, but is much shorter and wider. It is an ideal brush for producing thick straight lines and filling in colour on nails.

Fan brush

Technical Tip

Try using a fan brush with opalescent paints on a dark background or neon colours to brighten the design. It is good for sweeping across the nails vertically, horizontally or diagonally. Different types of paint create varying textures and finishes.

Fan brush

This is one of the most interesting brushes for creating texture and blending colours together without mixing. The bristles of this brush imitate the look of a fan. Make sure you use contrasting colours to give the best effect when using this brush.

Colour shapers

Colour shapers are now available in a wide range of sizes, shapes and hardness – the hardness is indicated by the colour of the head

- white – very soft, flexible
- grey – medium
- black – hard, inflexible

The pointed colour shaper creates dots and swirls; the cup colour shaper can create teardrops and half circles, while the angle chisel colour shaper can act like a windscreen wiper or define straight raised lines. The hardness of the colour shaper determines the definition of the design.

Sponge

Sponges come in various sizes and the texture ranges from small holes to large and some can be spiky. It is a good idea when choosing your sponges to buy smaller pieces, as they are better suited to nail art. If you have difficulty obtaining tiny sponges try the baby section of your local department store or chemist. Sponges are very good when used with two colours or with one colour over dry enamel. Try them with opalescent or pearlescent paints for an interesting effect.

Colour shapers

The equipment needed for your nail art kit

Carrying case

These should be strong and have a handle if you are a mobile technician/artist. Many mobile nail artists favour the use of a tool box from their local DIY store – these are made of strong, durable plastic but are usually lightweight and have many compartments that are handy for storing small items. They are normally a fraction of the price that you would pay for a purpose made beauty case. If you progress to becoming a photographic nail artist or work backstage at fashions shows, then you will need a much larger case, possibly with wheels. For such events you will need to take all of your equipment to cover every eventuality and this would be impossible to carry on the underground or bus. Choose a custom made nail trolley or use a wheeled suitcase that you can put all your other cases and equipment in.

Technical Tip

Remember, if using an orangewood stick to pick up any decals or flat-stones to have a small piece of Blu® Tack or some water handy. NEVER lick the end of the stick as this can spread pathogens from one client to another.

Pots and containers

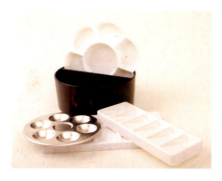

Artist's palette

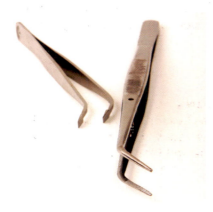

Tweezers

Blu® Tack

Inexpensive and indispensable, no nail artist should be without Blu® Tack. It is handy to use on the end of an orange stick for picking up and placing rhinestones precisely where required without the risk of dropping them. It can also be used to secure tips to a board when perfecting your nail art designs.

Orangewood stick

Orangewood sticks come in many sizes and lengths; they are useful for placing flat-stones, securing striping tape and polish secure decals. Pointed orangewood sticks can be used as dotting tools. These are disposable and if used on soft tissue or during the manicure process a new one is needed for each client.

Pots and containers

Small pots or containers with screw caps are ideal for storing tiny items, for example rhinestones, flat stones, glitter dust, bhindis, pearls, studs, rings, etc. There is nothing worse than purchasing these items only to find them mixed up at the bottom of your nail art kit because they have fallen out of their bags. Sorting them can be very time consuming.

Artist's palette

These are available from many art shops and some nail art companies. They come in a range of sizes, shapes and colours, but all you will need is a small one that fits easily into your kit. The bigger ones are for artists working on much larger areas than nails. If mixing two or more components together e.g. paint, glitter, etc., they are invaluable.

Tweezers

Tweezers come in various shapes and sizes. Pointed, curved tweezers are useful when picking up gems or objects to place securely into or on nail enhancements. Short tweezers are useful for picking up and securing striping tape and decals onto nails. These can be bought from nail art suppliers, art shops and hobby shops. Make sure that metal equipment is cleaned and sterilised between clients.

Scissors

Scissors should be sharp and used only for one specific purpose, for example if you use scissors to cut lace or material they must remain very sharp; if you use these same scissors to cut paper they will become blunt and useless for their original task. If you use a wide range of media, for example lace, tape etc., you should consider having several pairs. Scissors can vary greatly in price depending on their quality. It is worth having one pair of really sharp scissors for materials such as fibreglass, silk and other fine materials. Curved scissors are a good tool for cutting out designs on tips when creating 3D designs. You should also have one pair of scissors, which can be a cheaper pair, for cutting paper. Again remember to clean and sterilise between clients.

Combi drill

Transfers

Combination drill

In order to achieve a hole and secure posted, dangle or charm jewellery it is essential to have a small hand combination drill in your nail art kit. A combination drill has a screw thread with a sharp point at one end, and, at the other end, a tiny socket. This is a specialised tool that fits most post secure charms.

The range of products needed to perform basic nail art treatments

Transfers

Transfers come in a wide range of designs:

- flowers
- french
- lace
- picture themes that will run across all the fingers on one hand
- detailed pictures

Transfers are available as water release or self-adhesive. There are some terrific designs available which can transform nails in seconds. The designs can be intricate and far more detailed than anything that can be hand painted.

Water release transfers

Water release transfers tend to be more detailed and are very delicate. In order to use them you need to soak the required design or use a cotton bud dampened with water. Rub the reverse of the transfer to release it from the backing and then slide it off with your thumb or tweezers and position as required on the nail.

Self-adhesive transfers

Self-adhesive transfers tend to be thicker, less detailed and have an embossed appearance. To use them, you peel off the backing sheet

Foils and adhesives

Polish secure charms

Rhinestones

and place the design on the nail using a flat pair of tweezers. When storing this type of transfer, protect from dust and nail filings, as this could destroy the adhesion on the back and ruin the overall design.

Foil and adhesive

Foils can give some fantastic results. They have a metallic finish and come in various colours and patterns. They must be used with foil adhesive and placed with the pattern facing upwards, then rubbed gently onto the nail with your thumb.

For best results wait until the adhesive becomes translucent/invisible before placing the foil. Remember, wherever you place the foil adhesive the foil will attach. If there are gaps in your design after you have removed the foil then you can reapply the adhesive, but only where the gaps are, or you risk lifting the foil from your design.

Polish secure items

Using polish secure jewellery and gems can liven up any design. They are simple to use, apply and remove. There are many sizes and colours of gems available and the more adventurous may like to try out square, oval and oblong shapes.

Rhinestones

Rhinestones give a design a fantastic look because of the prisms. Look out for round, square, oval and triangle shapes that give your designs a 3D effect. The use of one stone in a simple painted flower or transfer can be really spectacular.

Rhinestones come in many shapes, sizes and colours. They are polish secure items and as such adhere to wet polish. The best way to pick them up is with an orangewood stick tipped with Blu® Tack or top coat.

Flat-stones

Flat-stones

Flat-stones come in a variety of shapes, sizes and colours. They are polish secure items and as such adhere to wet polish. The best way to pick up flat-stones is with a dampened orangewood stick, as Blu® Tack tends to be too sticky to let them go.

Flat-stones are a good alternative to rhinestones as they are not easily knocked off, are a lot smaller and are very competitively priced. Always try a sample before buying large quantities, as the cheaper makes lose their shine and colour when top coat has been applied.

Pearls

Pearls come in many sizes – from tiny to quite large. Be careful when designing your image, as large pearls can be very proud and not a good medium for the heavy handed client to wear. Pearls can look beautiful when applied to a bride who has had a French design hand painted or airbrushed onto her nails.

Technical Tip

Look out for flat-sided pearls – they are easier to apply to the surface of the nail.

Glitter dust

This is a fine, sparkly powder that looks great when applied to a nail design. It can be tailored to match a client's outfit for a special occasion and looks especially good with a dark background polish. Experiment with mixing glitter dusts on a palette.

Glitter dust

Glitter dust must be applied with a sable brush and glitter dust mixer. Dip a clean brush into the mixer and then take it out, allowing the first drop to drip back into the bottle. There should be a smaller bead on the end of the brush, which you then mix with the glitter. You must roll your brush with the mixer to pick up the glitter – not jut dip it in – or you will not be able to work as well when designing your required look.

Remember to clean your brush after each application of glitter before dipping it back into the mixer – use a dappen dish filled with polish remover.

Technical Tip

Try using glitter dust on toenail designs – it really adds a wow factor under bright light.

Technical Tip

Practise with the size of the beads and the ratio of mixer to glitter. It can make a difference to the overall look if there is not enough glitter in your bead to cover the area of the design and it could end up looking just like a top coat instead of a nice thick glitter mix.

Studs and leaves

These are polish secure shapes that come in silver and gold, or metal colours, and can create very interesting and detailed designs. The studs tend to be hollow and must be placed correctly into wet enamel – their adhesion to nails is very good due to their being hollow.

Technical Tip

When using studs the hollow must be placed down onto the surface of the wet polish, so make sure it is picked up with the domed side upwards. It is very hard to turn a stud over once applied and you might have to re-polish the nails. For longer lasting wear, for instance on toes, studs could be applied with a gel adhesive, but this process should only be carried out by experienced nail technicians and the polish needs to be completely dry.

Charms

Technical Tip

It is best to use a clasp fitting that can be removed by the client when required, e.g., for housework, washing hair, etc.

Safety Tip

It is best to inform your client about removal and recommend the appropriate type of charm suitable for their lifestyle. Remember if a dangle gets caught it could cause damage to the natural nail.

Striping tape

Striping tape comes in many colours, including metallic finishes. It is a fun way to create a simple but effective design with the minimum of fuss and can be used to enhance designs or to neaten the edge where two colours meet. Try using some of the patterned and textured finishes such as snakeskin, hearts, diamonds, holograms, etc. Non-adhesive striping tape needs to be pressed gently into wet polish and may need a small amount of nail adhesive to secure the ends once they have been cut. Some striping tapes come with an adhesive backing and just need to be cut and pressed onto dry polish and have a top coat applied to keep the tape in place.

Charms

Charms are available in two types: posted or dangle. They should only be fitted to nail enhancements or natural nail overlays.

Posted charms

Posted charms are generally placed through a hole in the nail made by a combination drill and are secured by tightening the nut with the socket at the other end of the combination drill. It is best to turn the client's nail upside down and use a corkboard as a cushion underneath. Gently rotate the drill backwards and forwards until a hole has been made. Make sure that you support the client's finger with your thumb to hold it firmly whilst drilling. It is better to make the hole in the nail before polishing or wait until the polish is thoroughly dry before attempting to drill the hole.

Dangle charms

Dangle charms are secured through a hole made in the nail by a combination drill and secured by a link. You may need tweezers to help you with this technique.

Paints

A nail artist should have a good selection of paint which includes primary, opalescent, neon, metallic, pearlescent, etc. Acrylic paints

Paints

Technical Tip

Not all manufacturers assume that their paints are going to be used on fingernails and although the paint may not be harmful it may not be possible to buy complementary products such as sealants, top coats and base coats. You may need to experiment with your designs and paints before performing treatments on your clients.

Technical Tip

Using the primary colours and black and white it is possible to create most colours in the spectrum.

Nail kit

are a good medium to work with and can create good colour depth. Watercolours can be less vivid and vibrant when applied in a nail art treatment. You should always consider the safety aspects when using paints on your clients. Check with your supplier that they can be used on human nails and that they will not have any harmful effects by being near the skin or in your breathing zone. If your supplier is not sure that the paint can be used on fingernails then contact the manufacturer to see if it is suitable and keep the letter on file to ensure that the manufacturer's liability remains intact. If buying your supplies from a nail art supplier or manufacturer you should not have to worry, but if you shop from an art, hobby or craft shop then you will probably have to do some homework on the safety aspects of the paints.

You must ensure when selecting your paints that you have the appropriate base and top coats. If they do not complement one another you may find that the paint cracks when top coat is applied or that the paint is dragged down the nail because the top coat has softened the paint. Although this may create an interesting design, it may not be the look you intended to create.

Complementary products for your nail art kit

Embossing kit

An embosser is like a syringe full of paint in various colours. It is held in the palm of the hand and the end part is pressed down to allow paint to come out of the small hole in the end. This tool allows the most precise control of paint but the designs you can create are limited. The results are unique 3D designs. Designs can be completed in as little as ten minutes and are achieved by combining the three basic strokes of dots, lines and commas. The designs are quite proud and some clients may want a design that is more subtle, so make sure that you have a good range of samples for your clients to choose from.

Marbliser kit

Every marbled design is different depending on the use of colours. A few drops of each colour are dropped into tepid water and mixed with a pin. The client's nail is then gently dragged through the water and pulled out leaving the design on the nail. The design is then top coated. It can be quite a messy treatment to perform. Care must be taken not to get paint on your client's jewellery or clothes. You will need to allow extra time for the oil-based paint to dry out.

Technical Tip

Remember that this is an oil-based paint and can be extremely difficult to remove from the finger. Make sure that you use the correct remover to get the paint off the skin without drying out the skin and that extra time is allowed for cleaning up.

Gold and silver leaf

Gold/silver leaf

Gold and silver leaf is extremely fine and delicate. It will adhere to wet polish with the aid of a pointed orangewood stick; it works best shredded into tiny pieces which will allow the enamel colour to show through. If used to cover the whole nail you will encounter creases that may detract from your overall design. Gold and silver leaf is a good medium to use in 3D designs. It is available from art, hobby, craft or nail suppliers, but shop around for the best prices as it can be quite expensive to buy. Make sure you price this treatment according to the materials used and the extra time that it takes.

Polishing techniques

Learning objectives

In this section we will learn about:

- **the tools, equipment and products needed**
- **achieving a perfect one colour polish**
- **using various techniques to create a perfect French polish**
- **shaping and shading techniques**
- **some useful technical tips**

Although it is the most basic treatment a manicurist or nail technician will perform, polishing is greatly underestimated. Polishing nails is an art form in itself and, as any new technician will tell you, it takes a great deal of practice to master it fully. It is not just about getting straight lines and not allowing polish on to the skin, but also about how much polish to take up on each brush application. It is like learning to drive a car; it takes co-ordination of a lot of skill. To perform a French polish perfectly takes even more skill.

Courtesy of Creative Nail Design

Products, tools and equipment

Oils

There are many oils on the market and most reputable nail companies market oils as a retail item. If you are using oil on your client within the treatment it gives you the opportunity to talk about homecare and the retail products every client needs. Oils can be used to help dry, split cuticles and also help to dry polish.

Put a thin layer of oil over the entire nail surface once the nails are 'touch dry'. Leave your client for 5 minutes by which time the nails should be dry and all the oil absorbed into the surrounding soft tissue. A good example to give a client on why they should use oil is to ask: 'How many times do you wash your hands in one day? Would you wash your hair or face as many times and not use conditioners or moisturisers?'

Make sure you use a good grade of oil that will absorb into the nail enhancement and soft tissue and not a cheap mineral oil that will just sit on the surface and do nothing. Check with the manufacturer what the key ingredients are in all products you are using, including oils. Oils can be referred to as fats and may have been extracted from animal or plant sources. Like all organic products, that is those derived from living matter (e.g. olive oil from olives), they can degrade with time and 'go off' or become smelly! They need to be kept in a dark, cool cupboard to ensure a longer shelf life.

Cotton wool and orangewood stick

If you wind a very small amount of cotton wool around the end of an orangewood stick, it can be used to clean any dust from underneath the nail. If the polish has 'bled' into the cuticle or sidewall, use a small amount of polish remover on the end of an orangewood stick tipped in cotton wool to remove it.

Enamel removers

Removers are used to dissolve and remove nail enamels from the nail. They can also be used to 'squeak' or de-oil the nail before applying polish on the natural nail, as the natural nail will hold oils on its surface.

The main ingredient in most removers is acetone and some organic solvents. However, the majority of nail companies use non-acetone removers, as acetone is believed to weaken tips, various wraps (i.e. fibreglass) and acrylics. Most removers now use solvents that are less drying and some may have added moisturising agents, such as aloe vera. Other ingredients include colourings to distinguish removers from other liquids, perfumes or fragrances, water and alcohol.

Base coat

Always use a good quality base coat specific to that purpose, that is, not one which can serve as a base and top coat. Base coat and top coat have different qualities and polish will last longer if these are used properly. Base coat is the first step in any polish procedure and a good base coat will stay sticky even when dry. This allows the polish to adhere really well and helps it to last longer.

Base coats usually contain more resin than coloured polishes, which gives them their tacky consistency and enable them to adhere to the nail. Most base coats are clear, although some may have a colour additive purely to distinguish them from other clear polishes such as top coats and nail strengtheners or hardeners. Some of the main ingredients are:

- resins and solvents
- nitrocellulose
- ethyl acetate and butyl acetate
- isopropyl alcohol

You may wish to use a nail strengthener or hardener as a base on a natural nail. Make sure you follow the manufacturer's instructions for application and consequently advise clients about continued use.

A ridge filler could also be used to help the appearance of the final polish look smoother. Ridge fillers are usually thicker than base coats and help to camouflage any irregularities or deep ridges in the nail. They take slightly longer to dry than normal base coats. Base coats usually have a lower viscosity and are lower in non-volatile ingredients which allows them to dry more quickly and be applied more thinly.

Courtesy of Creative Nail Design

Creative polishes

To apply the base coat

- Make sure the nail is free from dust and oil.
- Pull the brush out of the bottle, pressing against one side to get the correct measure of base coat needed.
- Press the bead into the middle of the nail about 3 mm away from the cuticle, towards the cuticle and then pull it down in a vertical line to the free edge leaving 1–2 mm margin at the cuticle area.
- Turn finger slightly to the left and repeat, leaving 1–2 mm free margin.
- Turn finger to the other side and cover the right side of the nail.
- Three thin strokes should be plenty to cover the entire nail.
- Allow a few minutes to dry, although the surface should stay slightly tacky.
- Nails are now ready to be polished.

Enamels and polishes

Coloured polishes, enamels or lacquers (pronounced *lack-er*) – the names all refer to the same item – are used to add colour or high gloss to the natural nail. Every week companies around the world design new colours and the choice we have as professionals is astounding and very beautiful. Nail polishes have been available since the early 1900s and were first made in the USA but various races have been decorating their hands and nails for centuries. Some of these include the ancient Indians, Egyptians and Chinese. They used natural products such as henna and other plant extracts.

The polishes we use today are made up of a mixture of various chemicals that allow us to produce beautiful, many coloured and long lasting nail designs. A brief description of some of the most used chemical ingredients in polishes follows.

- *Nitrocellulose* is a film-forming substance which is the bulk product of most polishes. It needs the addition of other chemicals to help with drying, to counteract shrinking and to stop discoloration with ageing.
- *Resins* are used to help reduce shrinkage when a polish dries, as well as improve adhesion and flexibility. Resins provide the finish gloss on the polish surface but unfortunately they reduce the hardness of the polish.
- *Solvents* are used to alter the consistency of a polish. The consistency must be right to allow even coverage with the brush. Butyl and ethyl acetate are the main solvents used to 'wet' the nitrocellulose. It is normally mixed with toluene to stabilise ingredients and regulate evaporation.
- *Plasticisers* are used to regulate evaporation and reduce shrinkage. Plasticisers can improve a polish's flexibility but can also prevent it from adhering to the natural nail.

- *Colorants*. There are two types of polish:
  – cream
  – pearlised

  Cream polish contains insoluble colours mixed with iron oxide and titanium dioxide. Pearl polishes get their effect from reflective transparent crystals of guanine. These can be obtained from the scales of fish or from synthetic products such as mica flakes that are coated with titanium dioxide. A cheaper alternative is to use bismuth-coated mica flakes.

Although it is traditional to use cotton wool to remove polish or to squeak the nail before the application of polish, you will sometimes find it leaves tiny fibres on the nail, no matter how careful you are. Lint-free pads are now available and are excellent for absorbing the right amount of liquid and leaving the nail free of fibres. This means that fewer pads and less polish remover are used. One pad will remove the bulk of the polish from all ten nails and a second will remove excess polish. A further advantage is that you are not constantly soaking your client's skin and drying it out with large amounts of polish remover. Try to purchase pads with a tab for you to hold, as this will prevent your fingers being overexposed to chemicals and the polish and nail design that you are wearing from being damaged.

It is always wise to test polishes before you buy, especially if you are buying in a whole range from one supplier. Either ask for a sample bottle or try a test on your own nails for a few hours or even a few days. See how the polishes stand up to the test of time and how easy they are to apply.

Here are a few qualities to look for in a good polish:

- even colour consistency
- good colour after two coats
- smooth flow with no streaks when applied
- dries to a high gloss finish
- colour pigment does not stain natural nail
- has a quick drying time
- no colour separation in bottle
- should dry to a hard, scratch-resistant coating

Nail polishes can be thinned with a solvent or a mixture of solvents that form the same base as the polish. You must use the thinner compatible with your range of polishes or one that your manufacturer recommends for your particular range.

Top coats

Top coats are used to seal polish in and provide a hard gloss protective cover for natural nails or coloured enamels. A top coat should be applied as a thin, even colour over the whole nail. However, remember to leave that tiny free margin around the cuticle and sidewall.

Some top coats might also act as quick dries, but it is always best to use products that are made specifically for that purpose. Don't forget, if a product makes a spectacular claim, always test it before buying.

Apply top coat in the same way as base and polish (see below). One thin coat only is required.

Quick dries

A nail quick dry is optional and doesn't need to be used for any other reason than that the client needs to be drier quicker. Quick dries can come in the form of:

- polishes/top coats
- sprays
- electric or battery blow-dryers
- oils

Creative polish rack

Application of polish

The application of base coat, polish and top coat are all basically the same. You will need to consider the size and shape of the nail when deciding on the amount of polish for each application and possibly how many strokes for each nail. Obviously a short, round nail will require a different amount of polish from a very long, square nail.

Here is the easiest way to hold the polish bottle.

- If you are right handed, hold the polish in your left hand and vice versa.
- Hold the bottle in the palm of your hand.
- Support the bottle with your ring and little finger against the pad of muscle at the base of your thumb.
- Tilt the bottle slightly – the less polish there is in the bottle the further down the palm you will have to tilt the bottle to reach the polish at the bottom.
- Hold client's finger in between your index and middle finger and your thumb.
- Rotate client's finger and hold back lateral sidewalls when polishing to get an even coverage without touching any soft tissue.

Technical Tip

Never use polish remover to thin down your polish. Remover may contain oils and water which would prevent the polish from hardening properly.

Technical Tip

The client's arm should be leaning on the desk for stability when polishing. It is much more difficult to achieve an even coverage if your client's hand is waving in the air.

There are various ways of applying polish but the easiest is the three-step method (see below). The first coat should be a thin layer, leaving a 1–2 mm margin free in the cuticle area and along the sidewalls.

1. Apply the first stroke as for the base coat, place the brush three-quarters of the way down the nail in the centre of the nail, pushing the colour slightly up to the cuticle without leaking into the soft tissue.
2. Slightly turn the finger to one side and cover the left side of the nail, making sure the brush is pulled all the way down to the free edge.
3. Proceed in the same way for the right side of the nail.

Polish application

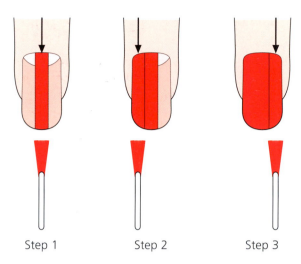

Step 1   Step 2   Step 3

You would apply a second coat the same manner, but use very slightly more polish for good coverage. Make sure all the edges are covered and the surface is smooth. You may need to add another coat, if the consistency of the polish is thin, to deepen the colour.

Here are a few more tips to help your polish application techniques.

- By placing the brush in the middle of the nail plate the majority of the polish will be in such a position that it can be worked evenly over the entire nail.
- Do not keep stroking the brush over the surface of the nail as the solvent is evaporating and the polish will become tacky and streaky.
- If mistakes like streaking or a missed area do occur, the second coat will usually rectify this.
- If a larger mistake occurs, the nail should be cleaned off and started again.
- Make no more than 4 strokes on a small nail and 6 on a larger nail.
- If a client has a wide nail, leave a free margin along the sidewalls to give the illusion of a slimmer and longer nail.
- If you have a client who constantly 'chips' their polish along the free edge, take a small nail art brush and remove 1–2 mm of the polish along the free edge.
- If a client smudges a nail before you have finished you can take a small amount of polish on the brush and work over the smudge to soften it and then brush over the entire nail to make it smooth.
- Sell a bottle of the same colour polish to the client for touching up or for matching their toes to their fingers.
- Suggest colours that complement skin tone as well as make-up and clothes.

Point to Remember

Ask your clients for payment, to get out their car keys, make their next appointment and help them put on their coats before polish application. This will avoid 'digs' and 'smudges' in the fresh polish.

Make sure your client does not bang his or her hands down on a dusty tissue or towel as this will cause the dust to rise up and land on the wet polish. There is no way to rectify this other than to start again.

Creating a perfect French polish

The French polish has got to be the most requested treatment within manicures and nail enhancement treatments. As a nail technician, you will either love it or hate it. A significant number of manicurists and nail technicians do not offer it simply because they find it difficult to perform. You will need to consider these points before attempting the French look:

- the nails have some free edge, but not too much
- your enamels or polishes are not thick and sticky
- you have a steady hand

Performing a French manicure can make a short nail look longer and slimmer if done properly. Whether you are using polishes or nail enhancement products, look at how a smile line makes the nail look as if it is smiling or how a line can look like a grimace or even make it look sad.

The easiest way to perform a French finish is by airbrushing, but this can be expensive to set up. A French finish can be done in three ways:

- chevron
- rounded – starting with chevron
- rounded

You will see that the white starts off as a chevron and then you turn it into a smile.

Chevron and rounded-chevron

- Apply your base coat as before.
- Apply white polish to the free edge of the nail starting on the left and sweeping the brush across and down to the bottom right hand corner.
- Repeat on the other side, working from right to left.
- If the smile effect is required, swipe the brush across the nail, but not in a straight line, dipping it slightly to achieve a curve.
- Apply clear, sheer pink, peach or natural polish over the entire nail using the 3-stroke method as before. Be careful to use the correct shade for your client's skin tone.
- Apply a top coat over the entire nail.

Rounded

- Pull the brush out of the side of the bottle and lose about half the polish.
- Take the side of the brush with enamel on and swipe across from one side to the other, dipping slightly in the middle to create a smile line.

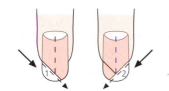

French polish – chevron

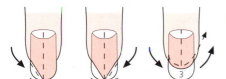

French polish – rounded

- Take the brush and work the bulk of the polish down the nail to the free edge in 3 strokes (less if it is a small nail). Work down the middle and then either side.

- Use the chosen colour on the rest of the nail, as above.

- Apply top coat, as above.

Technical Tips

Practise your smiles on tips or practice cards to achieve deeper curves. The French polish is so versatile you can incorporate it with other artistic designs such as flowers, pearls, rhinestones, lace and many other techniques.

Have some tips on a display board to show your clients. Remember not everyone will know what a French polish is.

You will see at this stage that the white is in the shape of a chevron, some clients prefer this to the smile line. You could always add a little flower, pearl or diamante in the 'V' for artistic effect.

You may use white polish on the back of the free edge if the natural nail is yellow or discoloured and your client wants to camouflage this. Make sure you also use a top coat if using white under the free edge.

Using a top coat on top of a colour will prevent chipping and peeling of the enamel.

Remember polish is drying so don't overwork it, as you will get streaking. Place the polish where you want it and let it find its own level.

You can always neaten a smile line with a small art brush and some polish remover or nail dehydrator.

Always allow a little longer for a French polish to dry.

Try not to let clients blow on their nails, as inevitably they will smudge one while their hands are wafting around.

Do not use polish driers between polish layers as this will cause the polish to peel or bubble.

Step-by-step freehand nail art designs

Learning objectives

In this section you will learn about:

- **basic hand painting techniques with various tools**

- **the basic procedures for using nail art products**

- **a number of step-by-step freehand nail art designs**

Everyone has to start somewhere, even those who are naturally artistic. We have called this section 'freehand nail art' because the products and techniques are easy for everyone to learn. They do not rely on the use of expensive equipment and you do not need to be artistic. If you want to experiment further, then just expand on the designs in the book or experiment with the products and techniques to design your own work. The cost of setting yourself up to perform these designs is minimal compared, for example, to setting up for airbrush treatments. We have found over the last five years that our salon clientele can be as young as 14 years old – they all love nail art and designing their own look. Hopefully in the near future this service will become a qualification that we can offer young people in colleges and schools. The teenage market for nail art is huge – you only have to look at teen magazines, books and TV shows to see that nails are very important to the 9–16 year old age group. These youngsters are our future clientele and as they mature, they will become more knowledgeable and demanding in the services they seek. It is therefore important that the industry takes note of what these clients want. It is also imperative that we listen to the needs of the young students wishing to come into the nail industry and do not discount the fact that teenagers themselves can provide basic nail art services to our clients. These teenagers can become very valuable Saturday staff or apprentices.

Chevron French with striping

Step-by-step designs

Name of design: Chevron French with striping

Equipment needed:

- Creative Stickey base coat
- Creative Time Square silver polish
- striping brush
- black and silver glitter paint
- top coat

1 Apply base coat to all ten nails.

2 Apply two coats of silver pearlised polish, ensuring good colour coverage on all ten nails.

3 Using the striping brush loaded with black paint, draw a line diagonally across the nail from the edge to just over half way at the base of the nail.

4 Mirror on the other side, taking great care that the centre of the chevron matches the centre of the nail.

5 Fill in the area below the chevron created with 1 coat of black paint followed by 1 of black and silver glitter.

6 Allow paint to dry thoroughly. Apply two coats of top coat for protection.

Name of design: Animal print with polish

Equipment needed:

- Creative Stickey base coat
- Creative Hollywood bronze polish
- liner brush
- black paint
- top coat

Animal print with polish

1 Apply base coat to all ten nails.

2 Apply two coats of Hollywood polish, ensuring good colour coverage on all ten nails.

3 Using the tip of the liner brush start 2 mm in from the side of the nail and pull the brush to the centre and lift. Repeat this down the length of the nail.

4 Repeat action from the other side meeting and joining with the paint in the middle. Repeat again using white paint on the edge of the black line.

5 Allow paint to dry thoroughly. Apply two coats of top coat for protection.

Technical Tip

Try using black and white to create and interesting zebra effect – vary the length of the lines and the angle – create a 'V' in the centre.

Holly leaves

Various designs

French bhindi

Name of design: Holly leaves

Equipment needed:

- Creative Stickey base coat
- Creative Pharoahs Gold polish
- white, green and red paint
- detail brush
- striping brush
- dotting tool
- top coat

1 Apply base coat to all ten nails.

2 Apply two coats of Pharoahs Gold polish, ensuring good colour coverage on all ten nails. Using detail brush and green paint outline two holly leaves in opposing corners and fill in.

3 Using the dotting tool and red paint, dot the red berries at the end of the holly leaves. Red rhinestones or flat-stones could be used instead of paint.

4 Using the striping brush and white paint, pull down the nail moving side to side to create a squiggle effect.

5 Allow paint to dry thoroughly. Apply two coats of top coat for protection.

Name of design: French bhindi design

Equipment needed:

- Creative Stickey base coat
- Creative Cream Puff white enamel
- Creative Moonlight and Roses sheer enamel
- bhindi
- tweezers
- top coat

1 Apply base coat to all ten nails.

2 Apply two coats of Moonlight and Roses polish, ensuring good colour coverage on all ten nails.

3 Using the Cream Puff polish, pull a line one-third of the way up the sidewall diagonally to the opposite corner.

4 Repeat on the opposite side to create a perfect chevron.

5 Allow paint to dry thoroughly. Apply two coats of top coat for protection.

6 Using the tweezers pick up and place the sticky back bhindi on the chevron. Ensure the corners are well pressed down.

Daisies

Name of design: Daisy flowers

Equipment needed:

- Creative Stickey base coat
- Creative Strawberry Smoothie pale pink pearl polish
- marbling tool or colour shaper
- white, blue, red and yellow paint
- top coat

1. Apply base coat to all ten nails.
2. Apply two coats of Strawberry Smoothie polish, ensuring good colour coverage on all ten nails.
3. Using the large end of the marbling tool, loaded with white paint, place five dots to create a flower shape. Reload the marbling tool between each dot so that dots are the same size. Repeat diagonally across the nail.
4. Create two more lines of daisies diagonally across, above the first line.
5. Using the different coloured paints, dot in the centre of the daisies. Rhinestones or flat-stones could be used instead of paint.
6. Allow paint to dry thoroughly. Apply two coats of top coat for protection.

Abstract dotting

Name of design: Abstract dotting

Equipment needed:

- Creative Stickey base coat
- Creative Chilled Champagne polish
- contrasting colour paint
- marbling tool or colour shaper
- top coat

1. Apply base coat to all ten nails.
2. Apply two coats of Chilled Champagne polish, ensuring good colour coverage on all ten nails.
3. Starting in the bottom left-hand corner, place the large end of the marbling tool into the paint and dot onto nail.
4. Create your abstract design using either the same size dots or decreasing.
5. Allow paint to dry thoroughly. Apply two coats of top coat for protection.

Technical Tips

- To create dots of the same size you must dot into the paint between dotting the nail
- If you want the dots to gradually decrease in size you should dot once into the paint and then dot three or more dots onto the nail before reapplying paint

Technical Tips

- Try using complementary colour dots that contrast with the base coat
- Dot the outline of a design and then fill in with different colours
- Swirls are very effective – you could shadow them with a contrasting colour
- Try using neon paints on a dark base colour

Neon paints

Technical Tip

To create dots of the decreasing size you must dot into the paint only once.

Heart with dots

Technical Tip

To create dots of the same size you must dot into the paint between each dotting of the nail.

Name of design: Neon paints using marbling tool

Equipment needed:

- Creative Stickey base coat
- Creative Voodoo black polish
- marbling tool or colour shaper
- neon paints: yellow, blue and red
- top coat

1 Apply base coat to all ten nails.
2 Apply two coats of Voodoo polish, ensuring good colour coverage on all ten nails.
3 Starting at the side or edge of the nail and using the large end of the marbling tool loaded with yellow paint, place a dot onto the nail and, without reloading with paint, place more dots in a curve shape so the dots decrease in size.
4 Reload marbling tool with red paint and repeat.
5 Reload marbling tool with blue paint and repeat.
6 Allow paint to dry thoroughly. Apply two coats of top coat for protection.

Name of design: Heart shape with dots

Equipment needed:

- Creative Stickey base coat
- Creative Tabloid red polish
- marbling tool or colour shaper
- white paint
- top coat

1 Apply base coat to all ten nails.
2 Apply two coats of Tabloid red polish, ensuring good colour coverage on all ten nails.
3 Starting in the centre of the nail and using the large end of the marbling tool loaded with white paint, create a heart shape on the nail.

4 Reload marbling tool with white paint and fill in the area outside the heart shape with dots.

5 Allow paint to dry thoroughly. Apply two coats of top coat for protection.

Diamond shape dotting

Name of design: Diamond shape dotting

Equipment needed:

- Creative Stickey base coat
- Creative Snakebite brown polish
- marbling tool or colour shaper
- white paint
- top coat

1 Apply base coat to all ten nails.

2 Apply two coats of Snakebite brown polish, ensuring good colour coverage on all ten nails.

3 Starting approximately two-thirds of the way up the nail, in the centre, place the large end of the marbling tool loaded with white paint, and dot onto nail.

Reload marbling tool loaded with white paint and repeat one-third up from the free edge.

Place a dot at the side walls between the two dots. Fill in with dots between these four points to create a diamond shape in the middle of the nail.

4 Using the large end of the marbling tool and white paint, place a dot the top of the nail just above the first dot. This time dot in a straight line towards the cuticle without reloading the paint, so that the dots decease in size. Repeat at the tip of diamond below.

5 Fill in the area surrounding the diamond with dots using the marbling tool loaded with white paint.

6 Allow paint to dry thoroughly. Apply two coats of top coat for protection.

Three colour strip with rhinestones

Name of design: Three colour strip from corner with rhinestones

Equipment needed:

- Creative Stickey base coat
- Creative Gypsy-a-Go-Go pink polish
- striping brush
- white, magenta and silver glitter paint
- orangewood stick with Blu® Tack
- diamond rhinestones
- top coat

1 Apply base coat to all ten nails.

2 Apply two coats of a Gypsy-a-Go-Go pink polish, ensuring good colour coverage on all ten nails.

3 With white paint and a striping brush, start at the left-hand corner and pull the striping brush vertically across the nail with a sweeping movement. Reload paint onto brush and make two smaller sweeping curves – one above and one below.

4 With a clean brush loaded with magenta, repeat the above step between the three white lines.

5 With a clean brush loaded with silver glitter, highlight the three white lines.

6 Allow paint to dry thoroughly. Apply two coats of top coat for protection. Using an orangewood stick tipped with Blu® Tack, pick up a single diamond rhinestone and place in the left hand corner of the design.

Name of design: Two colour strip from corner

Equipment needed:

- Creative Stickey base coat
- Creative Crusade brown polish
- striping brush
- white and black paint
- top coat

Two colour strip from corner

Technical Tip

Try substituting one of the colours with glitter paint for a more dramatic design.

1 Apply base coat to all ten nails.

2 Apply two coats of Crusade polish, ensuring good colour coverage on all ten nails.

3 With black paint and striping brush, start at the left-hand corner and pull the striping brush vertically across the nail with a sweeping movement. Reload paint onto brush and make two smaller sweeping curves – one above and one below.

4 With a clean brush loaded with white, repeat the above movements, placing the white stripes between the three black lines.

5 Allow paint to dry thoroughly. Apply two coats of top coat for protection.

Name of design: One colour strip with dotting from corner

Equipment needed:

- Creative Stickey base coat
- red polish
- striping brush
- gold and white paint
- marbling tool
- top coat

One colour strip with dots in corner

1 Apply base coat to all ten nails.

2 Apply two coats of red polish, ensuring good colour coverage on all ten nails.

3 With gold paint and striping brush start at the left-hand corner and pull the striping brush vertically across the nail with a sweeping movement. Reload paint onto brush and make two smaller sweeping curves – one above and one below.

4 Using the large end of the dotting tool, pick up white paint and starting in the left-hand corner dot 5 or 6 times in a curving movement between the gold lines without reloading marbling tool with paint. This will make the dots decrease in size.

5 Allow paint to dry thoroughly. Apply two coats of top coat for protection.

Name of design: Zebra print red and black with striping brush

Equipment needed:

- Creative Stickey base coat
- Creative Hollywood red polish
- striping brush
- black paint
- top coat

1 Apply base coat to all ten nails.

2 Apply two coats of Hollywood red polish, ensuring good colour coverage on all ten nails.

3 Starting from the left, pull striping brush loaded with black over two-thirds of the nail, getting thinner towards the end.

4 Repeat this action from the other side, in between the lines you have already created.

5 Allow paint to dry thoroughly. Apply two coats of top coat for protection.

Zebra print

Technical Tip

You could slightly curve the line for a more interesting design.

Name of design: Cross hatch two colour striping

Equipment needed:

- Creative Stickey base coat
- Creative Voodoo polish
- striping brush
- white and gold paint
- top coat

1 Apply base coat to all ten nails.

2 Apply two coats of Voodoo polish, ensuring good colour coverage on all ten nails.

3 Starting two-thirds of the way down the nail, use the white paint and striping brush to draw three diagonal lines. Repeat in the other direction.

4 Using a clean striping brush and the gold paint draw three diagonal lines between the white lines. Repeat in the other direction.

5 Allow paint to dry thoroughly. Apply two coats of top coat for protection.

Cross hatch

Technical Tip

You could substitute the striping brush and paint for flexi brushes.

Copper base with foil

Foil group

Red with gold foil

Name of design: Copper base with foil

Equipment needed:

- Creative Stickey base coat
- Creative Burning Embers polish
- foil adhesive
- foil
- foil sealant
- top coat

1   Apply base coat to all ten nails.

2   Apply two coats of Burning Embers copper enamel, ensuring good colour coverage on all ten nails.

3   Allow enamel to dry slightly, paint foil adhesive in the required design. Try different designs e.g. tiger, zebra or random.

4   Wait for the adhesive to become translucent, press the foil lightly so the design side is facing upwards and press.

5   Use the sealant to cover the design.

6   Apply coat of top coat for protection.

Name of design: Red with gold foil French design

Equipment needed:

- Creative Stickey base coat
- Creative Company Red polish
- gold foil
- foil sealant
- top coat

1   Apply base coat to all ten nails.

2   Apply two coats of Company Red, ensuring good colour coverage on all ten nails.

3   Allow enamel to dry slightly, paint foil adhesive in the French manicure design. Try a French chevron.

4   Wait for the adhesive to become translucent, press the foil lightly so the design side is facing upwards and press.

5   Use the sealant to cover the design.

6   Apply coat of top coat for protection.

Marbling red and white

Name of design: Marbling red and white

Equipment needed:

- Creative Stickey base coat
- Creative Cream Puff white polish
- red and white contrasting nail paints
- marbling tool
- top coat

1 Apply base coat to all ten nails.
2 Apply two coats of Cream Puff polish, ensuring good colour coverage on all ten nails.
3 Using the large end of the marbling tool, place drops of red and white contrasting nail paint onto the corner of the nail.
4 Clean marbling tool.
5 Using both ends of the marbling tool, swirl red paint into the other colour to create a marbling effect. Each end of the marbling tool will give you a different sized swirl.
6 Allow paint to dry thoroughly. Apply two coats of top coat for protection.

Group marbling

Technical Tip

- Use contrasting colours for a dramatic effect
- Use acrylic paints – these allow you more time to create your design; although nail enamel could be used you will have less time to perfect your design
- Do not overblend colours otherwise they become a third colour and you will lose the design

Name of design: Marbling blue, purple and white

Equipment needed:

- Creative Stickey base coat
- Creative Royalty polish
- 2–3 contrasting colour paints
- marbling tool
- top coat

1 Apply base coat to all ten nails.
2 Apply two coats of Royalty polish, ensuring good colour coverage on all ten nails.
3 Using the large end of the marbling tool place drops of first, second and third contrasting nail paint onto the corner of the nail.
4 Clean marbling tool.
5 Using both ends of the marbling tool, swirl one colour of paint into the other to create a marbling effect. Each end of the marbling tool will give you a different sized swirl.
6 Allow paint to dry thoroughly. Apply two coats of top coat for protection.

Marbling blue, purple and white

Black and red glitter heart

Name of design: Black with red glitter dust French and heart

Equipment needed:

- Creative Stickey base coat
- Creative Voodoo polish
- red glitter dust
- glitter dust brush – sable
- dappen dish
- polish remover
- top coat

1 Apply base coat to all ten nails. Apply two coats of Creative Voodoo polish, ensuring good colour coverage on all ten nails.

2 Put tip of glitter brush in mixer, allow the first drop of mixer to fall off the brush, then roll into the glitter and pick up the glitter dust.

3 Place onto the polished nail and press and work into the French smile design. Remember to flatten down the glitter or the design will be too proud. Clean the brush in the dappen dish filled with polish remover before placing back into the mixer or you will contaminate your mixer.

4 Repeat creating the heart shape just above the smile line.

5 Once the glitter has dried, apply coat of top coat for protection.

Metallic copper and gold glitter

Name of design: Metallic copper and gold glitter design

Equipment needed:

- Creative Stickey base coat
- Creative Burning Embers metallic copper polish
- gold glitter dust
- glitter dust brush – sable
- dappen dish
- polish remover
- top coat

1 Apply base coat to all ten nails.

2 Apply two coats of Creative Burning Embers, ensuring good colour coverage on all ten nails.

3 Put tip of glitter brush in mixer, allow the first drop of mixer to fall off the brush, then roll into the glitter and pick up the glitter dust.

4 Place onto the polished nail and press and work down the nail to create long swirls. Remember to flatten down the glitter or the design will be too proud. Clean the brush in the dappen dish filled with polish remover before placing back into the mixer or you will contaminate your mixer.

5 Repeat step, but this time work upwards on the nail.

6 Once the glitter has dried, apply coat of top coat for protection.

Cappucino and gold/silver glitter dust

Name of design: Iced Cappuccino with gold and silver glitter dust

Equipment needed:

- Creative Stickey base coat
- Creative Iced Cappuccino polish
- gold and silver glitter dust
- glitter dust brush – sable
- dappen dish
- polish remover
- top coat

1   Apply base coat to all ten nails. Apply two coats of Creative Iced Cappuccino enamel, ensuring good colour coverage on all ten nails.

2   Put tip of glitter brush in mixer, allow the first drop of mixer to fall off the brush, then roll into the glitter and pick up the glitter dust.

3   Place onto the polished nail and press and work down the nail into required shapes. Remember to flatten down the glitter or the design will be too proud. Clean the brush in the dappen dish filled with polish remover before placing back into the mixer or you will contaminate your mixer.

4   Repeat the process with different colour glitter to add dimension to the design.

5   Allow glitter to dry and apply coat of top coat for protection.

Glitter dust group

Name of design: Neon glitter dust

Equipment needed:

- Creative Stickey base coat
- Creative Super Sexy polish
- blue, pink and gold glitter dust
- glitter dust brush – sable
- dappen dish
- polish remover
- marble/dotting tool
- blue, gold and pink paint
- top coat

1   Apply base coat to all ten nails. Apply two coats of Creative Super Sexy enamel, ensuring good colour coverage on all ten nails.

2   Put tip of glitter brush in mixer, allow the first drop of mixer to fall off the brush, then roll into the glitter and pick up the glitter dust.

3   Place onto the polished nail and press and work into various shapes, leaving gaps in between. Remember to flatten down the glitter or the design will be too proud. Clean the brush in the

Neon glitter dust

dappen dish filled with polish remover before placing back into the mixer or you will contaminate your mixer.

4 Repeat with other colours, apply in different shapes.

5 Using the marble/dotting tool and follow the glitter dust shapes you have created with either blue, gold or pink paint.

6 Allow glitter and paint to dry and then apply coat of top coat for protection.

Flat-stone design

Name of design: General flat-stone design

Equipment needed:

- Creative Stickey base coat
- Creative Voodoo or Hotski to Tchotchske polishes
- flat-stones
- dampened orangewood stick
- top coat

1 Apply base coat to all ten nails.

2 Apply two coats of chosen Creative polishes, ensuring good colour coverage on all ten nails.

3 Using the dampened orangewood stick, pick up and place flat-stones or stars into wet polish.

4 Apply two coats of top coat for protection.

Name of design: Chevron metallic with studs/rhinestones

Equipment needed:

- Creative Stickey base coat
- Creative Cream Puff polish
- Creative Candy Apple polish
- studs/rhinestones
- orangewood stick tipped with Blu® Tack
- top coat

Group rhinestones

1 Apply base coat to all ten nails.

2 Apply two coats of Cream Puff white polish, ensuring good colour coverage on all ten nails.

3 Using the Candy Apple red polish, pull a line one-third of the way up the sidewall diagonally to the opposite corner.

4 Repeat on the opposite side to create a perfect chevron.

5 Allow paint to dry thoroughly. Apply two coats of top coat for protection.

6 Using the orangewood stick tipped with Blu® Tack place the rhinestones/studs in a line along the edge of the metallic red chevron. Alternatively you can follow the line down to the free edge as we have done in the pictures.

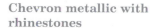

Chevron metallic with rhinestones

Polish secure design – square crystals

Name of design: Polish secure design using square crystals

Equipment needed:

- Creative Stickey base coat
- Creative King's Ransom gold enamel
- square crystals
- gold rhinestones
- orangewood stick tipped with Blu® Tack
- top coat

1 Apply base coat to all ten nails.

2 Apply two coats of King's Ransom gold polish, ensuring good colour coverage on all ten nails.

3 Allow paint to dry thoroughly. Apply two coats of top coat for protection.

4 Using the orangewood stick tipped with Blu® Tack, pick up and place a square crystal two-thirds of the way up the nail; directly below place a rhinestone.

5 Alternate square crystals and rhinestones until reaching approximately 5 mm from the free edge. Continue with rhinestones only until the free edge.

6 At the top of the design use rhinestones to create a lunula shape.

7 Ensure rhinestones and crystals are embedded into wet polish on each nail before proceeding onto next nail.

Polish secure – stud flower

Name of design: Polish secure stud flower

Equipment needed:

- Creative Stickey base coat
- Creative Voodoo polish
- striping brush
- gold studs
- orangewood stick tipped with Blu® Tack or a wet orangewood stick
- top coat

1 Apply base coat to all ten nails.

2 Apply two coats of Voodoo polish, ensuring good colour coverage on all ten nails.

3 Allow paint to dry thoroughly. Apply two coats of top coat for protection.

4 Using the orangewood stick tipped with Blu® Tack, pick up and place one stud in the centre of the nail.

5 Place a further seven studs around the centre stud to create a flower shape. Apply leaf shapes below and above flower.

6 Ensure studs are embedded into wet polish. Perform design on each nail before going on to next nail.

Jewelled cross

Name of design: Jewelled cross

Equipment needed:

- Creative Stickey base coat
- Creative Knight's Armour silver polish
- striping brush
- gold paint
- orangewood stick tipped with Blu® Tack
- four small and two large gold studs
- four red rhinestones
- top coat

1 Apply base coat to all ten nails.

2 Apply two coats of Creative Knight's Armour silver polish, ensuring good colour coverage on all ten nails.

3 Starting two-thirds of the way up the nail in the centre, use a striping brush loaded with gold paint. Pull down towards the tip of the nail ensuring that you lift the brush to create the point of the cross – practise on paper first. Starting 2 mm from the side of the nail, pull towards the centre and lift the brush – repeat on the other side to create the cross.

4 Allow paint to dry thoroughly. Apply two coats of top coat for protection.

5 While the paint is still wet, use the orangewood stick tipped with Blu® Tack to decorate the cross with gold studs and red rhinestones.

Polish secure – rhinestones

Name of design: Polish secure random design of rhinestones

Equipment needed:

- Creative Stickey base coat
- Creative Claret red polish
- red rhinestones
- yellow rhinestones
- orange rhinestones
- orangewood stick tipped with Blu® Tack
- top coat

1 Apply base coat to all ten nails.

2 Apply two coats of Claret red polish, ensuring good colour coverage on all ten nails.

3 Allow paint to dry thoroughly. Apply two coats of top coat for protection.

4 Using the orangewood stick tipped with Blu® Tack, start in the left-hand corner and place the orange rhinestones to create an abstract design.

5 Follow the design plan, but change to yellow rhinestones and finish off with red.

6 Allow to dry thoroughly.

Technical Tip

When performing a design with a lot of rhinestones, you may need to apply small dots of top coat or Gel Bond to keep the stones in place as you are working on each nail.

Black beads with gold outline

Name of design: Black beads outlined with gold beads

Equipment needed:

- Creative Stickey base coat
- Creative Wildfire polish
- black beads
- gold beads
- moist orangewood stick
- top coat

1   Apply base coat to all ten nails.
2   Apply two coats of Wildfire red enamel, ensuring good colour coverage on all ten nails.
3   Allow paint to dry thoroughly. Apply two coats of top coat for protection.
4   Using the moist orangewood stick, pick up and place four black beads to create a diamond shape – it is best to start in the middle of the nail, approximately 5 mm from the cuticle.
5   Repeat diagonally across the nail leaving a space for the gold beads. Outline each diamond shape with the gold beads.
6   Repeat the pattern over the required area.
7   Ensure beads are set into wet top coat for maximum adhesion.

Opalescent blending

Name of design: Opalescent blending

Equipment needed:

- Creative Stickey base coat
- client's colour choice of Creative polish
- opalescent paints
- marbling tool
- fan brush
- top coat

1   Apply base coat to all ten nails.
2   Apply two coats of the Creative polish of your client's choice, ensuring good colour coverage on all ten nails.

Technical Tip

For best results a dark polish should be used or the opalescent sheen may be lost.

3   Using the marbling tool, pick up and place a very small amount of the first opalescent colour onto the nail. Using the fan brush, make sweeping movements from one side of the nail to the other.

Technical Tip

The less paint you use the more opalescent the finish.

Group opalescent

4   Repeat step 3, placing a second opalescent colour slightly above the first.

5   Repeat step 3, placing a third opalescent colour slightly above the second.

6   Allow paint to dry thoroughly. Apply two coats of top coat for protection.

Opalescent blue sponge design

Name of design: Opalescent blue sponge design

Equipment needed:

- Creative Stickey base coat
- Creative Voodoo black enamel
- opalescent blue paint
- sponge
- top coat

1   Apply base coat to all ten nails.

2   Apply two coats of Voodoo black enamel, ensuring good colour coverage on all ten nails.

3   Using the sponge loaded with opalescent blue paint, press onto nail ensuring even distribution of paint.

4   Allow paint to dry thoroughly. Apply two coats of top coat for protection.

Gold and copper sponge design

Name of design: Gold and copper sponge design

Equipment needed:

- Creative Stickey base coat
- Creative Cream Puff white polish
- gold and copper paint
- sponge
- top coat

1   Apply base coat to all ten nails.

2   Apply two coats of Cream Puff white polish, ensuring good colour coverage on all ten nails.

3   Using the sponge loaded with copper paint, press onto nail ensuring even distribution of paint.

4   Alternate using the sponge loaded with gold paint, continue until area is covered.

5   Allow paint to dry thoroughly. Apply two coats of top coat for protection.

Freehand Chinese symbol

Name of design: Freehand Chinese symbol

Equipment needed:

- Creative Stickey base coat
- Creative Cream Puff polish
- fine detail brush
- red paint
- top coat

Technical Tip

Chinese symbols are a collaboration of straight lines and small curves. Take each stage one at a time, always starting at the top of the design so as not to spoil it.

1 Apply base coat to all ten nails.
2 Apply two coats of Cream Puff white polish, ensuring good colour coverage on all ten nails.
3 Using a fine detail brush and red paint, use a sweeping movement to create two small red lines – these two strokes will form the top of your design. Continue to copy design of chosen letters down the nail.
4 Allow paint to dry thoroughly. Apply two coats of top coat for protection.

Multi-coloured design

Name of design: Abstract multi-coloured striping design

Equipment needed:

- Creative Stickey base coat
- Creative Cream Puff polish
- striping brush
- green, brown, red, gold and blue paint
- top coat

1 Apply base coat to all ten nails.
2 Apply two coats of Cream Puff white polish, ensuring good colour coverage on all ten nails.
3 Using a striping brush loaded with the first colour, start from the top right-hand corner and pull down the nail, moving the wrist to create the desired shape.
4 Using a clean striping brush loaded with the second colour, repeat using the previous line as a guide.
5 Repeat the above step changing colour until the design is complete.
6 Allow paint to dry thoroughly. Apply two coats of top coat for protection.

Red flowers on green

Name of design: Red flowers on a green backdrop

Equipment needed:

- Creative Stickey base coat
- Creative Super Sexy enamel
- shading brush
- bronze paint
- top coat

1   Apply base coat to all ten nails.

2   Apply two coats of Super Sexy green polish, ensuring good colour coverage on all ten nails.

3   Using shading brush loaded with red paint, start in the right-hand corner at the free edge. Copy the petals pulling the brush downwards and into the corner.

4   Using shading brush loaded with red paint, start above the first flower in the centre. Copy the petals pulling the brush outwards so most of the paint is in the centre of the flower.

5   Repeat the first two flowers up the length of the nail.

6   Apply one coat of top coat for protection.

Name of design: Poppies and bees on white nails

Equipment needed:

- Creative Stickey base coat
- Creative Cream Puff white polish
- red, green, black and yellow paint
- liner brush
- detail brush
- top coat

Poppies and bees

1   Apply base coat to all ten nails.

2   Apply two coats of Cream Puff white polish, ensuring good colour coverage on all ten nails.

3   Using a liner brush loaded with green paint, start at the free edge on the right-hand side. Copy the stem and leaf design in the diagram. With a clean detail brush loaded with black paint, place a fine line down the stem to create definition to the design.

4   Using a detail brush loaded with red paint, outline the poppies. Fill in the poppies with red paint. Using a detail brush loaded with black, add definition to the poppies and outline the bees.

5   Using a detail brush loaded with yellow paint, fill in the bees and place a dot of paint to highlight the centre of the poppies.

6   Apply one coat of top coat for protection.

Name of design: Butterflies and flowers

Equipment needed:

- Creative Stickey base coat
- Creative Cream Puff white polish
- liner brush
- fine detail brush
- green, blue, black, yellow and orange paint
- top coat

Butterflies and flowers

1   Apply base coat to all ten nails.

2   Apply two coats of Cream Puff white polish, ensuring good colour coverage on all ten nails.

3   Using a liner brush loaded with blue paint, copy the butterfly to the left then load brush with black and paint body as in the diagram.

4   Using a detail brush loaded with blue paint, outline the large butterfly. Fill in the butterfly. Using a detail brush loaded with black, add definition to the body and paint in the antennae on both butterflies. Using the liner brush loaded with green paint, copy the stem and leaves of the flowers. Using the fine detail brush loaded with orange, paint in the first flower.

5   Using a detail brush loaded orange, paint the second flower. Using the detail brush loaded with yellow paint, place a dot to highlight the centre of the flowers.

6   Apply one coat of top coat for protection.

Name of design: Chinese lady

Equipment needed:

- Creative Stickey base coat
- Creative Cream Puff white polish
- striping brush
- liner brush
- fine detail brush
- black and red paint
- top coat

1   Apply base coat followed by Cream Puff white polish, ensuring good colour coverage on all ten nails.

2   Using a striping brush loaded with black paint, draw a thin line from the sidewall, about one-third of the way down the nail, towards the middle of the nail, then at a 90° angle down a few millimetres

3   Repeat on the other side but only take the line to the middle and not down the nail. A little below each line, paint an additional line at a slight angle to give the appearance of oriental eyes.

4   Using fine detail brush, apply black paint in blocks to create hair.

5   Using a striping brush loaded with red paint, draw a small mouth shape, use a fine detail brush loaded with red paint and colour in the mouth.

6   Allow paint to dry thoroughly. Apply two coats of top coat for protection.

Chinese lady

Name of design: Leopard print

Equipment needed:

- Creative Stickey base coat
- Creative Orange-a-Peel polish
- detail brush
- flat brush
- black and brown paint
- top coat

Leopard print

1 Apply base coat to all ten nails.

2 Apply two coats of Orange-a-Peel polish, ensuring good colour coverage on all ten nails.

3 Using the flat brush loaded with brown paint, randomly place the brush on the nail creating different shaped patches.

4 With black paint and using the detail brush, paint around the edge of the shape already created.

5 Allow paint to dry thoroughly. Apply two coats of top coat for protection.

Animal print

Name of design: Animal print

Equipment needed:

- Creative Stickey base coat
- Creative Snakebite polish
- detail brush
- flat brush
- black, taupe and white paint
- top coat

Technical Tip

Gentle pressure with a tiny wet pointed cotton bud will remove acrylic paint.

1 Apply base coat to all ten nails.

2 Apply two coats of Snakebite polish, ensuring good colour coverage on all ten nails.

3 Using the flat brush loaded with taupe paint, randomly place brush on the nail creating different shaped patches and outline with white paint.

4 With black paint and using the detail brush, paint around the edge of the shape already created.

5 Allow paint to dry thoroughly. Apply two coats of top coat for protection.

Freehand purple Aztek design

Name of design: Freehand purple Aztek design

Equipment needed:

- Creative Stickey base coat
- Creative Rebel with a Cause dark purple polish
- white and dark purple acrylic paint
- fine detail brush
- fine liner brush
- top coat

1 Apply base coat to all ten nails.

2 Apply two coats of Rebel with a Cause dark purple, ensuring good colour coverage on all ten nails.

3 Using a fine liner brush loaded with white paint, add the fine lines. You may need to practise this on paper first.

Technical Tip

Keep your acrylic paint diluted enough to flow freely from the brush; this will make things easier for you. Also try periodically cleaning your brush in water and reshaping the point to keep the lines controllable and fine. Be adventurous as you don't need to plan these designs at all, just let the brush fill in the surface of the nail line by tiny line.

4   As you approach the cuticle area of the base colour, gradually mix in some white to the purple you are using for your line work, to create a subtle shift in colour from white to darker purple. By the time you reach the opposite corner of the nail, you should be sure to use pure dark purple for your line work. A very lovely hand painted nail is the result.

5   Allow paint to dry thoroughly.

6   Apply two coats of top coat for protection.

Name of design: Freehand orange Aztek design

Equipment needed:

Freehand orange Aztek design

- Creative Stickey base coat
- Creative Pharoah's Gold polish or airbrush gold colour fade
- striping brush
- red paint
- top coat

1   Apply base coat to all ten nails.

2   Apply two coats of Pharoah's Gold polish or an airbrush blend from metallic gold to pink ensuring good colour coverage on all ten nails.

3   Using a striping brush loaded with red paint start the line work in the gold area using a very light touch from the free edge towards the centre of the nail.

4   Build the design by shadowing the first line very closely and repeat the lines until you have an astonishingly subtle design. This can create a hypnotic effect.

5   Allow paint to dry thoroughly.

6   Apply two coats of top coat for protection.

Name of design: Pencil face on nails

Equipment needed:

- Creative Stickey base coat
- Creative Cream Puff polish

Pencil drawing of face

- white block for buffing
- pencil
- top coat

1 Apply base coat to all ten nails.

2 Apply two coats of Cream Puff white polish, ensuring good colour coverage on all ten nails. Allow to dry completely. Gently buff the nail to get a smooth, but matt surface. Pencil will not mark a mirror smooth surface.

3 Begin to sketch the outline of the face and hair and work out the proportions. You may use a rubber to fix mistakes, just like on paper. If you find the sketch is not working, just remove it with a gentle buff and start again.

4 Once you are satisfied with your basic drawing, begin to work in the dark areas, such as hair and eyes. With an eraser or rubber, smooth out the work you have done so far. This gives an unmistakably photographic quality to the image. Add pencil and blend it in, just like putting on make-up.

5 Using a sharpened pencil for the final details, outline the eyes and lips and the darkest details.

6 Apply two coats of top coat for protection.

Alternative faces

Name of design: Goldfish design

Equipment needed:

- Creative Stickey base coat
- Creative Cream Puff white polish
- white block buffer
- light grey pencil
- dark grey pencil
- translucent red glaze
- white and black paint
- top coat

Final picture of goldfish

Step-by-step goldfish design

1   Apply base coat to all ten nails.

2   Apply two coats of Cream Puff white polish, ensuring good colour coverage on all ten nails. Allow to dry completely. Gently buff the nail to get a smooth, but matt surface. Pencil will not mark a mirror smooth surface. Carefully line up your nails to create a nice even working surface.

3   Begin to sketch the outline of the goldfish and work out the proportions. Use a light grey pencil. You may use a rubber to fix mistakes, just like on paper. If you find the sketch is not working, just remove it with a gentle buff and start again.

4   Once you are satisfied with your basic drawing, continue to use the grey to fill in the fish's body. Create the details and begin to work in the dark areas, such as the underbelly of the fish and the background fins. Using a dark grey pencil for definition, draw the scales. With an eraser or rubber, smooth out the work you have done so far. This gives an unmistakably photographic quality to the image. Add pencil and blend it in, just like putting on make-up.

5   Use a red translucent glaze for the goldfish. Finish by adding white highlights and a touch of black for the eye.

6   Allow paint to dry thoroughly. Apply two coats of top coat for protection.

Technical Tip

Don't hesitate to use all of the nail's surface. This adds to the overall effect.

Chapter summary

There are many companies that offer nail art courses; some are basic and others are more advanced. After reading this chapter and following the step-by-step guidelines you could incorporate some of the designs onto your own or your client's nails without having to attend a nail art course. Remember, though, that there is always value in someone else's experience and you may find that a nail art tutor can pass on easier techniques or designs for you to do. This chapter will also help those who think that they are not particularly artistic to get started on some simple designs. You may refer to this chapter throughout your training or career to help with polishing, tools of the nail art trade, and step-by-step designs to help you develop your own artwork. As a true professional you should make sure that you gain a professional government-recognised qualification in any area of nail technology where you intend to provide services, including nail art. For those who aspire to higher levels, read on to discover airbrushing, competition work and photographic and fashion work. This chapter is the beginning of your nail art path – have fun and good luck.

Designs by Katherine Marsden

Knowledge review

1   What are primary colours?

2   Why is it so important for a nail artist to have a good understanding of colour?

3   What is a tertiary or intermediate colour?

4   List three places that you could buy nail art kit.

5   List five different nail art brushes and what you would use them for.

6   What would you use a colour shaper for?

7   What safety measures would you take when using a combi drill?

8   What two types of transfer could you use?

9   What differences are there between using flat-stones and rhinestones?

10   How would you apply dangle charms and what safety measures would you take?

11   Why should you only use paints that are recommended for nails?

12   What is the best way to apply one colour polish?

13   What are the two ways of applying a French polish?

14   Why is it so important to use a base coat when applying polish?

15   What does a quick dry do to help the polish dry quicker?

16   What are the different ways of performing striping?

17   How would you perform a foil design?

18   What technical tips could help you to perform a marbling design effectively?

19   What colour polish would be best as a base for an opalescent blend design?

20   What are the first three steps to painting the goldfish design?

21   Which design would you use a rubber on?

22   Which design is spread across five nails? Can you think of another design you could use with this technique?

23   What other areas of work could you progress onto within nail art?

24   What tools would you need in your basic kit?

25   What is a flexi-brush?

26   What type of case is best to carry your nail art around in?

27   Why is Blu® Tack so indispensable to a nail artist?

28   How would you use striping tape in a nail art design?

29   How can you use polish to make a nail look slimmer?

30   Why is it so important to gain client agreement before applying your nail art designs?

31   How do polishes differ in colour and consistency?

32   What after care advice would you give your clients for these treatments?

33   What retail items would you recommend your clients use to keep their nails and designs in good condition?

4

The art of airbrushing

Learning objectives

In this chapter we will consider the following aspects:

- equipment and maintenance
- airbrush systems, paints and accessories
- pre-cut templates and how to design your own
- step-by-step designs – beginning
- step-by-step designs – intermediate
- step-by-step designs – advanced
- troubleshooting

This chapter intends to give nail artists the ability to make an informed choice when buying airbrush equipment, paints and tools. There are a number of companies who sell airbrush kits but you can make a very expensive mistake if you purchase this specialist equipment without doing some research. We have always followed one golden rule – whatever service we provide for our clients, we choose a specialist supplier who offers good training and then we use only their products. Mixing one company's products with another can cause problems. It is much safer to choose a company that specialises in airbrushing and nails rather than a company whose airbrush was designed for cake decorating or graphics. If you are purchasing a nail airbrush system, all the equipment and products will be complementary and compatible and you can use them on your clients with no problems.

Equipment and maintenance

Learning objectives

In this section you will learn about:

- **airbrushing compared to hand painting**
- **air supply and compressors**
- **hoses**
- **moisture trap**
- **maintenance and cleaning**

Airbrushing as an art form has been around for over 100 years, but for the nail technician it is a relatively new area. Airbrushing gives greater artistic freedom to the nail artist and allows the creation of 3D designs that are practically impossible to achieve with hand painting. The technique enables designs to be created on nails more quickly, cheaply and with greater artistic accuracy.

Sudo airbrush

Airbrushing compared to hand painting

Airbrushing is becoming very popular as a decoration for nails and more and more salons are investing in the necessary equipment; some have even totally replaced their polish bottles with airbrush paints. Airbrushing allows much more detailed designs in a fraction of the time hand painting would take. There are certain designs that are particularly popular with clients because they are so quick and the clarity of the designs are far better than with hand painting, for example:

- French manicure on fingers and toes – in a fraction of the time
- colour fades – difficult to achieve with hand painting
- animal prints – the clarity of the design and the use of many colours

The cost of performing an airbrush design is considerably lower for the airbrush artist than using hand paints or polishes. A small cup of colour paint can spray 20 fingers and toes for less than 0.01 of a penny. Airbrushing is much more cost effective than any other nail treatment; here are some of the reasons why:

- the price of the paint versus enamels
- it is quicker to achieve designs
- the shelf life of paint is longer than enamel
- colours can be mixed to suit clients' needs
- designs can be created to match clients' outfits
- once the equipment has been bought there is no further outlay
- it is difficult for clients to perform this service on themselves
- the paint dries instantly so intricate designs can take very little time
- airbrushes can be used for make-up, body, tanning and hair art

Simone body art

Most manicurists or nail artists provide nail treatments that include a polish within the price of the treatment. This means that for 10 or 15 minutes you are not earning any revenue. If you introduce your airbrush design, whether it be a simple colour fade or an animal print, you can charge from £5.00 extra but spend no extra time.

Even using one colour paint instead of enamel can be more cost effective because it is so much quicker. Remember that every day you airbrush your speed and skill will improve. We always say that our airbrush is our sixth finger and using our airbrush has become so natural that it has become a part of our hand and feels as if we are drawing. Imagine, after a year of using your airbrush on two clients a day, how much extra revenue you can earn as well as how skilful you can become.

Technical Tip

You may wish to add to your kit as time goes by and your skill level increases. It is important to try out an airbrush before you buy to see if you are comfortable with it; the wrong airbrush could be an expensive mistake. We have attempted to cover all types of compressors and the equipment needed so that you will be able to make an informed choice and ask the right technical questions before making a decision and purchasing your compressor and equipment.

Sudo Mist Air small compressor

Sudo TC5000 compressor

Don't be driven by price – consider your requirements:

Example 1: Are you mobile? – if the answer is yes you need a compressor that is lightweight and has a handle, and possibly runs for a shorter period.

Example 2: Are you working from home or do you rent space? – if so, you could probably use a bigger compressor that has a moisture trap and can run for longer periods.

Example 3: Many salon owners make the wrong choice to start with; they buy a compressor that is only suitable for running short periods of time *or* a compressor that is not suitable for running two or more airbrushes at any one time. A larger compressor will be able to run several airbrushes.

Having done your research and decided which of the three factors above refers to your situation we will now look at the various pieces of equipment you will need to purchase to set up your airbrush kit.

Equipment

We look at airbrushes in detail in the next section. Here we discuss the equipment you will need for your airbrush to work. It is usually best to buy all the various elements from one manufacturer to ensure compatibility.

Compressors

Compressors are the preferred source of air for most airbrush artists, provided you have an electricity supply. There has never been a better time to purchase a compressor as many are now specifically designed for the nail industry. The following types are readily available:

- Lightweight compressors suitable for mobile technicians and artists. Many manufacturers supply the compressor in a durable carrying case that also holds the paints and other accessories needed to perform the service. This type of compressor is typically not designed to run for more than 15–20 minutes, so would not be recommended for the salon user.

- Many compressors use a small piston to build up air pressure. This type of compressor can be noisy but they do vary: the cheaper ones tend to be the loudest. Sometimes the compressor has an automatic shut off so it will only run when the airbrush lever/trigger is pressed.

- Some of the older compressors have a large tank attached which shuts off when the correct pressure is reached. They can be very heavy, but in a salon environment they will not be moved often. This type of compressor can run several airbrushes at the same time, which makes it an ideal choice for the salon owner who wishes to purchase only one quality compressor. It is one of the most reliable models and usually quiet – an important consideration if other treatments such as facials and body massage are being performed in another room.

- Some compressors require little or no maintenance. Many of the older models need oil to keep the working parts lubricated and to stop them over-heating. The oil gauge should be monitored and the compressor filled regularly. This compressor should never be turned on its side as it may flood the motor. Other maintenance may include changing the oil, changing air filters and draining the tank of any water/moisture build up.

Before choosing your compressor you must decide on your individual requirements and anticipate what these may be in a year's time. If your needs are liable to be very different then it may be worth waiting or financing a larger compressor than the one you need at the moment. You should always think about training, support, and a complete system for total backup when buying an airbrush system. Otherwise, when problems occur, the paint manufacturer can try to blame the airbrush and the airbrush manufacturer can try to blame the compressor, leaving you with no solution to the problem.

Alternative air sources

Canister of air

This is a relatively cheap way to start, but is not sensible if you intend to do a lot of airbrushing, as it can prove to be expensive in the long term. Some of the problems you may experience are as follows:

- Can be unreliable if temperatures vary
- You always need to carry an extra canister of air, as it usually runs out before the can is empty. This makes anticipating whether there is enough left to start or finish a design difficult
- The pressure can vary as the canister is used, as the PSI (pounds per square inch) can drop as the contents reduce
- PSI can vary between manufacturers
- You will need an air hose adapter to use a canister of compressed air. The fitments may vary if you use an alternative manufacturer, making it expensive if you experience problems with your usual supplier
- The canister must be stored upright to prevent the loss of gas. The gas itself is freezing and could, on contact with the skin, cause frostbite. It is also important to remember this when fitting the adapter
- Canisters can spit moisture after being used for a few minutes due to moisture build up, perhaps spoiling the nail design

Cylinder of compressed air

This looks like an oxygen tank that you might see in a hospital. This type of air supply is not widely used by nail technicians/artists today, many of whom are mobile, and compressors are more readily available. However, a cylinder of compressed air is useful if electricity is a problem, and it is also a very quiet source of air supply.

To use a cylinder of compressed air you will need to find a retailer who will deliver, as the cylinders are very heavy. Normally a deposit is required for the cylinder, but to ensure you do not run out it would be wise to secure two so you always have a backup. You would also need to purchase a regulator, which should have a pressure gauge to ensure the correct pressure is set and maintained. An adapter and manifold is also required if you intend to use more than one airbrush.

There are many health and safety regulations to consider if choosing this type of air source.

- The cylinder must always be kept and secured in an upright position
- If the cylinder is knocked over, the stem may be broken so it should be returned to the manufacturer to avoid the risk of explosion. An air cylinder may be too unstable to be used by untrained personnel and you may find your local council will want to see that staff have been trained in the handling of this equipment
- You will need a locked cage outside the premises with access restricted to trained personnel only
- Extreme cold can cause a problem with the air flow regulator
- If using more than three airbrushes at any one time the amount of compressed air flowing through the regulator may cause it to temporarily freeze
- You should consider attaching a separate gauge to indicate the amount of air left in the tank

Moisture separator/trap

Compressors utilise the air from the room that you are working in, but wherever there is air there is moisture and even debris. If the moisture and debris are not separated from the air by a moisture separator/trap, it will collect in the hose and will come through your airbrush – remember that your paint should be sprayed dry and any moisture present could cause smears and runs that will prevent your design from drying and spoil it.

Sudo moisture trap

There is nothing more frustrating than creating a wonderful design – which is time consuming and uses a large selection of colours – only to find that one nail is spoilt.

Many of the problems associated with airbrushes are sometimes due to a system not incorporating a moisture separator/trap *or* the moisture trap not being emptied on a regular basis.

Air pressure regulator

Air pressure is measured in pounds per square inch (PSI). An air regulator controls the PSI and allows the technician or therapist to select the required air pressure, taking into consideration the treatment being provided.

In a salon environment, where the demands are greater to both justify and maximise the investment in a compressor, many nail technicians and therapists are providing new treatments such as body art, make-up, tanning, hair and airbrushed nail art. These treatments can offer a larger profit margin. However, to make this process cost effective it is a good idea to promote and utilise the equipment as often as possible.

It is important to consider when purchasing your compressor whether you will want to offer alternative airbrush treatments – either now or in the future – and whether you will require a pre-set or adjustable pressure. This could be reflected in the price of the equipment.

Hose

Treatment	*Pressure (PSI)*
Nail art	35
Body art	15
Tanning	20
Hair art	25
Make up	7

Hoses

The hose connects the airbrush to its source of air – compressor, canister or cylinder. Each manufacturer will have a fitting that is unique to its airbrush and its air source.

Hoses are generally manufactured from plastic and vary in length from 5ft (1.8m) to 10ft (3m). There are three types of hoses commonly used by today's manufacturers:

Sudo Compressor and kit

1 *Straight hoses* – these are usually used as a connection between the moisture trap and airbrush.
2 *Coiled hoses* – this type of hose is used by some manufacturers between the compressor and moisture trap. It is coiled and long in order to cool down the air travelling from the compressor to the moisture trap.
3 *Rubber hoses with braided fabric cover* – used to be recommended when using a metal airbrush, however many manufacturers have now changed to lightweight, durable plastic hoses which are more comfortable to use and do not affect the balance of the airbrush.

It is a good idea to purchase a complete system from one manufacturer; this will ensure compatibility and after sales service from your supplier. Many suppliers now offer training and maintenance advice with their set up kits. You may not get the support you require if you purchase from several manufacturers – remember a system works best if it is complete.

Technical Tip

If purchasing your airbrush and compressor from different manufacturers you will need to check that the connections at either end of the hoses are compatible with the compressor, moisture trap and airbrush.

Sudo airbrush kit

Adaptors and manifolds

There are a number of different adaptors on the market – they work in much the same way as a plumbing system, using thread and nut connections that can be male or female. Adaptors allow you to downsize or upsize your connections. This could be useful if you introduce a different type of airbrush to your existing system.

A manifold can be T- or Y-shaped and allows you to add any of the following to your system:

- an additional airbrush
- a regulator
- a moisture separator/trap
- a hose

Maintenance of your airbrush system

Airbrush cleaner

There are many airbrush cleaners available. You should always use the one recommended by the paint manufacturer whose products you have purchased. Water based cleaners tend not to contain as many strong solvents as acrylic based paint cleaners. There are also effervescent cleaners, which can be purchased in a spray can with a tube that attaches to the nozzle at the top of the spray can. This cleaner is usually recommended for use at the end of the day or once a week to give a thorough clean. We would not recommend using this cleaner between each client as it will be time consuming and you may risk spoiling your design.

Cleaning station

Most airbrush kits come with a cleaning station. If your kit does not, then you will need to purchase one.

Spraying into a bin or tissue can create a health and safety risk and you could find that the mist from the paint and cleaning fluid will give you a headache if not disposed of properly. A good cleaning station will have a paint reservoir to catch excess paint and possibly a filter to stop paint coming back out. It is important to make sure that your breathing zone stays as clear of vapours as possible. If you are not happy with your cleaning station then shop around for a better one. Make sure that your cleaning station is cleaned out every day with tissue. If you are a mobile nail artist, put some tissue into the station whilst travelling so as not to cause a spillage in your kit.

Technical Tip

When planning your design, try if possible to use the lighter colour first. You will only need to empty your paint cavity of your first colour choice and then add the next colour and you are ready to airbrush. You will use less airbrush cleaner and complete designs in a shorter time.

Cleaning station

Airbrushes, paints and accessories

Learning objectives

In the section you will learn about:

- **the various types of airbrushes**
- **airbrush paints**
- **pre-cut templates and how to design your own**
- **the accessories needed for airbrush services**
- **base coat, top coat and sealant**

The range of airbrushes on the market today is quite diverse. There are trade shows just for airbrush artists, although these tend to be in Germany. An airbrush can be used for many things and we have not only used ours on nails, but also on furniture, salon walls, ornaments and many other objects. We have been asked numerous times to spray designs onto our clients' mobile phones.

Sudo airbrush and paints

Technical Tip

You can use any airbrush paint in any airbrush but always make sure that you have the correct size needle and the appropriate cleaner for that particular paint.

Sudo double action airbrush

Technical Tip

To airbrush proficiently takes time and you should practise the technique of blending the paint and air using the lever/trigger. To start with, your mix will probably be too wet but you should persevere with this as the mix should be dry to the touch when airbrushed onto the nail.

Airbrushes

There are two types airbrush available: the single action and the more traditional double or dual action.

In a single action airbrush, the lever or trigger acts only as an on/off switch; the flow of air is controlled elsewhere on the airbrush – normally by a screw that adjusts the movement of the needle. When using this type of airbrush you need to open the screw fully to empty the paint when changing colour, then reset. When the screw is set correctly, it is easier to obtain the correct mix of paint to air so that when you have finished airbrushing the design it is dry.

In a double action airbrush, the lever/trigger has a dual use:

- The first action of the lever/trigger being pressed down allows the air to flow.
- The second action of the lever/trigger being pulled back engages the paint supply, and enables it to flow freely. The further the lever/trigger is pulled back, the more paint is pulled through the airbrush. To change the shade, you simply press down and pull the lever/trigger fully back and the paint will flow out. This type of airbrush can be more difficult to master but ultimately offers greater versatility and control.

When choosing an airbrush, there are a number of design features to consider:

- Single action or double action airbrush – think about which will be best suited to your requirements and budget, and don't be afraid to ask for a demonstration or to try it out yourself.

Technical Tip

Acrylic paint also contains some water but has a thicker consistency and dries to a water resistant finish. Water based paint also contains acrylic but has a higher content of water and will dissolve or wash off in water.

- Side feed or gravity feed – some airbrushes have the colour feeder on the top of the airgun – gravity feed – and others have a side feeder, usually a bottle. For nail work it is more economical to have a gravity feed with a smaller cup or aperture, allowing smaller amounts of paint to be used. The side feeder bottles are more widely used when larger amounts of paint or solution are required, for example for tanning, body and hair painting.

- Paint feeder or colour cup

  – Some airbrushes have a cone shaped colour cup which can be quite economical, as the cup does not need to be filled as it is tapered at the base.

  – A number of manufacturers use a bottle that screws onto the side of the airbrush. This can be economical if you keep the caps on and keep them clean.

  – Many manufactures use a reservoir in the centre of the airbrush above the needle; sometimes these are small if the airbrush is designed specifically for nails. However, they can be quite large and paint can be wasted as you will need to cover the bottom of the cavity to prevent spitting. Bear in mind whether the airbrush has been designed for the nails market or not.

- If weight is a consideration, look at systems that use a plastic hose. Airbrushes made specifically for the nail market tend to be lightweight and durable.

- Look at where the hose is attached to the airbrush – often it is underneath and you must ensure that it is comfortable to hold and well balanced.

- Decide which type of paint you prefer to use – acrylic based or water based – and check that the airbrush needle is suitable or can be changed.

- Maintenance of the airbrush is important. Many need to be stripped down, thoroughly cleaned and oiled on a regular basis, and several types have numerous moving parts. Ask the manufacturer for a demonstration.

- The diameter of the spray from the airbrush must be suitable for the nail artist, if the system is not designed specifically for nails. Check the diameter of the needle.

- Remember that for detailed work you want all your paint to be on the surface of the nail, not covering a large area around the finger or hand. Many airbrush manufacturers offer in their range of accessories a crown cap that is used for very detailed work. Some accomplished artists draw freehand with this and create beautiful designs.

Airbrush paints

There are two main types of paint used within the nail industry for airbrushing:

- Water based paint, containing acrylic for colour, but with a high water content. This type of paint will normally dissolve in water. Water based paints tend to be opaque, although

Technical Tip

When blending colours and paints you should always use one medium. Do not try to mix water and acrylic based paints as both have very different base coats and sealants and are usually not compatible.

some manufacturers offer pearlescent and metallic colours. However the finish is not as stunning as acrylic. It is a very good medium for beginners to gain confidence and control of the airbrush without clogging and blocking – this is the main reason why beginners give up on airbrushing as a technique.

- Acrylic based paint contains water but has a higher concentration of acrylic paint. This type of paint will not easily dissolve in water as it dries to a water resistant finish, hence the end result is much brighter, deeper and vivid in colour. It has more versatility in its colour range, for example opaque, translucent, iridescent, pearlescent, metallic, neon and shimmer finishes. It can be more difficult to wash off surrounding skin tissue and will not easily be removed if spilt or splashed on clothing.

Technical Tip

Always check the size of your needle if you change paint manufacturers. Some recommend 0.2 mm whilst others recommend 0.4 mm. Be patient, changing from acrylic based to water based paints takes practice – if you have a tendency to spray too wet, you could adjust your pressure slightly, alternatively spray dry before applying the top coat. When changing from water based to acrylic based, you may have a problem with clogging – this is due to not finishing on air before lifting the finger from the trigger.

Ask manufacturers if they can provide you with paint samples before committing yourself to their system. Remember to ask about base and top coats. Always use the appropriate cleaner for the paint system that you have chosen.

Water based paint has two main advantages: it flows through the airbrush easily without clogging it and it is easy to remove from the skin surrounding the nail. Some cheaper water based paints need a white base (on top of the base coat), otherwise when you spray a colour you will not see a vibrant finish. This can cause problems if you want to use a stencil on top of your first colour choice unless your colours are getting darker.

Acrylic based paints have a number of advantages: translucent, pearlescent, opalescent, opaque and metallic finishes are all achievable; colours are usually more varied and vibrant. Some of the better quality acrylic paints will allow you to cover black with white – this makes design and colour choices easier. The disadvantage is that you need to be proficient at spraying in order not to clog your airbrush.

Templates

Stencils and pre-cut frisket

Stencils vary greatly from basic French manicure designs to very detailed pictures that are built up in layers. They can be used either in part or as a whole image when creating a design. Stencils can be

Stencils

a soft pliable plastic or hard and rigid. It is easier to use the softer plastic stencils as these will bend with the curve of the nail and give a better finish.

Many successful nail technicians/artists use just the edge or part of a stencil to create a wonderful abstract design. Stencils allow beautiful pictures to be painted in a relatively short time: a French design can be achieved in minutes, whereas using frisket is more time consuming due to the cutting, placing and removal. Stencils are also re-useable, but need to be cleaned with the appropriate cleaner and tissue, not cotton wool. If you are using water based paints, the paint should just simply wash off the stencil.

Nothing should be dismissed, be imaginative and experiment with different mediums. There are many items that could become home-made stencils and be used to create various weird and wonderful designs on your client's nails. There have been many times when the authors have forgotten their stencil wallet and have had to revert to using a piece of A4 paper and a pair of scissors.

Consider the following when designing your airbrush images and always practise on paper or spare tips before attempting designs on your clients:

Technical Tip

It is very difficult to make each nail identical, because the stencil is transparent on the first application of paint, but once it has been sprayed you cannot see through it to place it in the correct position. Sometimes, for the best effect, position the stencil in different places on the nail, e.g. top, bottom, left, right. Aim to work a theme and colour scheme as opposed to an identical design.

- you could use the corner of a business card for a chevron French
- the thumb can act as a stencil when spraying a basic French
- a piece of net or lace can create a textured look
- torn tissue will create a very effective cloud if sprayed lightly along the edge
- a hole punched in a piece of paper or card can create planets, snooker balls and cat's eyes.
- a comb can create interesting designs
- you can cut the edge of a simple piece of paper into various shapes

Frisket/masking paper

Frisket is a single-sided adhesive material that can be customised or designed by the technician specifically for the client. This can be quite time consuming for some designs, but quicker for others. For instance, we have already pointed out that it is quicker to achieve a French polish with a stencil than with frisket/masking paper, but when performing designs such as a planet scene or the cat's eye it is quicker and technically better to use frisket/masking paper. Frisket/masking paper allows you to develop your own designs and stencils and this can be especially helpful if you are considering competition or photographic work and want to achieve a look that no one has done before. Some manufacturers sell punches, similar to a hole punch for the office, which can create crisp circles in the frisket/masking paper.

If tailoring a design, it is best to use a sharp blade to cut the frisket/masking paper. If using the old fashioned craft frisket, it is best to peel off the backing, press the sticky side down onto a piece of glass and use a steel rule to cut against if you want straight lines.

Pre-cut masks are also available in many sizes, shapes and designs and come in sheets of ten, one for each finger. This type of mask is an easy way to recreate exactly the same design on each nail. The backing paper is peeled off and the pre-cut mask is applied directly to the nail. Some manufacturers produce several sizes of the same design, which allows for smaller nails.

When placed on the nail, a pre-cut mask should be secured to the curve of the nail to ensure that there is no bleeding of the paint underneath the mask. This will give a really sharp, clean edge to the design.

Precision tools

When putting together your airbrush kit you will need to consider purchasing some tools. If you look at what is available in a hobby or art shop you will be amazed at the array of tools on sale. Most of these will be irrelevant to the needs of nail artists, but there are a few that are invaluable to designing stencils, frisket/masking paper and 3D nail designs. The following are just a few of the tools available and you may wish to add more to your kit as you progress further into the designing or photographic side of nail art. When we attend photo shoots, the photographers, make-up and hair artists and models sometimes look at the tools in our kits in horror and wonder whether we perform torture treatments! We have to explain that they are not for use on the human body. Here are a few of those tools.

Hobby knife

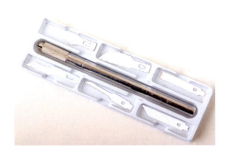

Hobby knife

This tool is invaluable for cutting frisket/masking paper. You will need a cutting board or a piece of toughened glass to attach your frisket/masking paper to. Hobby knives can come with different shaped heads or blades so that you can cut straight lines or curves. They can be relatively cheap throwaway items, or more expensive versions with replaceable blades and a variety of blade shapes. In our experience we find it easier to use the heavier, more expensive type with disposable blades as you will have more control over your cutting. Always buy a knife that has a safety cap to be used in storage and make sure that it is kept out of reach of children or animals. Also be aware of local bye laws that set down the rules for the disposal of 'sharps'; check with your local council.

Heated cutting blade

This tool must be used with care as it heats to over 300° centigrade and can cause serious burns. Never use it around children or animals and always ensure that it is clipped onto a stable surface. It can be used to cut your own stencils from hard plastic and gives a really crisp edge to stencils. This tool is really only for the serious airbrush enthusiast and not for the faint hearted.

Sharp scissors

These can be used to cut paper, frisket/masking paper or materials. There is a range of straight or curved scissors available, depending on the designs you want to achieve. Remember never to use the same scissors for paper and other mediums that require a sharper and more precise cut.

Colour palette

It is always a good idea to have a small colour palette so that if a client wants a certain colour mixed you can try it out first in your palette before mixing the colours in a mixer bottle or your colour cup on your airbrush.

Base coat, top coat and sealant

Base coat

Most paint manufacturers recommend the use of a base coat that is compatible with their paint system in order to achieve the best results.

Base coat should be applied extremely thinly. Remember that straight after application you may wish to use a stencil or frisket – you could find that you pull the paint off with the stencil if the base coat is too wet. If base coat is applied too thickly, you may experience problems with the design drying and peeling at the edges.

Following a nail extension service make sure that the nails are free of dust and oil – *squeak* nails if necessary. Airbrush designs should last until a client returns for their maintenance appointment – the life of this service is better on extensions than on natural nails.

Some manufacturers' base coat is crystalline, pearlescent, with good reflective qualities, and can be used with transparent paints. Others supply a clear base coat that is good for using with a French manicure design.

If using an acrylic based paint many nail technicians and artists do not use a base coat, but this depends on the quality of the paint you are using. If you use this method, the best results are not guaranteed.

When using a water based paint ensure that the base coat is used, otherwise you will pull the design straight off when top coating.

Spray sealant

Some paint manufacturers recommend the use of a spray sealant to seal the airbrushed design to the base coat. This should be misted lightly over all 10 nails. If applied thickly it can cause cracking and peeling. Do not confuse the word varnish with top coat – you still need to apply a recommended quality top coat or glaze coat to finish.

Brush on bonder or sealant

If a spray sealant is not recommended with your airbrush system you will find your manufacturer recommends a brush on sealant. When your design is completed you will need to seal or bond the airbrushed design to the base coat. Care needs to be taken when using a brush on sealant that the bristles of the brush do not drag the unsealed paint and destroy your design.

Technical Tip

Apply base coat to natural nails after a manicure and dehydration of the nail plate – this will extend the life of the design.

Technical Tip

Remember that if you have airbrushed your finished nail and the paint is wet, your design will spoil when applying bonder or sealant.

Technical Tip

You cannot miss this sealing step out – airbrush paint is not enamel, it is a dry powder that must be adhered correctly. Failure to do this will result in disappointment for both the nail artist and client.

Traditional bonding agents are specific to the paint system and should not be mixed and matched with alternative systems. Remember some paints are water based whilst others are acrylic mixes that require very different chemicals in order to adhere or bond to the nail.

When choosing your airbrush system, always ensure that you have a good supply of bonding agents or sealants. You can sometimes miss out the base coat if you are using acrylic paints, but you can never miss the sealant or bonder as your design will suffer. For the best results and longevity of your client's designs, which don't forget they have paid for, use the whole system.

Top coats

There are many top coats on the market but it is always best to use the top coat recommended by your airbrush system manufacturer. However, once the nails have been bonded or sealed you could use a traditional quick dry top coat or one that gives a high gloss shine. Always try out your favourite top coat on tips or yourself to assess wear and tear and to see how long the design lasts. This will also indicate whether your favourites are compatible with the paints and sealants of your chosen airbrush system. A good quality top coat is a great retail item and can help your client's designs lasts for weeks. Always recommend that a client purchase a bottle as part of their homecare pack, to reapply once a week, and advise the client to refresh their design and reseal the edges where there has been wear and tear from daily chores.

Step-by-step airbrush designs

Learning objectives

In this section you will learn about:

- **getting started**
- **progressive exercises to develop control of your airbrush**
- **step-by-step designs**

The art of airbrushing allows you the freedom to design the most beautiful works of art on your client's nails or to create wonderful designs for your photographic work, but, it takes practice. There are many nail artists who think they can learn airbrushing in a day and have thrown their airbrush into a cupboard after the first week of frustration. We have worked with the world's best airbrush artists who have performed designs on bodies, done portraits of the famous, painted cars and clothes – and they have taken many years to perfect their airbrush techniques. Learn to walk before you run: learn each stage of airbrushing and perfect your technique before moving onto the next. We have been taught by top artists and are still learning new techniques even though we have been airbrushing for over 10 years ourselves. The art of airbrushing is the same as

Sudo nail and body art

nail technology – it is ever evolving, with new equipment, paints and techniques coming on to the market all the time.

Remember that you can add the arts of body painting, hair and tanning to your list of treatments with your airbrush if you have the resources and the room. These treatments will bring in extra income for a small outlay.

Once you have mastered a good colour fade, where you cannot see where one colour ends and the other begins, then you are on the road to becoming a great airbrush artist. Once you can perform this practised technique, you can progress on to creating beautiful designs with stencils and frisket.

If you have problems with your airbrush it is usually through lack of proper cleaning, which was covered in the first section of this chapter. In addition, the final section of this chapter is devoted to troubleshooting tips.

Remember that practice makes perfect and you can practise on paper or tips. The designs you create on paper can be achieved on a nail, but may be on a smaller scale. Practise the following exercises and you will learn how to control the flow of air to paint ratio and find out how to hold your airbrush in the right position to spray effectively onto a surface. It is a good idea to get yourself a practice board and some Blu® Tack and keep practising on tips until you get your aim right.

Getting started

Ensure that you are wearing an old T-shirt or apron to begin with just in case you get into a mess with the paint! Acrylic based paints do not wash out of clothes. When first practising you will need a table, a comfortable chair, a good lamp, paints, cleaners, cleaning station and your airbrush equipment. Set up your airbrush and compressor as your trainer has taught you and make sure that you have a few undisturbed hours to keep practising your techniques. Have some tips ready with Blu® Tack for when you have finished your exercises and are ready to go on to airbrushing on nails.

Run a small amount of cleaner through your airbrush before putting paint through. Get used to using a spare piece of absorbent paper to spray onto before starting on your tips or clients as this will ensure that you have the correct pressure and mix of paint and air.

We are asked all the time by students 'Why can we not see the paint coming out of the airbrush'. The answer is that they are spraying correctly and have the correct ratio of paint to air. If you can see the spray then you will usually find that you are spraying too wet. Your wrist should remain straight whilst your arm moves up and down; this technique will give you an even, consistent coverage. If you move your airbrush with a wrist action, you will be spraying over all five fingers at once and have little control over your design. If you have difficulty with this technique, grip your wrist with your other hand whilst practising and you will find that after a little while you will get used to this technique.

Beginning exercises

Ready, set, go! When commencing spraying, hold the airbrush so it is comfortable in your hand; for some of us it is like holding a pen. Press down on the trigger for air flow and then pull back gently to engage paint. When paint comes through onto the practice board push the trigger forward slowly to disengage paint and end on airflow. Practice this a few times to learn control of the trigger.

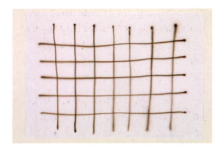

Beginners' exercise

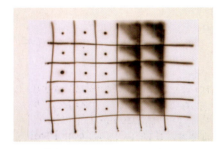

Beginners' exercise

Technical Tip

Remember to practise varying the distance between the nozzle and the paper to achieve a consistent colour and coverage without it looking stripy or blotchy.

Intermediate exercise

Using a bright paint, such as red or blue, spray onto the board in lines. Using the technique you have just learnt with the trigger, start at one end of the board and spray over to the end taking the nozzle nearer to the paper when you are in the middle and back up when you reach the end. This will show you that the closer you get to the paper with your nozzle the crisper the lines you achieve. Paint lines horizontally and vertically creating a grid effect.

Now practise making dots on your board. Try to aim for the middle of the boxes you have created with your lines. Try the same technique of going nearer and then further away and you will find that the closer the nozzle is to the board, the crisper the dot will be. Once you have practised this for a few minutes, you should find that your dots are in the centre of each box and not at the outer edges. This will show you how to direct your spray into the area where you want your paint to be.

Now you are ready to colour in the boxes. Take your airbrush and starting in the corner of a box, spray diagonally across towards the centre and then back up into the corner. Do this a few times, but each time you spray, do not come quite so far into the centre. This is the beginning of a colour fade. If you have achieved a softer colour in the centre and a bolder colour in the corner, then you are on your way to a good colour fade.

Intermediate exercises

It can take any time from a week to a few months to really master your airbrush. You should reach a stage where you can spray onto an area without worrying where the spray is going and whether the paint is too wet. Your airbrush should fit comfortably in your hand and the movement should feel free and natural, almost as if you have a sixth finger. Once the ratio of air to paint has been mastered and you can do a perfect colour fade then you are ready to attempt some more demanding designs. We can only show you a few designs in this book and fully recommend that you find a good nail art training centre that does advanced airbrush courses, or you could try contacting established airbrush artists to see if they will give you some one-on-one sessions. If you want to start thinking about competition and photographic work, then you will need experienced airbrush artists to guide you in the right direction. Experience in any field is worth a lot!

Take the skills you learn from this following section and experiment with your own designs. Find time to sit and play and you will be surprised at what you can create.

Take an A4 piece of paper or pad. Using black paint in your airbrush, spray from one side of the paper to the other and back again without releasing your finger from the trigger. Keeping your finger depressed on the trigger, pull back for paint as you sweep across the page, then as you get nearer to the middle of the page push trigger forward to disengage paint, but keep finger still depressed on trigger. As you get towards the other side of the page pull back the trigger again to release the paint. The idea is to fill the page with lines without taking your finger off the trigger.

This will help you to develop control of your trigger finger and help with your speed. It will also help you to learn how to start spraying in the middle of a design instead of sweeping your paint through. This technique is really important when designing pictures and trying to do any freehand work without stencils or frisket.

A second exercise that you can try is to once again keep your finger depressed on the trigger and take the airbrush around in a figure of eight. As you come around the loop for the second time go in closer with your airbrush. Keep your finger depressed until you reach the bottom of the page. You will see that the nearer the paper your nozzle goes, the crisper the line will be. This exercise is not only excellent for developing trigger control but it also helps you to control soft and crisp spraying.

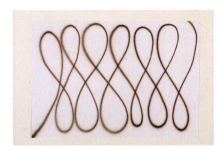

Intermediate exercise

Advanced exercises

This section is not for the faint hearted but mainly for those who wish to go onto competition or photographic work. There are not many salon clients who would want designs at this level, as they would be too costly and time consuming. Airbrushing at this level creates the most fantastic work and we have worked with airbrush artists who have never worked on nails and are amazed at what the world's top nail artists can do on such a small area. The techniques involved in airbrushing can create the most inspiring 3D designs. As with competition nail enhancements, this level of work is usually performed by experienced artists, and not beginners.

Take your A4 paper with the figures of eight and load your airbrush with black paint. Using the techniques that you learnt in the previous exercises, spray circles in the end of each figure of eight. When spraying, practise going closer to the paper to create a crisper line and then pull back to fill in with a softer spray. Leave a small circle of light in the centre of circle to give the illusion of light and make it look 3D.

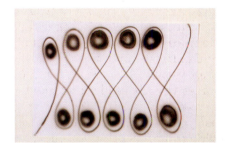

Advanced exercises

Take another piece of paper and, keeping your finger depressed on the trigger, spray in wavy lines backwards and forwards across the page until you reach the bottom.

Once you have completed your waves, go back to the beginning and spray again further back with softer lines. Spray more heavily at the lower wave to give an illusion of depth.

Advanced exercises

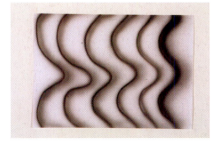

Advanced exercises

One colour tips

With another piece of A4 paper, spray lines from the centre of the page at the top to the bottom of the page in a fan shape. Once you have done this, keep your finger depressed on the trigger and spray in between the lines in a sweeping motion to give an illusion of a spider's web. Remember to use the technique of going nearer and further away to get crisper and softer lines. Fill in to give a 3D effect. You are now ready to spray on your tips.

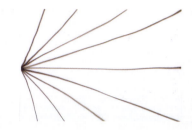

Advanced exercises

Advanced exercises

Step-by-step designs

Name of design: Silver colour fade

Colour fade step by step

Colour fade using contrasting colours

Equipment needed:

- Sudo base coat
- Sudo pearl silver, pearl grey and pearl black airbrush paints
- Sudo airbrush sealant
- Sudo top coat

1   Apply base coat to all ten nails.
2   Airbrush pearl silver colour on all ten nails ensuring good even coverage.

Colour fade using pearlescent paint

3   Starting on the right-hand side at the free edge and using pearl grey, work from side to side diagonally half way up the nail and back to the free edge. Repeat, but this time work only a quarter of the way up the nail and back to the free edge. Repeat on all ten nails.

4   Airbrush pearl black paint just at the corner, barely touching the nail. This will give the illusion of length. Repeat on all ten nails.

5   Seal the design with airbrush sealant.

6   Apply top coat for protection.

Technical Tip

Some pearl paints may not give good coverage, so use opaque white as a base.

Contour nails

Name of design: Contouring of colour

Equipment needed:

- Sudo base coat
- Sudo contrasting coloured airbrush paints
- Sudo airbrush sealant
- Sudo top coat

1   Apply base coat to all ten nails.

2   Airbrush all ten nails using the lighter colour of the paints.

3   Airbrush the darker colour down the sides of each nail taking care to ensure both sides are even in size and match all ten nails.

4   Seal with airbrush sealant.

5   Apply top coat for protection.

Technical Tip

Practise straight even lines on paper before attempting to perform the treatment. The closer to the nail the spray the more control you have, but remember to keep the airbrush paint dry or you could risk spoiling your design.

Name of design: Blue colour fade with clouds

Cloud step by step

Equipment needed:

- Sudo base coat
- Sudo pale blue, pearl mid blue, dark blue and white airbrush paints
- Sudo airbrush sealant
- piece of tissue torn
- Sudo top coat

1 Apply base coat to all ten nails.

2 Airbrush pale blue colour on all ten nails ensuring good even coverage.

3 Starting on the right-hand side at the cuticle and using mid blue, work from side to side diagonally half way down the nail and back to the free edge. Repeat, but this time work only a quarter of the way down the nail and back to the free edge. Repeat on all ten nails.

4 Airbrush dark blue paint just at the top corner, barely touching the nail. This will give the illusion of length. Repeat on all ten nails.

5 Using the torn edge of the tissue, mist white paint over the tear with the majority of the paint going on the tissue rather than the nail surface. Work the tissue down the nail to give a layered look. As you get closer to the bottom, spray more white for denser clouds.

6 Seal the design with airbrush sealant.

7 Apply top coat for protection.

Name of design: Red zebra stripe

Red zebra stripe step by step

Equipment needed:

- Sudo base coat
- Sudo red, pearl yellow gold and black airbrush paints
- zebra stencil
- Sudo airbrush sealant
- Sudo top coat

1 Apply base coat to all ten nails.
2 Airbrush red colour on all ten nails ensuring good even coverage.
3 Airbrush pearl yellow gold in opposite corners for definition. Repeat on all ten nails.
4 Place zebra stencil as flat as possible to the curve of the nail and airbrush with black paint, ensuring the paint is dry when spraying so the design is not spoiled. Repeat on all ten nails.
5 Seal with airbrush sealant.
6 Apply top coat for protection.

Name of design: Camouflage design

Camouflage step by step

Equipment needed:

- Sudo base coat
- Sudo pale green, light brown and translucent green airbrush paints
- stencil or pre-cut design mask
- Sudo airbrush sealant
- Sudo top coat

1 Apply base coat to all ten nails.
2 Airbrush pale green on all ten nails ensuring good even coverage.
3 Lay the stencil as flat as possible over the curve of the nail and airbrush translucent green paint. Repeat on all ten nails.
4 Lay the stencil as flat as possible over the curve of the nail and airbrush dark green paint. Repeat on all ten nails.
5 Seal design with airbrush sealant.
6 Apply top coat for protection.

Name of design: Blue colour fade with snowflake and rhinestones

Snowflake step by step

Equipment needed:

- Sudo base coat
- Sudo pale blue, dark blue and white airbrush paints
- snowflake stencil
- rhinestones
- orangewood stick tipped with Blu® Tack
- Sudo airbrush sealant
- Sudo top coat

1 Apply base coat to all ten nails.
2 Airbrush pale blue colour on all ten nails ensuring good even coverage.
3 Airbrush dark blue over pale blue to create a colour fade.

4   Lay snowflake stencil over the nail and airbrush white snowflakes over the nails until the design is evenly balanced.

5   Seal the design with the airbrush sealant.

6   Apply two coats of top coat for protection. Using the orangewood stick tipped with Blu® Tack pick up and place the rhinestones in the centre of the snowflakes.

Name of design: French white design pearl white base

French pearl design step by step

Equipment needed:

- Sudo base coat
- Sudo pearl white and white opaque airbrush paints
- Sudo airbrush sealant
- stencil with straight edge or paper
- Sudo top coat

1   Apply base coat to all ten nails.

2   Airbrush pearl white colour on all ten nails ensuring good even coverage.

3   Lay the straight edge of stencil or paper diagonally over the free edge at the corner of the nail and spray with opaque white airbrush paint, ensuring that the spray is dry so as not to spoil your design when moving the stencil. The concentration of paint should be on the edge of the stencil or paper so there is no over spray beneath the edge. Follow this step on all ten nails.

4   Move the stencil to the opposite corner of the free edge and repeat the last step.

5   Move the stencil up the nail and repeat from alternate sides until design is complete.

6   Seal with airbrush sealant.

7   Apply top coat for protection.

Name of design: Alternative purple French design with lilac base

Alternative purple French design step by step

Equipment needed:

- Sudo base coat
- Sudo opaque lilac and opaque purple airbrush paints
- Sudo airbrush sealant
- stencil with straight edge or paper
- Sudo top coat

1   Apply base coat to all ten nails.

2   Airbrush opaque lilac colour on all ten nails ensuring good even coverage.

3   Lay the straight edge of stencil or paper diagonally over the free edge at the corner of the nail and spray with opaque purple airbrush paint, ensuring that the spray is dry so as not to spoil your design when moving the stencil. The concentration of paint should on the edge of the stencil or paper so there is no over spray beneath the edge. Follow this step on all ten nails.

4   Move the stencil to the opposite corner of the free edge and repeat the last step.

5   Move the stencil up the nail and repeat from alternate sides until design is complete.

6   Seal with airbrush sealant.

7   Apply top coat for protection.

Name of design: Colour fade with leopard print

**Colour fade with leopard print
step by step**

Equipment needed:

- Sudo base coat
- Sudo French beige, light brown and black airbrush paints
- Sudo animal leopard stencil
- Sudo airbrush sealant
- Sudo top coat
- orangewood stick tipped with Blu® Tack
- rhinestones

1   Apply base coat to all ten nails.

2   Airbrush French beige colour on all ten nails ensuring good even coverage.

3   Create colour fade with light brown airbrush paint, starting from the right free edge.

4   Lay the leopard stencil flat across the light brown area taking care to block the French beige colour to prevent over spray. Airbrush the black leopard spots.

5   Seal the design with airbrush sealant. Apply two coats of top coat for protection.

6   Using the orangewood stick tipped with Blu® Tack to pick up rhinestones, place in a row along the edge of the colour fade.

Alternative animal prints

Name of design: Green and white edge design

**Green and white edge
step by step**

Equipment needed:

- Sudo base coat
- Sudo pale green, white and mint green airbrush paints
- fine edge stencil
- Sudo airbrush sealant
- Sudo top coat

1 Apply base coat to all ten nails.
2 Airbrush pale green colour on all ten nails ensuring good even coverage.
3 Lay stencil randomly over the edge of the nail and airbrush white paint. Repeat on all ten nails.
4 Lay stencil randomly over the edge of the nail and airbrush mint green paint. Repeat on all ten nails.
5 Seal the design with airbrush sealant.
6 Apply top coat for protection.

Name of design: Striking black zig zag

**Striking black zig zag
step by step**

Equipment needed:

- Sudo base coat
- Sudo yellow, orange and black airbrush paints
- zig zag edges stencil or pre-cut design mask
- Sudo airbrush sealant
- Sudo top coat

1 Apply base coat to all ten nails.
2 Airbrush yellow colour on all ten nails ensuring good even coverage.
3 Airbrush orange paint to create a colour fade on all ten nails.
4 Place stencil or pre-cut design mask and airbrush black over the exposed area. Repeat on all ten nails.
5 Seal design with airbrush sealant.
6 Apply two coats of top coat for protection.

Name of design: Variegated green lace design

Green lace design step by step

Equipment needed:

- Sudo base coat
- Sudo pale green, metallic green, dark green and gold airbrush paints
- plastic wire lace stencil or piece of lace
- Sudo airbrush sealant
- Sudo top coat

1 Apply base coat to all ten nails.
2 Airbrush pale green colour on all ten nails ensuring good even coverage.
3 Lay plastic wire over the nail as flat as possible and airbrush metallic green paint. Repeat on all ten nails.
4 Move plastic wire and airbrush dark green paint on all ten nails. Then repeat using gold paint.
5 Seal design with airbrush sealant.
6 Apply two coats of top coat for protection.

Colour fade using frisket

Name of design: Colour fade design with frisket

Equipment needed:

- Sudo base coat
- choice of two or three Sudo airbrush paints
- pre-cut design mask or frisket
- Sudo airbrush sealant
- Sudo top coat

1   Apply base coat to all ten nails.

2   Airbrush first colour choice on all ten nails ensuring good even coverage.

3   Place pre-cut design mask or frisket on the nail and airbrush second colour choice over the exposed area.

4   If using three colours, airbrush the third colour choice over only half or less of the exposed area.

5   Remove design mask or frisket and seal with airbrush sealant.

6   Apply top coat for protection.

Name of design: Abstract white and purple design in opposite corners on pearl white base

Abstract white and purple design step by step

Equipment needed:

- Sudo base coat
- Sudo pearl white and purple and white airbrush paints
- stencil with pattern and edge design
- Sudo airbrush sealant
- Sudo top coat

1   Apply base coat to all ten nails.

2   Airbrush pearl white colour on all ten nails ensuring good even coverage.

3   Lay stencil over the corner of the nail and spray with opaque white airbrush paint ensuring that the spray is dry so as not to spoil your design when moving the stencil. Spray all ten nails in the same position. With purple, lay the stencil just above the first airbrush design on the nail. This will create a white shadow effect.

4   Repeat step three in the opposite corner.

5   Layer the design in this way to create the total look.

6   Seal with airbrush sealant.

7   Apply top coat for protection.

Name of design: Abstract white design in opposite corners on purple base

Abstract purple and white design step by step

Equipment needed:

- Sudo base coat
- Sudo white and purple airbrush paints
- stencil with pattern and edge design
- Sudo airbrush sealant
- Sudo top coat

1   Apply base coat to all ten nails.

2   Airbrush purple colour on all ten nails ensuring good even coverage.

3   Lay stencil over the corner of the nail and spray with white airbrush paint, ensuring that the spray is dry so as not to spoil your design when moving the stencil. Spray all ten nails in the same position.

4   Repeat on all ten nails in opposite corner.

5   Layer the design over the nail to complete the required look.

6   Seal with airbrush sealant.

7   Apply top coat for protection.

Edge design step by step

Name of design: Random edge design in blues and silver

Equipment needed:

- Sudo base coat
- Sudo white, pale blue, metallic silver, turquoise and mid blue airbrush paints
- rounded edge stencil
- Sudo airbrush sealant
- Sudo top coat

1   Apply base coat to all ten nails.
2   Airbrush white colour on all ten nails ensuring good even coverage.
3   Lay the stencil over the nail, only exposing the edges of the nail, and airbrush pale blue paint. Move the stencil around randomly and repeat. Airbrush all ten nails in the same way.
4   Repeat, moving the stencil around the nail and changing the colour of paint to complete your design.
5   Seal the design with airbrush sealant.
6   Apply top coat for protection.

Name of design: Leaf and grass design on a red background

Leaf design on red step by step

Equipment needed:

- Sudo base coat
- Sudo red, white, silver and black airbrush paints
- leaves and grass stencil
- Sudo airbrush sealant
- Sudo top coat

1 Apply base coat to all ten nails.
2 Airbrush red colour on all ten nails ensuring good even coverage.
3 Lay the stencil over the nail, only exposing the edges of the nail, and airbrush with white paint. Move the stencil around randomly and vary the leaf and grass design. Continue the design over all ten nails in the same way.
4 Continue to repeat the design, changing colour as required. Repeat on all ten nails.
5 Seal with airbrush sealant.
6 Apply top coat for protection.

Name of design: Leaf and fern design

Leaf design on white step by step

Equipment needed:

- Sudo base coat
- Sudo pale blue, white, pink and purple airbrush paints
- leaf and fern stencil
- Sudo airbrush sealant
- Sudo top coat
- orangewood stick tipped with Blu® Tack
- rhinestones

1 Apply base coat to all ten nails.
2 Airbrush white colour on all ten nails ensuring good even coverage.

3   Lay the stencil over the nail, only exposing the edges of the nail, and airbrush with pink paint. Move the stencil around randomly and vary the leaf and grass design. Continue the design over all ten nails in the same way.

4   Continue to repeat the design, changing colour as required. Repeat on all ten nails.

5   Seal the design with airbrush sealant. Apply two coats of top coat for protection.

6   Using orangewood stick tipped with Blu® Tack, pick up rhinestones and place in the design as required.

Name of design: Splats

Splats step by step

Equipment needed:

- Sudo base coat
- Sudo white, blue, pink, lilac and purple airbrush paints
- Sudo airbrush sealant
- Sudo top coat

1   Apply base coat to all ten nails.

2   Airbrush white colour on all ten nails ensuring good even coverage.

3   Holding the airbrush at a 90 degree angle and loaded with the first colour place airbrush directly on the nail. Press the trigger down and lift the airbrush straight up and release the trigger at the same time. This will create a splat effect.

4   Repeat the first colour randomly over the nail and then on the other nine nails.

5   Change colour and layer the splats over the entire nail. Change colours if required to balance the design. Be sure the splat is completely dry before airbrushing the next or you may lose definition.

6   Seal with airbrush sealant.

7   Apply coat of top coat for protection.

Name of design: Pale blue base with dark blue and white sunburst design

Sunburst design step by step

Equipment needed:

- Sudo base coat
- Sudo pale blue, white and dark blue airbrush paints
- pre-cut design mask
- Sudo airbrush sealant
- Sudo top coat

Designs using the negative and positive sides of the design mask

1 Apply base coat to all ten nails.

2 Airbrush pale blue on all ten nails ensuring good even coverage.

3 Place pre-cut design mask from the edge of the nail – you may use the negative or positive side of the mask. Airbrush your first colour and repeat randomly over the nail, ensuring you only keep to the edge of the nail plate for a sharper design.

4 Move the design mask towards the edge of the nail plate so the first sunburst is only slightly visible. Airbrush your second colour choice. When the mask is removed the first sunburst should look like a shadow of the second.

5 Seal the design with airbrush sealant.

6 Apply top coat for protection.

Name of design: White and red design

**White and red design
step by step**

Technical Tip

This is a selection of designs using the same French frisket, placed in different places and angles over the surface of the nail.

Equipment needed:

- Sudo base coat
- Sudo red and white airbrush paints
- Sudo airbrush sealant
- positive frisket of stencil
- Sudo top coat

1 Apply base coat to all ten nails.
2 Airbrush white colour on all ten nails ensuring good even coverage.
3 Place the frisket or stencil above the free edge to create a French design and airbrush with red paint
4 Move frisket or stencil above the last application of paint and repeat up the nail until the design is complete.
5 Seal the design with airbrush sealant.
6 Apply top coat for protection.

Name of design: White French with negative red frisket design

**White French frisket design –
negative step by step**

Equipment needed:

- Sudo base coat
- Sudo red and white airbrush paints
- Sudo airbrush sealant
- negative frisket or stencil
- Sudo top coat

1 Apply base coat to all ten nails.
2 Airbrush white colour on all ten nails ensuring good even coverage.
3 Place the frisket or stencil above the free edge to create a French design and airbrush with red paint.
4 Seal the design with airbrush sealant.
5 Apply top coat for protection.

Name of design: White French with positive red frisket design

White French frisket design – positive step by step

Equipment needed:

- Sudo base coat
- Sudo red and white airbrush paints
- Sudo airbrush sealant
- positive frisket or stencil
- Sudo top coat

1 Apply base coat to all ten nails.
2 Airbrush white colour on all ten nails ensuring good even coverage.
3 Place the frisket or stencil at the free edge to create a French design and airbrush with red paint
4 Seal the design with airbrush sealant.
5 Apply top coat for protection.

Name of design: White and red frisket design

**White and red frisket
step by step**

Equipment needed:

- Sudo base coat
- Sudo red and white airbrush paints
- Sudo airbrush sealant
- positive frisket or stencil
- Sudo top coat

1   Apply base coat to all ten nails.

2   Airbrush white colour on all ten nails ensuring good even coverage.

3   Lay the frisket diagonally across the nail and airbrush red on the edge of the frisket to create a crisp line with a shadow. Repeat until desired effect is achieved.

4   Seal the design with airbrush sealant.

5   Apply top coat for protection.

Name of design: Union Jack

Union Jack step by step

Equipment needed:

- Sudo base coat
- Sudo red, white and blue airbrush paints
- frisket cut into thin even strips
- Sudo airbrush sealant
- Sudo top coat

1   Apply base coat to all ten nails.

2   Airbrush white on all ten nails ensuring good even coverage.

3   Place one thin strip of frisket down the centre of the entire nail. Place second strip across the middle of the nail creating a cross. Place two strips diagonally across each corner. Airbrush the entire nail with blue paint then remove frisket.

4   Place two larger pieces of frisket in parallel lines down the centre of nail just within the edge of the first white line and airbrush with red paint. Lift and repeat this along the centre of each white line.

5   Seal design with airbrush sealant.

6   Apply top coat for protection.

Technical Tip

When spraying the red line in the centre of the white, use a new frisket each time to ensure correct placement.

Name of design: Fawn and burgundy plaid design

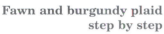

Fawn and burgundy plaid step by step

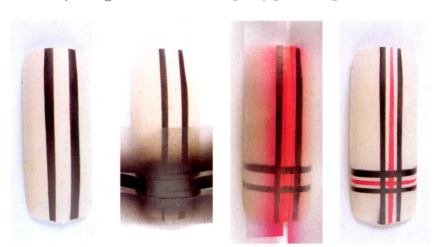

Equipment needed:

- Sudo base coat
- Sudo beige, red and black airbrush paints
- frisket cut into thin strips
- Sudo airbrush sealant
- Sudo top coat

1   Apply base coat to all ten nails.

2   Airbrush beige on all ten nails ensuring good even coverage.

3   Place a thin piece of frisket down the centre of the entire nail, then place two pieces of frisket evenly either side of the first piece and airbrush with black paint. Remove frisket. Repeat,

this time placing the frisket across the nail to create a cross. Remove frisket.

4 Place two pieces of frisket in parallel lines very close together down the middle of the nail and airbrush with red paint. Remove the frisket. Repeat across the nail. Remove frisket.

5 Seal design with airbrush sealant.

6 Apply top coat for protection.

Name of design: Flames

Flames step by step

Equipment needed:

- Sudo base coat
- Sudo black, red, yellow and orange airbrush paints
- pre-cut design mask frisket or stencil
- Sudo airbrush sealant
- Sudo top coat

Technical Tip

To ensure sharp crisp flames, always start at the top of the nail and layer flames down the nail or you may cover the previous application of flames.

1 Apply base coat to all ten nails.

2 Airbrush yellow on all ten nails ensuring good even coverage.

3 Place design mask frisket or stencil two-thirds of the way up the nail and airbrush black over the edge of the frisket.

4 Move the frisket down the nail and airbrush red; move the frisket again and airbrush orange paint. Add more black if required to add depth.

5 Seal design with airbrush sealant.

6 Apply top coat for protection.

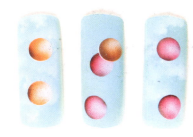

Bubbles

Name of design: Bubbles

Equipment needed:

- Sudo base coat
- Sudo pale pink, pale blue, yellow, purple, white and black airbrush paints
- bubble stencil or pre-cut frisket
- Sudo airbrush sealant
- Sudo top coat

1 Apply base coat to all ten nails.
2 Airbrush pale blue on all ten nails.
3 Place bubbles stencil or frisket on blue nail and airbrush yellow bubbles. Airbrush contrasting colours on the top and bottom of bubbles to create a 3D design. Remove frisket and repeat on all ten nails. Ensure you only spray lightly on the edge of the frisket to give a shadowed effect.
4 Seal design with airbrush sealant.
5 Apply top coat for protection.

Name of design: Bubbles over candy stripe

Bubbles and candy stripe step by step

Equipment needed:

- Sudo base coat
- Sudo pale pink, magenta, pale blue, yellow, purple and black airbrush paints
- stripe stencil or pre-cut frisket or stencil
- bubble stencil or pre-cut frisket
- Sudo airbrush sealant
- Sudo top coat

1 Apply base coat to all ten nails.
2 Airbrush pale pink on all ten nails, place pre-cut striping frisket or stencil on to nail then, using magenta paint, airbrush candy stripe and remove frisket. Repeat on all ten nails.
3 Place bubbles stencil or frisket on candy stripe and airbrush yellow bubbles. Airbrush contrasting colours on the top and bottom of bubbles to create a 3D design. Remove frisket and repeat on all ten nails.
4 Seal design with airbrush sealant.
5 Apply top coat for protection.

Name of design: Gold metallic clouds and bubbles

**Clouds and bubbles
step by step**

Equipment needed:

- Sudo base coat
- Sudo metallic gold, white, blue and black airbrush paints
- frisket or stencil
- Sudo airbrush sealant
- Sudo top coat

1. Apply base coat to all ten nails.
2. Spray all ten nails with metallic gold.
3. Using tissue or stencil, airbrush edge with white paint to create clouds.
4. Lay bubble frisket or stencil on the nail and airbrush bubbles with blue paint.
5. Leaving frisket in place, airbrush white and black to create a 3D image.
6. Seal the design with airbrush sealant.
7. Apply top coat for protection.

Name of design: Three-dimensional shapes

**Three-dimensional shapes
step by step**

Technical Tip

This design is much easier to achieve if a pre-cut design mask is used.

Technical Tip

You will need a fine needle for this type of work. Try adding a shadow underneath all of the shapes for an extra 3D effect.

Equipment needed:

- Sudo base coat
- Sudo metallic gold, pink, blue and light green airbrush paints
- Sudo airbrush sealant
- Sudo top coat

1 Apply base coat to all ten nails.
2 Using a four-colour blend with metallic gold, pink, blue and light green, airbrush all ten nails.
3 Lay stencil flat on the nail. Airbrush the desired shape with white paint.
4 Leave your stencil in place and add the metallic pink to give definition. Remove your stencil and freehand airbrush highlights in white and dark shadows in black onto the shapes.
5 Seal the design with airbrush sealant.
6 Apply top coat for protection.

Name of design: Eagle in sunset

Eagle in sunset step by step

Equipment needed:

- Sudo base coat
- Sudo pale blue, white, yellow, red, black and light brown airbrush paints – more colours can be added depending on your theme
- torn tissue
- stencil or pre-cut frisket
- Sudo airbrush sealant
- Sudo top coat

1 Apply base coat to all ten nails. Airbrush pale blue all over the nail for background. Using the torn tissue and white paint, create clouds.

Technical Tip

You could change the background scenery to create mountains and trees.

2 At the tip of the nail, airbrush the ground using light brown. Using a stencil or pre-cut frisket, airbrush a yellow sun. Do not remove the stencil or mask.

3 With a stencil or mask still in place, use red paint to highlight one side of the stencil; this will give the sun a 3D effect and add definition. Remove stencil or mask.

4 With a stencil or mask and black paint, airbrush an eagle and tree branches.

5 Seal the design with airbrush sealant.

6 Apply top coat for protection.

Name of design: Sunset with cat

Sunset with cat step by step

Equipment needed:

- Sudo base coat
- Sudo pearlescent red, orange, yellow, blue, black, green and opaque pink airbrush paints – more colours can be added depending on your theme
- stencil or pre-cut frisket
- Sudo airbrush sealant
- Sudo top coat

1 Apply base coat to all ten nails. Colour fade from red to blue at tip – incorporating all of the desired colours to create the design.

2 Place stencil or pre-cut frisket to create sunset using pink. At the tip of the nail airbrush base for cat – this could be a fence or solid base – and airbrush with pearlescent black paint.

3 Place the cat stencil or pre-cut frisket onto the fence or solid base and airbrush black paint to create the silhouette of a cat. Using the same stencil as the sunset, airbrush a shadow over the top of the sun to give definition.

4 Seal the design with airbrush sealant.

5 Apply top coat for protection.

Technical Tip

Try substituting these colours with darker ones to create a moonlight night time scene.

Name of design: Sunset, palm tree and island

Sunset with palm tree step by step

Equipment needed:

- Sudo base coat
- Sudo blue, white, red, yellow, black and green airbrush paints – more colours can be added depending on your theme
- stencil or pre-cut frisket
- Sudo airbrush sealant
- Sudo top coat

1 Apply base coat to all ten nails. Mask the top half of the nail and airbrush blue paint onto the bottom half of the nail. This will become the sea. Using white, mist the sea and create light reflections.
2 Turn the mask around and colour fade from top to bottom using yellow and red. Where two colours meet, this will create a sunset orange effect. Airbrush a light blue frame for the sky on all ten nails.
3 Lay the stencil over the side of the nail and airbrush with green paint to create the palm tree and island. Vary the colours but keep them a to similar tone as the palm tree and island are shaded. If you place the palm tree and island to the side you have the opportunity to incorporate other images in your design such as boats, animals, buildings, etc.
4 Seal the design with airbrush sealant.
5 Apply top coat for protection.

Alternative sunsets

Silver medal Nail Olympics

Troubleshooting

Learning objectives

In this section you will learn about:

- **the most common problems encountered with airbrush equipment**
- **some of the difficulties of airbrushing technique**
- **tips on how to solve most problems**

Most airbrushing problems are caused by nail artists not cleaning their airbrushes properly. It is vital that before you turn everything off for the day, you give your airbrush a good, thorough clean, including all the parts. Always make sure that you follow the manufacturer's instructions and use your instruction manual. Treat your airbrush as a precious tool and always keep it in good condition. There is nothing more frustrating and time consuming than turning your system on and being faced with a blocked airbrush at the beginning of your day. This will lose you respect from your clients and time spent cleaning at this point is time you could be earning money. In this section we will look at the most common problems and how to deal with them.

Paint is spitting out of the airbrush

1 Check that the hose is attached to both airbrush and compressor properly
2 Check that the PSI on your compressor is correct, especially if it is used for more than one purpose, for example body art or tanning
3 Check that your needle is clean and not bent
4 Check the nozzle for any damage, for example splitting, and replace if necessary
5 Check that nozzles or crown caps are tightened effectively
6 Check that your colour cup or paint reservoir is clean and free from dried paint
7 Fit a moisture trap/separator if your compressor does not have one or empty it on a regular basis. Wherever there is compressed air there is moisture. This will always ruin your design if spraying for more than a few minutes

Paint is bubbling in the colour cup

1 Check that the hoses are attached to both airbrush and compressor properly
2 Check that the PSI on your compressor is correct
3 Check that the needle is clean and the colour cup is not blocked
4 Check that nozzles or crown caps are tightened effectively
5 Check that the needle is not bent

6   Make sure that the nozzle and the nozzle cap are correctly fitted

7   Make sure that the nozzle and the nozzle cap are not damaged

No air coming out of airbrush

1   Check the hose is not trapped and stopping the air coming through, for example your chair leg may be on the hose!

2   Check that the hoses are attached to the airbrush and compressor properly

3   Check that the needle is not blocked or bent

4   Check your power supply and all relevant switches are turned on

Too much air coming out of airbrush

1   Check that the PSI on your compressor is correct for your treatment

2   You could be pulling the trigger back too far on your airbrush. If using a single action airbrush, reset the thread of the needle

3   Check that you have not damaged your airbrush by dropping or knocking it

Colours coming out too wet

1   The air pressure could be too low

2   You could be pulling the trigger back too far, too quickly

3   Make sure you shake your paint bottles before decanting into airbrush

4   Do not work too close

5   Ensure you press the trigger down before pulling back for paint

Some colours are not vibrant enough

1   Transparent, fluorescents and some pearl colours need to be sprayed over an opaque colour to give good colour depth or try using a crystalline base coat. For the best results use opaque white

2   Try spraying more layers to give extra depth

3   Make sure that you shake your colour pots as the chemicals can separate in storage

4   Check that your top coat is not contaminated with darker colours

Why does the paint peel off when stencilling or using mask?

1   Spray is much too wet

2   You are spraying too close

3   You are building the paint too thick

4   The base coat is applied too thick

Why does the paint bleed when using stencils or mask?

1   Spray is too fast and too wet

2   You are not holding the stencil down properly over the curve of the nail

3   The edges of the mask might not be properly adhered to the nail

4   Try to spray onto the stencil or mask at a 90° angle. Hold your client's finger at the correct angle to achieve this

How do I avoid overspray on to a client's skin?

1   Work about 1–2 inches (3–5 cm) from the nail surface

2   Direct the spray at the area you want to colour

3   Learn to control your trigger finger so that you do not use too much paint, and then finish with air to dry the paint

4   Hold client's finger at correct angle to airbrush

5   Some overspraying paint could be blocked with your own thumb

6   Use lighter colours at the top of the nail; darker colours are harder to remove from the skin

7   For clients who have sensitive skin use a sculpting form or a barrier cream, although this is not ideal as it could come into contact with your design

Chapter summary

After completing this chapter you should have a clear understanding of all the equipment needed to set up an airbrush service, how to keep your equipment in good condition and some idea about the possible problems you might encounter and how to solve them. It is important to keep practising a colour fade so that you cannot see where one colour ends and another begins. Also, remember to spray dry. Once you have achieved these skills, you will be able to tackle all the designs in this section. There is no other art form as versatile as airbrushing so learn your techniques, practise, become totally familiar with your airbrush and never stop learning. Remember that it is always better to have a professional government-recognised qualification, so try to find a training centre that can offer this.

Knowledge review

1 How long has airbrushing been around?

2 What are the benefits of airbrushing compared to hand painting?

3 What points would you consider before buying an airbrush system if you are a mobile nail artist?

4 What are the alternative air sources available?

5 What does a moisture trap do?

6 What pressure (PSI) would you use for nail art?

7 List the three types of hose you could use with your compressor.

8 What are the two types of airbrush available?

9 What points would you consider when buying an airbrush?

10 When should you clean your airbrush?

11 What is a 'crown cap'?

12 Which paints can you use in an airbrush?

13 Why is it so important to use your manufacturer's recommended airbrush cleaner?

14 What is the difference between a stencil and pre-cut frisket?

15 Why do you need to 'seal' the airbrush paint before applying top coat?

16 What are the reasons for the airbrush exercises?

17 What is the difference between highlighting and contouring?

18 How would you recognise a good colour fade?

19 How many different mediums could you use to create cloud designs?

20 Describe how you would perform an animal print with a stencil.

21 Describe how you would perform the step-by-step Union Jack design.

22 What are the first three steps in any sunset design?

23 Why is it so important to ensure that frisket/masking paper is laid down with all edges onto the nail?

24 What are the most common causes of airbrush blockages?

25 What could cause bubbles in the colour cup?

26   What would be the cause of no air coming out of the airbrush?

27   Why would the colours come out too wet?

28   How could you avoid over-spray on your client's skin?

29   How often would you have your compressor serviced?

30   What other airbrush services could you offer?

Mixed media nail art

5

Learning objectives

In this chapter we will consider the following:

- **products, tools and equipment**
- **cut out nail designs**
- **embedding**
- **coloured acrylics**
- **three-dimensional designs**

In the nail industry there have been many new products and techniques in the last five years that have given nail artists considerable creative freedom. With the advent of coloured acrylic powders and gels we can now provide previously impossible services for our clients. When Creative Nail Design launched their Mosaic Powders it opened up a whole new world not only for nail artists entering competitions and doing photographic work but also for salon clientele who wanted to be a little more adventurous. Our classes are always full of enthusiastic students and experienced nail technicians wanting to stretch their skills to the next level. Our previously neutral colours have been supplemented by a whole range of vibrant colours as well as glitter powders and Mosaic Powders that are all colour stable. The new HABIA Nail Standards published in 2004 include mixed media nail art and this chapter will help you to gain that qualification and also inspire you to create a new level of designs for your clients, competitions and photographic work. This chapter is where The Untouchables – the authors' nail art business – started and for us it is the most versatile and exciting chapter in the book!

Some nail artists may never wish to try the designs in this chapter but for those who want to take their designing skills into the salon, competitions and photographic work, this one is for you. We have tried to show you all of the techniques and some designs and you can take these ideas and work on them for yourselves, creating your own wonderful nails.

Note

For more information on the new Nail Standards for 2004, contact HABIA.

Products, tools and equipment

Learning objectives

In this section you will learn about:

- **the various products needed to perform mixed media nail art**
- **the tools and equipment needed for your kit**
- **working safely**

Group powders

It is impossible for us to list all of the products, tools and equipment that you would need for mixed media nail art, as every time we design a new set of nails we use something new or different. As you go through this chapter you will find that you may discover new techniques and tools yourself. We would encourage you to visit hobby shops, look at home in your kitchen and garage and not restrict yourself to nail products and tools. Anyone who has been on an Untouchables Play Day will have seen the kit that we carry is really obscure. On some photographic shoots the models and photographers have looked on in horror when we have taken pliers out of our kit!

Mixed media products

Creative Mosaic powders

There are many coloured acrylic powders and UV **gels** on the market today. All we would advise is that you never buy products without some training in how to use them, and make sure that you have technical back-up. The products should be tried and tested and approved by the Health and Safety Executive.

We use the Creative Nail Design Mosaic Powders and find these the most colour stable powders on the market. There are six colours in this range but Creative also have a perfect black powder, perfect white, pink, natural and clear as well as two glitter powders called Glimmer and Twilight. All of these colours can be mixed to create other beautiful colours. The Mosaic collection has the following colours:

- red – Spanish Tile
- yellow – Golden Glass
- blue – Cobalt Glass

These are all primary colours.

- orange – Terracotta
- purple – Quartz Crystal
- green – Jade

These are called secondary colours.

The new Creative collection of coloured powders is called Metro. The colours are beautiful and create the most amazing designs. The colours in the collection are:

Metro powders

- white – City of Peace
- copper – City of Angels
- bronze – The Melting Pot
- gold – The Golden City
- black – Sin City
- silver – City of Light

We would encourage you to sit down and experiment with mixing your powders rather than spending money on a large colour range. It can be very relaxing to create new colours by mixing powders yourself, and the same applies to your airbrush paints.

Technical Tip

Refer to the first section of Chapter 3 – Colour theory – if you need ideas or help with your colour choices.

Technical Tip

We would always recommend that you lay a thin coat of clear acrylic on the natural nail and nail tip before using coloured powders or gels for maximum adhesion, strength and also to prevent overexposure and discolouration of the natural nail.

Here are a few ideas to try:

- 1 part blue + 3 parts white = pastel blue
- 1 part blue + 3 parts white + 1 part Glimmer = pastel blue hologram glitter
- 1 part blue + 3 parts clear = translucent blue
- 1 part blue + 3 parts clear + 1 part Glimmer = translucent blue hologram glitter

You will need clean, dry containers with lids that are easy to open and big enough for you to shake the powder so that it mixes well. Always make a note of the proportions used or label your 'recipe' so that you can recreate your favourite colour combinations. You can use black to give your colours more definition or darken them slightly.

It is a good idea to attend trade shows and have a good look at what is on the market. We would recommend that you ask to have a demonstration nail before purchasing powders or gels so that you can see whether the clarity of the colour is what you expect and also how well it will last. If it does not wear well on you then it will not last on your clients.

We will now look in detail at some of the most important products in our own kits. The items we would never do without are liquid and powder. It is the most versatile medium for any nail art work and, as you will see throughout this chapter, some incredible arts of work can be created with liquid and powder.

Safety Tip

Never be tempted to mix one company's products with another as it could have disastrous results. Products are made to complement one another and should never be mixed.

Mosaic powder fairies

Liquid and powder

We use Retention + and the Perfect Colour Powders as they are colour stable and set quickly. This is important if you are in a competition and time is limited. You can create fantastic works of art just using colour acrylics, as you can see from the picture.

Tips

You will need a selection of different tips for various looks and occasions. If you are working on salon clientele, you will find normal tips are adequate but you may want to try Creative Clear Tips. It is possible to create beautiful designs with these tips, such as embedding lace and feathers or creating designs with coloured acrylics. If you are entering a competition where you can attach the nails just before you start or you are doing nails for a photo shoot, then you may want to use Kiss Tips Long Curve. These tips are versatile because they are so long you can use them for cut outs and airbrushing. They also fit quite neatly into most models' cuticle area.

Gel bond

This jelly-like adhesive has been a lifesaver on many occasions at photo shoots, backstage at London Fashion Week and when we have entered competitions. Because it has a thick consistency you can use very small amounts to great effect. We would only use a liquid adhesive when applying a set of nail enhancements or a resin when performing any fibreglass work.

Rhinestones

Rhinestones/flat-stones

We have a great relationship with Swarvosky Crystal and have done many jobs for them, including the Harrods Knightsbridge department store window. We would always recommend that you use good quality crystals and make sure that you have a good colour range to select from. Never put adhesive or top coat over the top of your crystals in photographic work or competitions as it will take away the shine and depth of the look. Flat-stones can be incorporated within your design and this can prove to be very cost effective. Check the quality, as some flat-stones lose their colour when top coat is applied or they are embedded within a design. These are available in a wide colour range and are a cheap item to add to your kit.

Materials, lace, ribbons

It is a good idea to visit a material shop, department store or hobby craft shop to acquire small samples and pieces of different materials. Lace, for instance, can look really stunning. It can be embedded on top of clear tips and into the acrylic. Black and red colours look beautiful but white can lose its definition.

Material can be used on top of nails as well as in the acrylic. Designs such as gingham on toes and a flower material can look really stunning. Ribbons can be used to great effect as well.

Materials and lace

Paints

We covered paints in great detail in Chapters 3 and 4. We do advise that you carry a selection of the primary colours, plus black and white and a few others such as silver and gold. We would also recommend the flexi-brush as it is easier to perform designs that need lines with these than with a liner brush. Using a flexi-brush gives greater control and speed.

Glitters

You should have a selection of coloured glitters in your kit. These can be used as explained in Chapter 3 or mixed with other media such as acrylics or gels.

Files and buffers

A selection of various files and buffers should be included in your kit. Once they have been used, keep them in a container or plastic bag so that the dust does not contaminate other items in your kit.

Base/top coats

Make sure that you have a spare of each just in case there is an accident – this is especially important if you are working on location somewhere. There are top coats with different finishes such as Northern Lights with a Hologram Glitter and Satin Top Coat with makes the polish go very dull and matt. There are also high gloss top coats such as Creative Super Shiney or Designer Nails Looks Wet.

Creative polishes

Enamels/polishes

Every nail art kit should have a good range of polishes. You should also carry a few empty polish bottles in case you need to mix polishes to create a specific colour requested by an editor or photographer. You could consider carrying polishes in clear plastic make-up cases. We have one for reds and browns, one for pinks and blues. It is much easier for a client, editor, model or photographer to look through a clear bag than for you to empty them all on to the desk or floor to find the right colour.

Polish remover

Ensure that you have a good quality polish remover and one that will not stain the skin with the polish. Make sure that the container has a screw top and will not leak in your kit when moved around. Always take a spare bottle in case you have to leave early and need to leave a bottle with the models to take off their polish themselves.

Sundries

Make-up wipes

Invaluable if you do not have access to washing facilities.

Disposables

Cotton wool, orangesticks, couch roll, lint free pads, tissues, etc.

As well as the above you might want to add a few items like transfers, bhindis and other nail art products that you like using.

Tools and equipment

Designer Nails wallet of tools

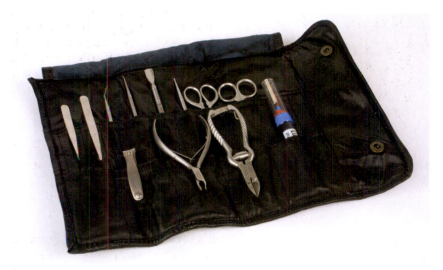

Most of these items have been explained in Chapter 3 so rather than repeat ourselves we will just list the items that we feel you need in your kit. There are a few specialist tools that you may want to use and we will explain their use further on in this section.

Here is a basic list of the tools and equipment you will need:

- scissors/tip cutters/cuticle pusher/nippers/tweezers
- a selection of nail art brushes
- acrylic and gel brushes
- pots/dappen dishes/mixing palette
- Blu® Tack
- lamp/UV gel lamp
- safety glasses
- hobby knife and small cutting board

The items that make people look on in horror at our kit are things such as a glue gun, drills, wire cutters, etc.

Safety Tip

Safety glasses should be worn when performing cut outs or drilling tips.

Glue gun

This is a tool that would not be used on a client. We would use this when designing a set of nails for a photo shoot or competition. A glue gun can be a lot easier than traditional nail adhesives when fixing objects or materials to nail tips. Glue guns are available in hot or cold varieties and care should be taken when using them. You must cover any surfaces that you are working on and make sure you have a heat resistant surface to put the gun on to when working. Ensure that there are no children or animals around when working with this tool. Take care to use a little glue rather than a lot, as most of the time you will be working on a very small surface such as a nail tip, unless of course you are creating a costume for a competition.

Drills

We would *never* advocate the use of drills for nail enhancement services but there are times when designing nail art tips that a drill

A drill

Technical Tip

Remember when using a drill on a plastic tip that the tip will become very hot. You will find that you need to practise your technique to do very fine work. You may wish to find a drill that has a speed control so that you can start slowly and build up your speed as your technique improves.

is a valuable tool. We would only ever use the drill on tips that we are preparing to put onto a client. A drill can be a handy tool for cut out designs and can create some beautiful shapes on the free edge of Kiss Tips Long Curve. You will not need many drill bits as you will probably only use a maximum of three different shapes. If you do buy yourself a drill for the purpose of designing nails then we would recommend finding your local hobby craft shop and looking at different makes. You do not need an industrial drill from a DIY store or a nail drill. You may find a nail drill will not have the power or bits to cut out the shapes that you want. A hobby drill is really your best option. Shop around for different makes and prices.

Another item mentioned above was wire cutters. Sue used these to create the Barbed Wire Nails for London Fashion Week. Rather than using real barbed wire we created our own with garden wire. You can see further details on this in the step-by-step instructions for this design on p. 213.

Checklist of safety tips

We would just like to list a few important safety tips for you to bear in mind, as the nails you will be doing in this section could be potentially dangerous to create or wear.

- Always apply your nail art designs on tips at the last minute before a show starts or a photo is taken
- Always keep your equipment and tools in a safe place both when you are using them and when they are not in use
- If using electrical equipment, make sure that there are no trailing leads and that all equipment is checked annually by a professional
- Store your equipment in proper storage and allow any heated items time to cool down before putting them away
- Keep lids on bottles at all times
- Dispose of your own waste
- Ensure that models wearing designs are warned of any potential dangers and that you are available to remove nails at the end of the photo shoot or fashion show
- Always apply nails in a safe manner and do not put your model at risk of any potential dangers such as overexposure or nail plate damage
- Look around you when you have finished to make sure that all tools and materials have been packed away or disposed of
- If disposing of blades or sharp items you need to have a sharps box or follow Local Council guidelines
- Wear personal protective equipment when necessary

Before we close this section we would just like to reiterate that you need not restrict yourself to nail tools. Look upon yourself as a designer and use the tools and equipment you need to create an image. Most of the time the nails will be finished before you apply them to human hands. We always say, anything goes!

Cut out nail designs

Learning objectives

In this section you will learn about:

- **cutting out tips with scissors**
- **using a drill to create shapes**
- **designing different looks with cut out shapes**
- **using different media once a shape has been cut**
- **step-by-step designs for you to follow**

Performing cut out designs on tips is one of the least technical and easiest areas to work in, but can still create stunning looks. You could work your designs out with pen and paper first, although anything too elaborate may not work as it could be too difficult to cut out. Once you have designed the look on paper you could use a pencil or pen on your tips if you need a guideline to work to.

Sudo Hair, Nail and Body Art

Cutting out with scissors

This is the easiest way of cutting a tip into different shapes but can be limiting when trying to achieve curves and circles. The hardness of the tips you are using will affect how easy they are to cut out. You will need to look at the following points to effectively obtain good clear cut outs:

- make sure your scissors are sharp
- depending on the look required, use straight or curved scissors
- always use tips with enough length
- use good quality tips, not ones that are too brittle
- have spare tips to hand to practise on or to allow for mistakes
- cut with the scissors straight on and not at an angle
- remember it is difficult to create exactly the same look on every nail
- take advantage of the possibility of creating various shapes for each nail, it makes the design more interesting
- remember when designing tips for the opposite hand the design must be a mirror image
- always cut a few extra designs in case your next step goes wrong or you need extra tips to make up for losses at a fashion show
- use a fine file like Creative Nail Design Kanga Board, which is thin and sharp, to file away any inconsistencies and neaten edges
- remember if you use a finishing block on top of the tip to finish, you will need to file with a shiny buffer otherwise the finished tip will come out looking scratched
- if you have not got a drill then you could use a hobby knife with different blades to cut out different shapes, but use a cutting board and protect your fingers

Once you have finished your cut outs remember to tidy up and remove all of the dust before progressing to your next stage. If the next step is airbrushing and there is any excess dust around it will completely spoil your design. The cut outs are only the first stage of your design process and it may be a good idea to do a few dozen of the same shape and try different media on top.

Using a drill to create shapes

We have already talked about the different types of drills that you could use for cut outs but one point to remember is if you are going to work on location you might need a battery operated drill as you may have no access to electricity. Some drills on the market use rechargeable batteries and others can be used with either batteries or mains electricity supply. Choose the drill which best suits your purposes.

Even though you will not be drilling when your client or model has their nails on, you still need to take care and follow all safety precautions. This includes such things as working on a surface that

Technical Tip

When drawing your designs on paper always draw to scale and do not make the tip size too big otherwise your design will not be true and could be difficult to achieve.

is appropriate and not your mum's best dining table or your antique coffee table! Using a drill can create beautiful shapes that you cannot do with scissors or a hobby knife, but if you drill into an area and make it too thin your tip will snap. Also remember that the heat produced by the drill will also affect the strength of the tip and make it more flexible whilst it is hot. Here are a few guidelines you may wish to follow:

- always work on a suitable protected surface
- do not allow children near you when working
- always disconnect the drill from the electricity supply when finished
- always switch the drill off when it is not in your hand
- remember that drills can become quite hot when used for long periods
- if you have long hair, tie it back when using a drill
- make sure you remove jewellery such as necklaces or earrings that could get in the way
- always take out your drill bits when you have finished with them so they do not become bent or twisted in storage or when being transported
- consider the value to you of a drill that has a variable speed facility
- ensure that your drill is electrically tested once a year by a professional
- do not allow the lead to trail across floor where people walk
- when drill bits become dull or blunt, replace them or have them sharpened

Technical Tip

You could also use your hobby knife or a sharp pair of scissors, but you need to be very careful when doing it this way, we do not want any cut fingers!

You may just use your drill to cut out all of the shapes you need in your design or you could start with scissors and use the drill to give definition with circles and curved edges. Always use your scissors first and then finish with the drill to produce definition. You may find that a lower speed will be better when you first start practising on tips with a drill. When cutting out with a drill frayed edges sometimes occur and you may, with skill, use your drill to get rid of these. This does take practice and there has been many a time when we have done this only to destroy our whole nail and have had to start all over again. You could use a white block or Creative Koala Buffer to get rid of the excess but you will then need to ensure that the tip is buffed back to a shine so that the scratches do not show through when it is finished.

Designing different looks with cut outs

You can do designs using the cut out method and then polish or airbrush on top or continue into 3D and embedding to give extra dimension. When planning your cut outs, remember that the simplest shape can look stunning with the right design on top.

You need to plan your shape before you start cutting. We have found that if we just cut without direction we end up with odd shapes or bits that drop off! Sometimes we have even done a design on paper only to find that it is impossible to create as a practical cut out.

If you are stuck for ideas then look in art books, especially at geometric shapes and designs. It is always more interesting to see a set of nails where each nail is a different shape than a set that are all the same and when we are judging competitions we always give higher marks for originality and expression.

The pictures here show a few examples of shapes that can be cut and in the next sections you will see these designs developed further when other nail art media are added.

The basic tips in the pictures shown here look very boring and plain, but once your designs have been finished you can see from the completed designs shown that they really don't look like the same nail tips.

Pointed nail   Diagonal cut   Curved cut   Hole cut

Technical Tip

It is important to remember that if your work is for a photo shoot or competition you will need to make sure that all the edges are neat and tidy and that your design has clear cut outs with defined shapes. The camera will pick up every little detail and judges will mark you down for untidy work.

Blue/gold/green cut outs

Using various media on your cut outs

Once your cut outs have been finished and are neat and tidy, you will either have decided which medium you are going to use to decorate them or you may be intending to try a few different looks to see how they turn out. Here are some of the options that you can choose from:

- airbrushing
- hand painting
- coloured acrylics and gels
- materials
- jewellery
- rhinestones and decals
- glitters

Of course you can use a mixture of all of the above and if you were entering a competition like The Nail Olympics in Las Vegas you would need to use a minimum of three of the above media otherwise you would lose points. If you are entering any competition, we would always recommend that you obtain the rules and regulations beforehand so that you can be prepared. Refer to Chapter 7 on Competition nails for more information.

It may seem from the designs in this book that most cut outs would be unsuitable for your salon clients, but this is untrue. Many of our clients wear diagonal or pointed nails on a daily basis and have maintenance visits every three weeks. Remember that when acrylic is put over the tip the sharpness of the tip is lost in the acrylic and these nails become wearable. We have many clients who want something different for special occasions and remember that whatever clothes designs you see on the catwalk are scaled down for the public – we do the same with our nail designs. Think of your nail art as catwalk and your salon nails as street wear. You can adapt many looks, although obviously not all.

Point to remember

Remember that a nail that has holes or cut away sides is going to be much weaker even with acrylic on the top, so warn your clients or the models wearing your designs that they need to be extra careful when using their hands.

Gold cut outs

Green cut out step by step

Step-by-step cut out designs

Name of design: Green cut out/airbrush and rhinestones
Equipment needed:

- long curved tips
- drill
- scissors
- files and buffers
- dark green and black Sudo paints
- orangewood stick with Blu® Tack
- crystal rhinestones
- Sudo airbrush sealant
- Sudo top coat and base coat

1   Cut tip into a point. Refine with thin board such as a Kanga Board.

2   Drill holes into side to form a perforated edge, decreasing in size towards the tip. Then drill holes into the top; use a cone shaped drill bit to give different size holes.

3   Tidy tip up and ensure that all edges are neat. Make sure that your working area is totally dust free.

4   Base coat the nails and allow to dry.

5   Airbrush the nails with green paint first and then spray the edges and the holes with black to give dimension to the design. Seal the design with airbrush sealant.

6   Use the top coat to embed the rhinestones. Make sure that you use at least two coats of top coat quite quickly and that the rhinestones do not have any top coat applied over them.

Blue cut out step by step

Name of design: Blue cut out/airbrush and rhinestones

Equipment needed:

- long curved tips
- drill
- scissors
- files and buffers
- blues and deep blue/purple Sudo paints
- orangewood stick with Blu® Tack
- crystal rhinestones
- Sudo airbrush sealant
- Sudo top coat and base coat

1 Cut tip into a diagonal point. Refine with thin board such as a Kanga Board.

2 Drill holes into side to form a perforated edge, decreasing in size towards the tip. Drill the other side with bigger perforations and less of them.

3 Tidy tip up and ensure that all edges are neat. Make sure that your working area is totally dust free.

4 Base coat the nails and allow to dry.

5 Airbrush the nails with the palest blue paint first and then spray the edges and the holes with darker blues to purple to give dimension to the design. Seal the design with airbrush sealant.

6 Use the top coat to embed the rhinestones. Make sure that you use at least two coats of top coat quite quickly and that the rhinestones do not have any top coat applied over them.

3D cut out step by step

Name of design: Three-dimensional cut out

Equipment needed:

- long curved tips
- drill
- scissors
- files and buffers
- Creative liquid and powder kit
- sculpting brush
- blues and lilac and purple Sudo paints
- orangewood stick with Blu® Tack
- crystal rhinestones
- Sudo airbrush sealant
- Sudo top coat and base coat

1   Cut tip into a soft point. Refine with thin board such as a Kanga Board.

2   Drill holes into side to form a perforated edge, decreasing in size towards the tip. Then drill holes into the top; use a cone shaped drill bit to give different size holes.

3   Tidy tip up and ensure that all edges are neat. Make sure that your working area is totally dust free.

4   Using small bead of acrylic work designs from the free edge up to the cuticle area. Be careful not to add too many at once; start off with a few and add to them as you build your design.

5   Base coat the nails and allow to dry.

6   Airbrush the nails with lilac first, then the darker colours to give dimension to the design. Seal the design with airbrush sealant.

7   Use the top coat to embed the rhinestones. Make sure that you use at least two coats of top coat quite quickly and that the rhinestones do not have any top coat applied over them. Do not add too many rhinestones otherwise you will lose the beauty of the design.

Steps 1–4

Step 5

Step 5

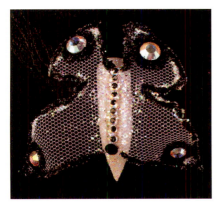

Cut out butterfly – final look

Name of design: Cut-out butterfly

Equipment needed:

- long curved tips
- scissors
- files and buffers
- pearlescent glitter polish
- pearlescent and black glitter
- orangewood stick with Blu® Tack
- large and small crystal and jet rhinestones
- Creative gel bond
- fine white net
- top coat and base coat

1   Cut tip into a point. Refine with thin board such as a Kanga Board.

2   Tidy tip up and ensure that all edges are neat. Make sure that your working area is totally dust free.

3   Base coat the nails and allow to dry.

4   Polish nails with 2–3 coats of glitter polish

5   Cut out net into butterfly shape and fix to centre of nail with small Creative gel bond dots down the nail. Press firmly into place with an orangestick.

6   Use black glitter and glitter dust mixer to edge the butterfly and give outline. Place small amounts of top coat on the net and randomly place pearlescent glitter over net.

7   Place small beads of gel bond along the centre and place small jet rhinestones along the line. Then place a slightly larger bead of gel bond at the outer corners of net and place large crystal rhinestones on top.

Embedding

Learning objectives

In this section you will learn about:

- **media that can be used for embedding**
- **safety techniques**
- **specific after care**
- **step-by-step embedding designs**

You may have seen the growth in embedding services in the nail industry over the last couple of years. We have been embedding objects and materials for well over seven years now, as have other nail artists, so it is not really a new service. The first year that the Creative Nail Designs Alternative Nail Awards were held, the winner was a Japanese entrant who embedded tiny shells into acrylic. Another artist embedded computer bits and another created a capsule nail holding oil.

This service is one that can easily be incorporated into your salon services. You need to make sure that you price this service according to the time you spend and also include the cost of the products that you are embedding.

Media that can be used for embedding

You can embed practically anything as long as it is small enough to fit on a nail plate. Remember that if you are embedding, it will make the nail proud so it is a good idea to place your objects into the apex area. This way the natural nail and the nail enhancement can cope with the extra thickness without undermining the health of either. You will need to look at whether the addition of your objects will change the shape and balance of the nail enhancement and make it look too bulky and thick and, if this is the case, choose smaller items or something different.

Here are a few items that could be successfully embedded:

Bhindis

- rhinestones and flat-stones
- studs and pearls
- bhindis
- gold and silver charms
- lace and other materials
- feathers
- shells or crushed shells
- sand, glitter, tiny glass beads
- striping tape or ribbons
- stars and sequins
- pictures
- stamps and pieces of paper money
- silver and gold foil
- gold and silver rings

Feathers

All of the above can be used on their own or in combination. If you are not sure what the end result will be, try it on yourself or practise on tips. It is a good idea if you have a client who wants a set of tips with lace (and you know their size) to prepare the tips beforehand. When the client comes in for their appointment all you have to do is apply the already prepared tips, cut to size and shape and then apply the acrylic over the top and finish off. This can save your client at least an hour and you can still charge the same, as you have had to spend the time preparing the tips. You will see that we have done this with the feather design and the rhinestones.

Safety techniques

It is imperative that you follow all your hygiene and safety rules. We have discussed health and safety in some detail in Chapter 1. Here are a few points that you should consider when preparing and performing an embedding service:

- Make sure that the natural nail is thoroughly cleansed before tip application
- Ensure that if you have prepared your tips in advance that you wipe over the contact area with an appropriate cleaner before application
- All products to be embedded should be sprayed with a disinfectant spray and left to dry before application
- Apply a very thin layer of clear acrylic before laying the object on the nail plate and tip
- Objects should be placed with tweezers and not fingers, as you could contaminate the object or nail with your bodily oils and bacteria
- After application of the tips, apply one object and apply acrylic before going on to the next nail
- Ensure that the stress area or apex is thick enough to cover all of the object so that when you buff down it does not protrude through the acrylic and spoil the design

There are many other safety issues, such as not overexposing your client to liquid and powder, ensuring your mix ratio is correct, not getting product on the skin, as well as waste disposal but these are all covered in depth in Chapter 1. We fully recommend that you do not skip that chapter, as it is critical for any nail artist to work safely and within the law.

Specific after care

Because we are providing a treatment and applying a product to our clients' nails, we need to ensure that we give the correct after care and maintenance advice to every client. We have covered general after care advice in Chapter 1, but we would like to reiterate some points – and add others that are specific to this treatment.

Unlike a normal maintenance treatment for liquid and powder clients, after a period of time you will need to either replace the objects or maintain them in such a way that the thickness of the nail does not start to put too great a weight on the free edge. This could seriously damage your client's natural nail health and you may see splitting or breaking across the nail enhancement if the nail is too top heavy. Some designs, as they grow out, can carry on looking quite nice – bhindis or rhinestones for instance – others can become ugly and need removing. It is really up to your client to decide what they want to do, but it is your responsibility to point this out when they first have their nails applied.

Here are a few points to consider discussing with your client before they have their nails applied:

- the longevity of the design
- the frequency of the maintenance programme
- the cost and time of the initial treatment
- their homecare routine and the retail items they will need for this
- possible contra actions

- the fact that their extensions must be professionally removed
- they should ring you if there is a problem
- that it might not be easy to replace a broken nail
- they must follow the manufacturer's or supplier's after care instructions

Once you have talked these points through with your client, they should sign a treatment card to say that they understand and agree to the treatment.

If you follow all of your guidelines for after care and educate your client as well as providing them with an after care leaflet in case they forget what to do, then you should have no problems. *Always* ensure that your client has signed their record card at the end of their treatment to say they are happy.

Step-by-step embedding designs

Technical Tip

With all of the following designs you have a choice of pre-preparing the tips. This will, of course, only work if you know what design your client wants to have and what their tip size is. Although it is time consuming to prepare the tips it does mean that you can fit making the tips into spare moments. It also means that your client is not waiting for possibly 2–3 hours while you perform the artistic work.

Name of design: Feathers on clear tips

Equipment needed:

- Creative liquid and clear powder kit
- Creative clear tips
- Creative gel bond and resin
- files and buffers
- fine feathers
- scissors and tweezers
- gold studs

Step 2

Step 3

1 Ensure that the client has had their nails thoroughly prepped.

2 Cut out the contact area of the clear tips to match the client's natural nail shape.

3 Apply tips to the client and cut to desired shape and length. Ensure that all nails are prepped again.

4 Pre-cut feathers to the basic shape and length that you require. Apply a small amount of resin on the area where the feather is to lie. With tweezers, place the feather in place and gently push all hairs down into the resign with an orangestick. Add a small gold stud for effect if desired with a small dot of gel bond.

Step 5

Feathers – final look

Step 2

Step 3

Step 5

Technical Tip

If you work slowly at first and find that the resin is dry, then apply small amounts, controlling the flow with the nozzle, onto the hairs of the feathers and push down again with an orangestick.

5   Once you have finished five nails, then overlay with liquid and powder.

Technical Tip

If you find you are working really slowly, then ensure that each nail is prepped, the feathers laid and the overlay applied, then repeat on each nail.

Name of design: Red lace with red rhinestones

Equipment needed:

- Creative liquid and clear powder kit
- Creative clear tips
- Creative gel bond and resin
- files and buffers
- red lace and rhinestones
- red glitter

1   Ensure that the client has had their nails thoroughly prepped.

2   Cut out the contact area of the clear tips to match the client's natural nail shape. Pre-cut lace to match nail shape.

3   Apply tips to the client and cut to desired shape and length. Ensure that all nails are prepped again.

4   Apply a thin coat of red glitter over the free edge and up to the smile line. Apply a thin coat of resin and gently push the pre-cut lace down onto the natural nail bed, hold down with an orangestick till dry.

5   Apply a thin coat of acrylic over the red glitter area and embed the rhinestones whilst the acrylic is wet. Add another bead of acrylic when all rhinestones have been embedded to cover up to the smile line. Then add your beads in **Zones 2 and 3**.

6   Perform the same steps on the other nine nails. Finish the nails to a high shine using your files and buffers.

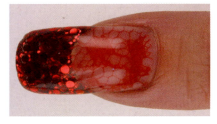

Red lace with red rhinestones – finished look

Step 2

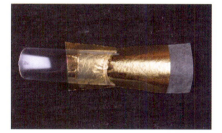

Step 2

Step 2

Step 3

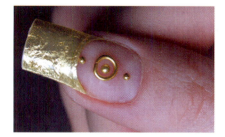

Gold foils on clear tips – final look

Design name: Gold foils on clear tips

Equipment needed:

- liquid and clear powder kit
- Creative clear tips
- gel bond and resin
- files and buffers
- gold foil (silver could be used as an alternative)
- scissors and tweezers

1 Ensure that the client has had their nails thoroughly prepped.

2 Cut out the contact area of the clear tips to match the client's natural nail shape.

Apply a thin coat of resin to the tip and lay foil over the entire area. Do not worry if the foil is overhanging the contact area slightly because you can file this away gently before application. If there are any areas where the foil has not taken, then just reapply a small piece with resin.

3 Apply tips to the client and cut to desired length. Do not shape the nails until after the acrylic has been applied or you will spoil the foil. Ensure that all nails are prepped, again being careful not to touch the gold foil.

4 Once you have finished five nails then overlay with your liquid and powder.

5 Perform the same steps on the other five nails. Finish the nails to a high shine using your files and buffers.

Coloured acrylics

Learning objectives

In this section you will learn about:

- **products, tools and equipment**
- **tips for designing nails for your salon client**
- **step-by-step designs for coloured acrylics**
- **maintenance of designs**

Products, tools and equipment

Many technicians who offer coloured acrylic designs find that their application on regular or normal services improves immensely because of the very nature of this medium – improved product control is required to achieve sharp, crisp lines for definition and clarity. If this is not achieved, the design will look very cloudy and be undesirable.

Your product mix should be a little drier than normal. The way to achieve this is to:

1 Soak the brush in monomer liquid.
2 Pull the excess against the edge of the dappen dish – one way only.
3 The opposite side should be placed on to the powder for bead collection.
4 The brush should be turned and placed on a tissue to remove all excess liquid.

Technical Tip

Various sizes and shapes of brush can help to create an intricate design – the brushes should be the same quality as the brushes used for creating nail enhancements.

This procedure will give you greater control, as the product will not run or spread. If the bead is too big, wipe it on to the tissue and then scoop from the bead the amount required for the intricate design.

As we mentioned in the first section of this chapter, the colour range of acrylics is quite diverse and very exciting, as you can mix any colour you want to. When using coloured gels you will find the colour range is more limited. Coloured acrylics and gels can be used on clients who always choose the same colour as it is permanent, rather than using polish colours that have to be reapplied each time. This will also work with a funky French design. With coloured acrylics life becomes much more exciting and interesting, especially when working in three dimensions.

Here is a list of the products, tools and equipment that you will need for this nail art service:

- acrylic liquid and coloured powders or gels
- tips and adhesives, if you are not sculpting
- sculpting forms – indispensable if you are creating 3D nails
- sculpting brushes of various sizes
- a gel lamp if coloured gels being used
- all nail preparation products
- files and buffers

Basically, you will need all of the normal nail enhancement kit with a few additions such as coloured powders. You can incorporate other media in with the coloured powders, such as adding rhinestones along the smile line of a red French manicure or embedding a crystal rhinestone flower into a blue French manicure.

Tips for designing nails with coloured powders

Here are a few techniques that we have used which can also be incorporated into designs with coloured powders:

Marbling

Pick up a small bead of white and then dip again into blue, picking up on top of the white bead a small blue bead. Place on the free edge of the tip and gently press into the smile line as if doing a French. With a little bit of practice you can create some beautiful marbling designs using a range of various colours. Red and yellow, blue and white, red and white all look good together. You can mix more than two colours together but be careful not to overdo it.

Colour fade

Choose complementary colours for a colour fade. Pick up a small bead of your darkest colour and place onto the free edge and push lightly up the nail until the bead is thin and translucent. Pick up the next colour bead and repeat again, working from the thinnest part of the last colour to where the smile line is. Work your way up

Creative Mosaic acrylic butterfly

Technical Tip

When applying coloured powders in the cuticle area it is important to ensure that you have the correct mix ratio and that you are not working too wet or too thin, as this will create a watered down effect and you will see the natural nail through the colour.

the nail with each colour until you reach the cuticle. We would recommend using around four colours as a maximum. You could finish with a thin layer of glitter over the top or mix a little glitter powder in with each colour.

French

You can use coloured powders to create a traditional French polish look with any of the colours, or be more adventurous and try something different. Using clear tips, apply clear or glitter powder up into the shape of the smile and then use a colour on the natural nail plate. Black could have a dramatic effect, or for something more subtle use a pastel pink or blue.

Valentine

Apply pastel pink with glitter in it to the free edge creating a crisp smile line. Place a very small bead of clear over the natural nail and leave for a minute to set. Create a small heart using red powder just above the smile line, or you could do two to three small hearts trailing down from the cuticle towards the free edge.

If you have any spare time, and the inclination, sit and practise on tips. You will be surprised what you can produce.

Step-by-step designs for coloured powders

Name of design: Coloured French manicure

Equipment needed:

- Creative Mosaic powders/liquid kit
- prep products
- files and buffers
- tools
- Creative clear tips
- sculpting brushes

1   Prep the natural nails.

2   Pre-tailor, apply, cut and shape clear tips.

3   Take up bead of chosen coloured powder and apply to Zone 1. Press out from side to side to create a French tip. Ensure that your mix ratio of liquid to powder is correct and not too wet.

4   Apply clear or pink to Zones 2 and 3 as you would normally. If you want to keep the clarity of the colour, then put a small bead of clear over the colour.

5   Finish all ten nails to a high shine.

6   Ensure that your client has the recommended retail items, good sound after care advice and a maintenance appointment. When maintaining this design you would follow the same steps as if you were doing a backfill on a white French design.

Red and white Mosaic designs

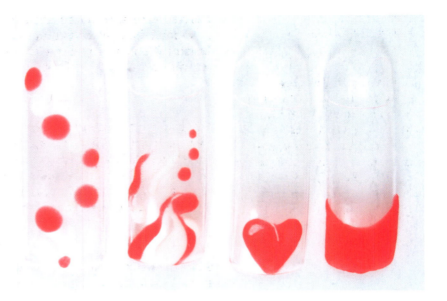

Name of design: Hearts and coloured shapes

Equipment needed:

- Creative Mosaic powders/liquid kit
- prep products
- files and buffers
- tools
- Creative clear tips
- sculpting brushes

1 Prep the natural nails.

2 Pre-tailor, apply, cut and shape clear tips.

3 Coat the area of the natural nail with a small bead of clear powder if you are going to do a design on that area. This will prevent overexposure to the natural nail when you are playing with your shapes. This will also safeguard the strength and longevity of the product.

4 Take a small bead of red powder and put on to the free edge of the clear tip. Take off excess liquid by dipping brush on to tissue. Shape the heart with your brush, keeping the sides working as if you were sculpting a nail on a form. Wait until the product is nearly dry and with the end of your sculpting brush make an indent to give the heart shape. Apply a tiny bead of white powder to give a shadow at the top of the heart.

5 If you want to do something different then try small to medium beads of different colours over the surface of the nail or diagonal lines to create an animal print. Practice with different shapes and colours. After you have finished your shapes, proceed to apply product in the other zones depending on the designs you have done.

6 Finish all ten nails to a high shine.

7 Ensure that your client has the recommended retail items, good sound after care advice and a maintenance appointment. When maintaining this design you would follow the same steps as if you were doing a backfill on a white French design.

White glitter flower

Name of design: Glitter flowers

Equipment needed:

- Creative Mosaic powders/liquid kit
- prep products
- files and buffers
- tools
- Creative clear tips
- sculpting brushes

1 Prep the natural nails.

2 Pre-tailor, apply, cut and shape tips.

3 Apply overlay of chosen colour powder to all three zones.

4 Finish all ten nails to a high shine.

5 Using twilight powder and a medium sculpting brush, apply a small bead on to the nail and allow the bead to settle for 30 seconds. Once it has flattened, shape with the tip of the brush into a point. Bring your brush up and round and bring the point into the centre of the nail. Do the second petal and then go back to the first and with an orange stick or the end of the brush press into the middle of the petal to create the fold. Repeat this until you have five or six petals in a group. Take a small bead and place in the centre and allow to settle. Repeat if your client wants more flowers.

6 Ensure that your client has the recommended retail items, good sound after care advice and a maintenance appointment.

Technical Tip

You may, if you wish, apply the coloured powdered designs on top of a colour polish. This technique is handy if you have a client who is in a rush or just wants the design for a few weeks.

Flowers and ladybirds

Maintenance of designs

In exactly the same way as we would advise our clients who wear natural nail enhancements we have to advise our nail art clients to return for maintenance. All the same after care rules apply as does the use of the same homecare products. The only difference is, if you have colour in the cuticle area how are you going to rebalance to bring the nails back to their original condition? If you have just used a block colour then you would rebalance in the normal way. If your client is wearing a French or a marbling design on the tips then you would again just rebalance in the normal way. If they are wearing a colour fade then you need to decide which way you are going to grow the colours, darker or lighter. If you are going darker then you will need to cover Zone 1 and 2 in clear to give clarity to the colours rather than re-do the whole colour fade. Add the darker colour in Zone 3.

If your client is wearing a funky design, then they need to decide if they want to grow it out as the nail grows down or pay you for your time in following the design through into the re-growth area.

Please refer to Chapter 1 for the homecare advice for your clients.

Three-dimensional designs

Learning objectives

In this section you will learn about:

- **what a 3D nail is and what you would design them for**
- **techniques for building designs with coloured acrylics**
- **the use of embellishments to create designs**

This section covers the exciting world of 3D artwork, which some nail artists may never wish to enter, while others will want to take their skills to the highest artistic level. This type of work will take a lot of time, experience, skill and patience.

What is a three-dimensional nail?

People may argue with us over this point, but we consider that, within the nail industry, many people provide 3D services within their salons and others enter competitions with their designs. The two categories that 3D nail art falls into are:

- encapsulated 3D artwork
- surface 3D artwork

The first category of encapsulated art is basically any nail enhancement or natural nail that has been overlaid with product to enclose nail art objects. This is a service that can be, and is, provided to many salon clients very effectively. We call this embedding and it was covered earlier in this chapter.

Kelly – bhindis

Geisha

The second category is the one we have had the most fun with and is really our favourite as we can really let our artistic creativity flow, and that is surface work. You can design the most incredible nails and people will not believe that they have been made by you and contain objects you have bought and stuck on! Surface 3D work means that your artwork will be sitting on the surface or coming out of the nails and protruding through the surface. This type of design is very hard for a client to wear – and in some cases is dangerous.

Who would you design these nails for, if not for your salon clients?

- photographers
- trade magazines
- consumer photo shoots
- fashion shows
- trade show competitions
- photographic competitions

This area of work is very time consuming and you will find that you need to set time aside, not only work out the design but just to sit and play and find the best way of making the nails. Embedding is the easiest way of creating 3D nails but on other occasions you may have to make objects to apply on the surface or apply items you have bought. This takes time and patience so make sure that you set aside some quiet time and a space, preferably away from the salons and training schools, where you can work out what you will be doing next. It often helps to bounce ideas off someone else – colleagues, friends or even your clients.

We have not included a list of products, tools and equipment in this section, as it is difficult to define what you really need for this service. You will obviously need your nail enhancement kit and your

Dragon

**Nails from Harrods
Knightsbridge Christmas
display**

Yellow acrylic flower

Fairy

nail art kit but you may add items from art shops, hobby shops, bead shops and many other obscure places. We have found the products we use most in 3D work are our gel bond (totally invaluable), our Creative Retention + liquid and Creative mosaic powders and our Sudo airbrush system. Our airbrush is now used not only on nails but on the hair and body as well, as we can carry our theme from the nails onto the body with the same artwork.

Because some of your designs will not only take hours but days to make, buy some storage boxes so that you can keep them safe. Jacqui made some snake nails four years ago that took two days to make and put them in a plastic bag. Needless to say, at some point, they were squashed so Sue has spent that amount of time again making another set for this book. If you keep your nails safe then you may reuse them at some future point. We often get calls from editors or make-up artists who want to 'borrow' a set of nails for a shoot, so they go off in their own taxi across London and return later in the day!

Techniques for building designs

You will see some of the materials we have used for making our 3D nails in the step-by-step instructions below. As we have said before, a lot of our work is done with acrylic because it is so versatile, can be moulded into any shape and can be easily fixed together. It is much harder to achieve this with gel and virtually impossible with fibreglass, although both of these systems have advantages elsewhere in the nail industry.

If you want to work with acrylics in an artistic way and would like some guidance then we would recommend finding a training school that will help you. I know that all three of us teach many students who have gone on to become competition winners and it is not necessarily our skills that they have needed but our experience. The three authors have over 50 years of experience in the industry between them!

Working with acrylics in this way requires some skill and we would not recommend it to the student who has only just completed nail technology classes. This work is really for the experienced technician who can handle mix ratios and sculpting brushes.

You may have seen in magazines or at trade shows some of the wonderful work that nail artists do with coloured acrylics. Some of the work is encapsulated and some on the surface. If you are going to encapsulate and build your design into the nail you will need to protect the surface of the natural nail with a thin layer of acrylic and allow that to set before proceeding with your design. Failure to do this could seriously overexpose your model or client to the monomer or liquid whilst you are working on your design.

You have two options when working designs into the acrylic: to work on the nail surface or to make your designs beforehand. This depends to an extent on the design you are creating. A tropical scene, for example, would be hard to create beforehand so it needs to be done on the nail, and probably only one nail on each hand for a salon client otherwise it could take hours. If the design

Technical Tip

When we were making the dragons and fairies, every part was made separately and put together on the nail. Remember to base your nail in your chosen medium first whether that be hand painting, airbrushing or even using your coloured acrylics to make a garden or colour fade.

Mosaic colour fade with 3D dragon

incorporated little flowers, hearts or shapes however these could be made beforehand and set into the acrylic.

If you are entering a competition and want to make your design to sit on top of the nail then it will be much easier, and will give the design more clarity, if you make all of the pieces and attach them on to the basic design on the nail.

Here are some tips for creating shapes and designs with acrylic:

- Use sculpting forms to create your designs on, as they will peel off easily when you have finished
- Remember that you can build parts of a design and use small beads of product or gel bond to attach them together on the nail, for example the Fairies
- Have a range of different sized brushes: although we normally work with the biggest, our 'Ultra Sculptor', you may find you need to work on an intricate object with a more pointed and smaller brush
- Practise your bead technique
- Learn when to work wet and dry for different looks
- Always allow the bead to settle for at least 10 seconds before pulling into shape; in some cases – like flower petals – you would wait until the product is nearly set
- Use a hobby knife, orangewood stick, tooth picks and other implements to help create different textures and shapes whilst the product is still wet
- Bend your sculpting form whilst the product is still wet to produce a flowing shape
- Be creative with your powders and mix them on the brush to make a marble effect which looks great on flowers
- For tiny areas like the eyes of insects use paint with a dotting tool

The use of embellishments

Many of the nails we have designed have had more than one medium on them and most of the time we like to mix mediums to give shape and texture to a design. The Harrods nails were made from acrylic, rhinestones, cut outs, materials, airbrushing, glitters and some hand painting. All of those on two sets of nails.

We know that sometimes people wonder about the ideas that we come up with – barbed wire on nails? Remember that each set of your nails should tell a story and we can certainly say there is a story behind each of ours. The Barbed Wire nails were made to match make-up. The make-up artist had drawn barbed wire across the models' faces, so the nails matched perfectly.

The Untouchables were asked to do a front cover for *Nails Plus* magazine and the remit we had to work to was 'anything goes as long as it is fibreglass nails'. We did not want to just do a set of normal fibreglass nails as we are not known for 'normal'. However, what could we do that was different with something as neutral as

Sam with fibreglass

fibreglass? We felt that there was nothing artistic that we could do with the fibreglass nails themselves so we had to make a feature of fibreglass within the picture. Many technicians rang us to congratulate us, but just did not understand the cover. We made Sam, the model, into an Egyptian Mummy with her hands coming through the material. One hand was as a mummy, the other had reels of fibreglass attached to the nails. It looked as if her nails were coming undone with the fibreglass unravelling as she tried to come through her shroud. It certainly made people talk and we gave the magazine what they wanted – a cover that people were talking about, good or bad.

Whether you are doing a photo shoot, competition or fashion show, do not set yourself any boundaries. Try to take your nail technician's hat off and look around you, bounce ideas off other people, you will be surprised what you come up with.

Embellishments include the more normal nail art items, such as rhinestones, charms, etc., or it could include other materials:

- cottons, ribbons and materials
- sandwich bag ties or kitchen wire
- wire mesh
- foils
- shells

The list is endless.

The message that we are trying to get across is *be creative*, look around you, take inspiration from competitions, books, the TV, nature and every other place. Never discount any of your ideas, try them all out on practice tips and you will be amazed at your creations.

Technical Tip

We recently judged a competition where a very forward thinking nail artist used bath crystals on her nail design, creating a quartz crystal cave. It looked stunning and we thought it was extremely clever.

Lace nails

Step-by-step three-dimensional designs

Name of design: Burgundy nail with lace

Equipment needed:

- Creative Stickey base coat
- Creative Spike burgundy polish
- gold studs
- piece of lace
- Creative gel bond adhesive
- orangewood stick or tweezers
- top coat

Name of design: Red nail with lace

Equipment needed:

- Creative Stickey base coat
- Creative Candy Apple red polish
- gold studs
- piece of lace
- Creative gel bond adhesive
- orangewood stick or tweezers
- top coat

Technical Tip

If using material on your design, you should pre-cut it to fit the nail before application. Place small dots of gel bond adhesive along the sides and middle of the nail and secure by holding for 10 seconds. If you are not coating the whole nail, just place small dots where you want the material to go. When pressing the material into place ensure you press down and into the centre of the nail. It is advisable to use gel bond adhesive to secure rhinestones and studs on top of material – if top coat is used you may find that the material will curl at the edge. Remember, this design is only for temporary wear.

Materials

Denim and studs

Technical Tip

This design can be used for a photograph or special occasion – it is not suitable for everyday wear. You could attach this design to extensions or under natural nails.

1   Apply base coat to all ten nails.

2   Apply two coats of enamel ensuring good coverage on all ten nails.

3   Apply gel bond adhesive to just the free edge under the nail extension. Apply pre-cut piece of lace, press to secure and hold for 10 seconds with an orangewood stick not your fingers!

4   Apply two coats of topcoat – avoid coating the lace.

5   Using an orangewood stick tipped with Blu® Tack pick up and place the studs in the required design.

Untouchables crystal nails

Name of design: Fabio jewel encrusted nail

Fabio nails step by step

Equipment needed:

- Creative Stickey base coat
- long curve tips
- glitter polish
- diamond rhinestones – assorted sizes
- silver flat-stones
- crystal dangle
- combi-drill
- Creative gel bond adhesive
- orangewood stick tipped with Blu® Tack
- Creative Super Shiney top coat

Technical Tip

This design is for occasional wear only.

1   File or cut tip to a point. Using the combi-drill make a hole in the end of the nail.

2   Apply base coat.

3   Place small beads of gel bond where you want the larger crystals to be placed and put them into position with an orangewood stick tipped with Blu® Tack. Fill in the gaps with smaller rhinestones and flat-stones using Super Shiney top coat. Work a small area at a time, otherwise your top coat will dry before it has adhered to the embellishments.

4   Allow to dry. Attach dangle.

Name of design: Ruby jewel encrusted nail

Red ruby nails step by step

Technical Tip

As your guideline and to keep the lines of rhinestones straight, first put a line down the centre and then work from side to side. This design also looks good with just the polish underneath, but remember that the glitter adds texture.

Equipment needed:

- Creative Stickey base coat
- long curve tips
- deep red polish
- red glitter and glitter dust mixer
- ruby rhinestones
- Creative Super Shiney top coat
- orangewood stick tipped with Blu® Tack

1 File or cut tip to a point.
2 Apply base coat. Apply two coats of deep red polish.
3 Apply red glitter over the whole nail.
4 Apply two coats of Super Shiney and embed the ruby rhinestones from the cuticle end down to the free edge.

Barbed wire nails

Name of design: Barbed wire nails

Barbed wire nails step by step

Equipment needed:

- long curve tips
- Creative gel bond
- kitchen wire
- Sudo airbrush equipment
- gun metal Sudo paint
- pliers
- airbrush sealant
- Sudo base coat and top coat

Technical Tip

If you are using these nails for a photo shoot or fashion show ensure that the model is aware of the dangers. Although it is not real barbed wire the nails could still leave a nasty scratch.

1 Cut tips diagonally across at an angle.

2 Using kitchen wire, cut a length of wire, double over, and twist.

3 Take two pieces of wire and twist around one another around one-third of the way down one piece of wire to create a barbed wire effect.

4 Base coat all ten nails. Place small beads of Creative gel bond down and along the middle of the nail and gently place wire into gel bond. Hold into place for at least one minute for the gel bond to set. Remember to apply some pressure but do not allow the wire to move once you have placed it.

5 Once all ten nails have had the wire attached then spray with your airbrush and Sudo paint across the whole nail ensuring good coverage on the wire. You really need to spray underneath as well.

6 Seal with airbrush sealant and top coat designs.

Step 1

Step 2

Step 3

Step 4

Step 5

Japanese 3D nail art

Name of design: Lily pond

Artist: Teruko Kobayashi

Equipment needed:

- usual tools and equipment needed for creating nail enhancements
- Aurora glitter
- nail art sealer

1 Using clear powder with Aurora glitter and liquid, make a sculptured nail. Shape and finish in the normal way.

2 Make a frame using coloured and white powder.

3 Using white powder and liquid for the flower design, place on the clear section and around the frame. Build tiny petals on a piece of foil so the size can be perfected.

4 Transfer the blue petals from the foil to the frame edge attaching with a small amount of clear powder and liquid.

5 Finish with a glitter polish and nail art sealer.

Lily pond – final look

Name of design: Japanese traditional cards

Artist: Kaoru Suzuki

Equipment needed:

- usual tools and equipment needed for creating nail enhancements
- fine nail art brush
- silver glitter
- nail art sealer
- cup of water
- purple and white enamel
- top coat
- orangewood stick

This design is applied to a finished nail enhancement.

1 Using acrylic paint and a fine nail art brush, paint only the centre with a white colour leaving the base and free edge clear.

2 Paint the edges in red creating a square, leaving the free edge still clear.

3 Draw in the small leaves and branches of the flowers using the fine point of the brush with red and green paints.

4 Place a red curtain in the centre of the tree and flower.

5 Prepare a cup of water, then add a light purple polish, white polish and top coat. Using an orangewood stick, mix all the colours together to make a water marble. Place a nail tip into the water to pick up the design. Attach this second nail to the first using adhesive.

6 Cover the seam with a silver glitter and use nail art sealer to finish.

Step 1

Step 2

Step 3

Step 4

Step 5

Japanese traditional cards – final look

Step 1

Step 2

Step 3

Step 4

Step 5

Name of design: Chandelier

Artist: Kaoru Suzuki

Equipment needed:

- usual tools and equipment needed for creating nail enhancements
- cigarette lighter
- tweezers
- orange and yellow rhinestones
- clear tape
- small lights

1 Using a cigarette lighter, warm up the free edge of the tip and make a curved shape while the tip is warm.

2 Position tiny beads of white acrylic powder mixed with glitter to create the curved lines. Build couple of thin tiny lines using glitter mixed with clear powder.

3 Attach the lines using the tweezers on top of the design.

4 Place orange and yellow rhinestones in the gaps using an orangewood stick and top coat. Add a coloured powder to the free edge.

5 Attach the small lights to the underside of the nails with clear tape.

Chandelier – final look

Step 1

Step 2

Step 3

Step 4

Step 5

Name of design: Pretty

Artist: Teruko Kobayashi

Equipment needed:

- usual tools and equipment needed for creating nail enhancements
- coloured powders
- nail sealer

This design is created on top of a finish nail enhancement.

1   Using liquid and white powder, create a half moon.

2   Use liquid and black powder to fill out the rest of the nail plate.

3   Use liquid and clear powder to make the free edge shape and finish nail enhancement.

4   Between the black and clear sections create a design sculpture such as ribbons.

5   Create a couple of circles on the free edge using liquid and white powder then place a third circle on top of the first two using liquid and glitter powder.

6   Finish with nail sealer.

Pretty – final look

Chapter summary

There are many designs that you can incorporate for your salon clients and designs that can only be used for photographic or fashion work. You must be aware of all safety measures and know what is safe for your clients to wear and what measures to take at fashion and photographic locations. The treatments in this chapter will be incorporated into the new HABIA Nail Standards published in 2004, so look out for training centres or colleges that can offer you training in these areas with the professional qualifications to back up the training. We have found our work in these specialist areas very exciting and they have certainly stretched our capabilities as we hope they stretch yours. Enjoy designing, practise lots and we hope to see your work in magazines or competitions.

Knowledge review

1 Which techniques does this chapter cover?

2 What is the name of the Creative coloured powders?

3 How many colours are there?

4 What other colours are available?

5 How would you make a pastel blue hologram powder?

6 Why would you lay a thin coat of clear powder on the nails before creating designs with the coloured powders?

7 Which tips and adhesive is best to use for art work?

8 Which materials could you use for embedding and designs on top of the nails?

9 Give three other products you would need to perform coloured powder designs.

10 What personal safety equipment might you need?

11 What types of drills are there for use with nail art?

12 Give six general safety tips for performing mixed media nail art services.

13 Give two ways of cutting out a design on tips.

14 What points must you consider when cutting out tips with scissors?

15 List six guidelines for cutting out tips with drills.

16 List the four designs you can do with cut out tips.

17 What nail art media can you use on top of your cut outs?

18 List the steps you would take to perform the blue cut outs with airbrushing and rhinestones.

19 What media could possibly be used for embedding?

20 List five safety techniques you need to consider when performing embedding designs.

21 What specific after care would you give a client having embedded designs?

22 How could you ensure that your mix ration of liquid to powder was drier when working with coloured powder and performing designs?

23 What tools and equipment would you need to perform a coloured acrylic or gel design?

24 List four simple designs that you could perform with the coloured powders.

25 How would you maintain your client's coloured acrylic designs?

26 What are the two types of three-dimensional nail art?

27 When would you perform three-dimensional nail art?

28 Give six tips for creating shapes and designs with acrylic.

29 What do we mean by the term 'embellishments'?

30 What type of wire did we use for the barbed wire nails?

Fashion and photographic nails

6

Learning objectives

In this chapter we will consider the following aspects:

- **photographic work**
- **professional photo shoots**
- **catwalk and fashion work**

This chapter is for the experienced technician who would like to get out of the salon or for the student who wishes to make a career out of this type of work. Performing photographic and catwalk nails is a highly skilled area and one where, in some situations, you will become a 'designer' in your own right. The work is demanding and very exciting and you will be working very closely with other professionals from other areas such as make-up and hair, so good communication skills and lots of confidence are needed. We have found our work in the fashion industry an interesting journey and hope to take you through that journey with us in the following sections.

Photographic work

Learning objectives

In this section you will learn about:

- **how to design and style your own pictures**
- **how to find the perfect model**
- **working with other professionals**
- **planning your pictures**
- **using additional materials and props**
- **building a portfolio of work**
- **making contact with agencies**
- **working at a photo shoot**
- **the critical differences between salon nails and photographic nails**

Nail artists are good at designing nails or even copying an intricate design and changing it slightly, but to put those nails into a picture is another skill in itself. If you look in consumer and trade magazines at hand shots there are many occasions when the nails look great but the picture lets them down or vice versa. Photographic nails are not just about the nail design but the whole picture, which needs to be carefully thought out. Of course the nails are the focal point of the picture, but they must not be lost in the overall look of the picture, unless that is your intention.

Your nail design should be natural, creative and inspiring to the audience. Be creative, if it is a simple nail shot of natural nails, use a background that complements the nails. Study other nail artists' work; think about what you like and what you don't. This section will guide you through designing your own pictures and the skills you will need if you are thinking of becoming a professional photographic nail artist attending photo shoots.

Designing and styling your own pictures

When planning a photo shoot you first need to draw up a plan. If you do not plan your day, the shoot could become a very expensive mistake. It can be extremely upsetting to find that your shots have not come out the way you wanted them to. If you stick to your plan then you have a good chance of producing some beautiful shots.

First, do some research. Make a scrap book of cuttings from magazines, trade journals, film and television and every time you see a picture that inspires you, keep it safely in your scrap book. Explore the internet sites that you think may excite you. Do not always think nails, look at jewellery and make-up pictures and sites. When working in fashion, photography or for a competition, the nails are not the only medium you need to think about and without a good plan of everything you need to consider, you could lose time, money or even a top prize!

Here is a simple outline of what to do when planning your nail shot. Initially you will need to:

Sudo airbrush design board

- design your nails
- decide on a theme for the picture
- work out a budget
- decide if you need to involve other professionals
- look realistically at what props you can use

With these decisions made, look at your budget and work out how much props and other professionals could cost. You will find that most up and coming make-up and hair artists will be happy with a credit or a copy of the picture for their own portfolio. If you do not know any other professionals, contact your local college and talk to the fashion, hair, beauty and photographic departments. Tell them what you want to do and see if there are any final year students who would like to work with you. In the past we have used

Salisbury College as a studio with props, young talented photographers and hairdressers for free. But they have raised their own profiles as a result of the work they have done with us, so it is a two-way relationship. You may already have friends or family who work in these fields or you may perform some of them yourself. If you decide to hire a studio, photographer, make-up and hair artist you will find it very expensive. We have been on a shoot where one front cover has cost in excess of a million dollars – the Hollywood Special Edition of *Vanity Fair*, featuring stars such as Sophia Loren, Cate Blanchett, Kate Winslet and many others – but, believe it or not, the photographer was the most expensive!

The next step is to look at the props you wish to use. It is possible to hire a person called a stylist who will source the items you want for you. This can be very costly and most artists start out by styling their own pictures. Props can make all the difference to a picture, but if you cannot afford expensive items of jewellery, ornaments or clothing then consider hiring them. Look in local phone books for hire agencies. Local shops may consider lending items to you; again a credit with your photo is free advertising for them.

Unless you are going to do a whole body shot, you will probably not need a photographic studio. Most hand shots can be done in a small space but remember that you will need to allow room for lighting. You will save yourself hundreds of pounds by not using a studio. If you have no room at home see if you can use a salon or training room; it will still be cheaper than a studio.

When designing your nails initially you will probably already have a theme in mind. However, there have been times when we have made some beautiful nails with the final picture in mind, but when we have tried to put it into practice it just has not worked or has been totally impractical. When working on your theme try to be as realistic as possible. If the picture is going to be taken digitally remember that it can be played around with and the background changed, but always check that this is allowed if you are entering a competition.

Most designs, whether hair, make-up or nails, fall into three categories:

- natural and commercial
- fashion or avant-garde
- fantasy

Decide which category your picture falls into. If you are entering competitions you will need to be very clear on this – see Chapter 7. There have been many disappointed nail artists who have entered their work in the wrong category and have been told they might have been in with a chance if their picture had been in the right one.

You can create opportunities for your own future and career by entering competitions, helping at photo shoots and fashion shows, even if initially you work for free.

Your blueprint for a successful picture

Be organised; it will save you time and money. Look at the following points:

- your nail design
- colour theme
- how are the props going to complement the nails?
- how will the nails be the main focus of the picture?
- the position of the hands
- what is the overall theme of the picture?
- can the hands be photographed in different positions?

You do not have to be an artist to draw a plan of your picture. Try to visualise the final look. Do you think it is going to work? If you are unsure then plan for a few different looks with the same nails. Unless you are using hair and make-up, it should be quite simple to change a picture around for a different look. Remember to choose a theme, otherwise your public will be confused by the message you are trying to convey. Every picture carries a message, everyone will interpret it in a different way. Ask friends and family what they think, sometimes others can make very valuable input and see something that you are missing. We get extremely useful inspiration from our students and colleagues all the time. Colour is very important. If your nails are going to be bold, choose a background that complements rather than clashes with the colours. If the nails are natural or pastel, make sure you do not lose them in the background or among the props. Sometimes the simpler colours and pictures have the most dramatic effect.

Choosing the right model

Besides your beautiful nail creations your model will be the most important feature. The wrong hands can make beautiful nails look really awful and spoil a whole picture. You only have to look in nail magazines to see the effect of a good or bad model. If you are going to use more than the hands, then you should consider the other body parts too! If the model's face is going to be used, try to look at some of her previous pictures to see how she looks through a camera lens. If you are going to use body parts make sure they have no distinguishing marks that will spoil the picture.

Here is a list of points to look for when choosing your hand model:

- young skin is better than old
- light body hair
- even skin tone
- long, slender fingers
- small bone structure
- no scars, cuts or bruises
- nice healthy cuticles

Technical Tip

Ensure that all jewellery is taken off the night before the shoot so that there are no indentions on the fingers, neck or other parts of the body.

Groom your model a few weeks before on how to look after their hands and cuticles, give them a free hand cream and cuticle oil to use.

- long, slender, pink and healthy nail bed
- medium size nail plate
- flat to slightly arched nail beds
- medium 'C' curve

Checklist for success

When you have drawn up your initial plan of theme, props and people then you can start organising the shoot itself. If you are using other professionals, they will need to be booked and props will have to be bought or acquired. Sometimes making a costume can take days and if your nails are fantasy or avant-garde they will also take considerable time to make.

Technical Tip

Sue spent 40 hours making ten of the corkscrew nails. You must make sure that your work is absolutely perfect. The camera will show up any inconsistencies and could spoil your picture. Take time to create your designs, it is worth it.

Sudo backstage, London Fashion Week

Make a list of things to do and tick them off as you do them to ensure that nothing is forgotten. Here is a list of jobs to consider:

- make your nails
- decide on a theme
- create a blueprint of the overall look of the picture
- choose your model – use the checklist as a guide
- book hair and make-up artists if being used
- hire, buy or borrow the props a few days before the shoot
- decide on the location of the shoot and book it in advance
- ensure the photographer is aware of what background and lighting you will need for the day
- make sure that all the key people involved have written confirmation of the time, date and location of the shoot and warn them it may take more than a few hours

Technical Tip

We have been on shoots where even the photographer thought it would take only a few hours, but in fact one shot alone took over 12 hours to get right. The poor model had a real arm ache!

- arrange for refreshments and food for everyone if it is going to be a long day
- if the photo is being taken as a competition entry, check the rules of the competition to see that you are adhering to all the regulations

If you are considering becoming a professional nail artist and joining an agency in order to go out and work on professional paid shoots, you will need to have a portfolio of work. Everyone has to start somewhere and by entering competitions, doing local fashion shows and working with other professionals you will gain experience of what it is like to work with a camera.

Professional photo shoots

Learning objectives

In this section you will learn about:

- **the importance of working as a team**
- **the key professionals you will be working with**
- **the types of work involved**
- **the kit you will need**
- **your personal portfolio**

Photographer

Technical Tip

You can already obtain qualifications for Manicure/Pedicure and Nail Extensions, but there are new qualifications in the pipeline for Basic and Advanced Nail Art, Photographic and Fashion Work. Read trade magazines or contact the Association of Nail Technicians or HABIA for more information.

From experience, we can say that it took quite a while to build up a good reputation within the photographic and fashion world. It required a lot of hard work with very little return in the beginning. We have met some fantastic people, especially in the hair and make-up field, who have inspired us and helped us to grow as a nail art team. The Untouchables as a business was launched in 1996 and has grown from a team of two to a team of eight nail artists. The fashion industry has gradually realised, over the past five years, that there are nail technicians who provide an excellent service and are artists in their own right.

Our work has taken us all over the world and we have been given opportunities that have been ground breaking in the professional nail industry. This type of work is not appropriate for a novice nail technician, but it could be considered by those who have experience and a high level of skill. Here are a few of the qualities we feel an agency would be looking for when taking a nail artist on to their books:

- friendly
- confident
- approachable
- diverse
- talented
- experienced
- hard working
- qualified

You will need to have a confident and friendly personality as you will be put into situations where you are meeting people, often for the first time.

Some of these could be people with a very high profile and they need to have confidence in your abilities so that you do not let teams of other professionals down. In the case of the people you are working on, they will want to know that you are qualified and experienced in your field so that their fingernails and toenails look their best. Anyone in the fashion, TV or film world knows that their image is their most important asset and you will be contributing to that for them.

It is important that you are approachable and open to suggestions. You will be working as part of a team, and the other team members need to know that they can rely on you. You will need a certain amount of talent and be able to diversify your skills, as there will be situations when you think you are to perform a basic polish and it turns out to be a very complicated nail design. Lastly, you should aim to get the relevant professional qualifications for the areas of work you are doing. It may not appear important at the moment, but as health and safety laws become more stringent we believe it is something that agencies could be looking for in the future.

Teamwork and other professionals

Good communication skills are essential when working in the media. There are no situations where you will not be interacting with somebody else in one way or another. You may come across:

- photographers and their assistants
- make-up artists and their assistants
- hair artists and their assistants
- stylists
- dressers
- editors and their assistants
- designers and their representatives
- public relation companies
- other nail technicians
- and, of course, your agent

Make-up artist, London Fashion Week

Technical Tip

If possible – perhaps you already know the make-up artist you are working with – ring them the day before and ask what they are planning, as this will give you an idea of what colours and equipment to take with you.

It can be quite daunting to go into a shoot on your own knowing that there are no familiar faces. However, we have never been on a shoot and come away without making new friends and valuable contacts. Even if you are nervous, always keep a smile on your face as this makes you approachable. Remember that other people there could be as nervous as you. It is a good idea to make contact with the make-up artist, if there is one, as they will usually choose – in conjunction with the stylist or photographer – what the look for the shot is going to be.

When an agency books you for a shoot, they will want to send you an e-mail or fax of all the details. This is like a call sheet and it is imperative that you have access to one of these methods of receiving information. The call sheet will tell you who the main contact is, what other professionals are involved on the shoot and their contact numbers, the location and the call time. If you have any problems and think that you cannot do the job or are going to be late, you *must* inform the agency or main contact on the call sheet straight away. Good communication will earn you a good reputation. Always make sure that you are honest and if you think a job is out of your league, tell your agent rather than getting a bad reputation for poor work. People do appreciate honesty.

When you are at the shoot and your equipment and kit are set out, sometimes in impossibly tight spaces, make sure that all the key people know who you are. Do not wait to be made tea or coffee, go and make it yourself. Introduce yourself, as you may find that other people on the shoot assume you are part of the studio group. Try to get five minutes with the make-up artist or photographer to clarify what exactly it is they require. If they are not sure, and you would like to pass some ideas by them, then take some tips on sticks to present some colours or looks for them to choose from. Some shoots will be very laid back – you may only have to perform one manicure or polish on one model, but you may be asked to stay all day 'just in case'. On others, you may have up to five or six models who all need their fingers and toes manicured.

We did a shoot for a teenage magazine where we were told the three young models all wanted very simple nail art. When we got there, two of them were nail biters and needed nail extensions. The models then decided to have Fawn and Burgundy plaid, Union Jack, Zebra Stripe and a complicated Glitter Design (one of the models was done twice). It took a considerable time and the photographer was under pressure to get all the shots done, but the end effect was brilliant and everyone was extremely happy. So be warned, expect the unexpected!

Here are a few golden rules to stick to when attending a photo shoot:

- always be prompt
- introduce yourself to the make-up artist, hair artist and photographer and they will introduce you to the others
- do not dress up, dress down
- make sure you have your call sheet
- keep a smile on your face
- have a comprehensive kit for all eventualities
- make sure you plan your route whether it be by train, bus, underground or car, and allow plenty of time
- make sure that you can stay until the end, which could be many hours later
- talk to the others and make good contacts for further work
- always carry your own or your agent's business card

Sudo London Fashion Week

Types of work

Unless you are also a make-up or hair artist, the treatments you will be asked to perform on shoots will come from the following list:

- manicure
- pedicure
- nail extensions
- nail art, be it basic or advanced

Most of the work we do, at least 80 per cent, is manicures and pedicures. It is very difficult to do a set of nail extensions. First of all they are very time consuming and second you may never see that model again, so if you cannot recommend a good technician for her to go to for maintenance or removal, you will earn yourself a bad reputation. If models wear nails without being properly educated about them, they will often let them drop off or pull them off. This causes so much damage to their natural nails that it could affect their modelling careers and you do not want to be associated with that eventuality.

Make sure that you use professional products and that you have a small stock in case the model wants to keep what you are using. We have always used Creative Nail Design products as much as we can and we find now that the models we work with time and time again ask us for cuticle creams, oils and hand lotions as well as their

Technical Tip

We have found that taking some 'colour pops' in our kit is the perfect way to do designs to show at the shoot. Or you could make some colour pops at home or in the salon and keep them in your kit as pre-prepared examples. Colour pops look so much more professional than tips on sticks or just tips on their own.

Colour pops

favourite polishes. If you find a company whose products you are happy with, try approaching them for some freebie items for your kit. If they say no, you have not lost anything, but they should see it as free advertising and hopefully even be grateful to you.

Whichever treatment or service you are providing, make sure that it is the best it can be. Remember that models, TV and music celebrities all have regular manicures and pedicures in their work and you want your work to stand out. Use products that they can feel make a difference, go a bit deeper on that massage and always make sure your 'polish job' is immaculate. Do not be afraid to re-do a nail or two if you feel they are not perfect. The photographers will only tell you to do so anyway when they look through the camera.

There have been times when the shoot has been slow and we have offered the make-up artist, hair stylist or photographer a manicure or pedicure too. This really does earn you brownie points!

It is possible that you are booked to perform a nail art treatment and the make-up artist, editor or photographer is not sure what this is. They may want to liase with you a few days beforehand or ask you to send in some designs. It is a good idea to have some already made up so that you can send or email pictures of work.

You may find that you can use pre-prepared stick-on designs that you have made at home or in the salon. Be careful if you are going to stick plastic nails onto natural nails that you protect the natural nail from damage. There are professional courses for fashion and photographic nails where you can learn the techniques to do this. You will quickly earn a bad reputation if you leave people's nails in bad condition with no after care. If you do have to use stick-on nails, make sure that you are there to remove them safely; do not let the client or other professional just pull them off.

If your agent lists you as able to perform nail art services, make sure that they know how far your artistic abilities stretch. On some shoots we are told what to do and on others we are left to 'design' the look ourselves. This can be quite daunting, especially when the photographer has an idea of what they want but cannot understand the restrictions that we have to work to as professional nail technicians.

On one very high profile shoot, the photographer was adamant that long beautiful nail extensions were wanted on a model who had terrible bitten nails. They wanted nine perfect nails, but one to stay as the bitten nail with dirt under the edge as if the false nail had fallen off. We tried to explain to the photographer that even the most skilled nail technician could not make these severely bitten nails into anything beautiful, certainly not beautiful enough to have close up photographs taken. They insisted that was what they wanted and when the pictures came out they realised that it had not worked. A further shoot was scheduled for later that week and the photographer took our advice on the styling of the nails in the picture. We were also allowed to take our own model. If you are experienced in nail technology, you will know what is possible and what is not. Make sure that you are always honest with the people you are working with – they do not understand the limitations, you do.

The professional nail kit

As we have mentioned before, always take a full working kit with you on every job. Whether you just perform manicures and pedicures or the whole range of nail services, including airbrushing, will determine how big a kit you carry.

Creative products

Here are a few points to remember:

- use a case on wheels with a carry handle
- you may need to get on and off the underground, so make sure your kit is easy to carry
- a case with different sections that stack can be good, so that you do not have to take everything if you do not need it and do not have to spend hours sorting out your case.
- make sure that your case is sturdy
- make sure the case has compartments in which bottles can be stored upright
- use see-through plastic zipper cases for polishes – these can be colour coded to make choosing colours easier
- do not rely on the studio for pedicure baths or washing up bowls!
- take a little of everything rather than a lot of a little
- take clean towels and tissues
- make sure you have a good range of manicure and pedicure tools
- take sterilising wipes or solution in case you are working on more than one model
- always use clean files
- keep a stock of your agent's business cards in your case
- remember nail art paints can be mixed, so rather than take a whole selection of colours take a small selection and a mixing palette instead

Technical Tip

Remember that if you are going out on location you may not have access to an electricity supply. So if you depend on a lamp, UV gel lamp or airbrush compressor, you may have to change your plans.

Your kit should include everything that you need for that particular shoot but remember that some items can double up. For instance, if you are tight for space, your hand/foot lotion can also be used as a cuticle cream, your nail dehydrator can be used as a polish remover and also to tidy up polish along cuticle lines. You may have to work in poorly lit conditions so you may wish to take a small lamp with you.

Sudo kit

Remember that even if you have been told the shoot is natural nails, make sure you take polishes and some nail art kit with you. Here is a basic list of items needed in your kit, but obviously you can add other items if you feel you need them.

- towels and tissues
- cotton wool, cotton buds, gauze pads
- clean files and buffers
- orangewood sticks
- manicure and pedicure tools
- manicure bowl – possibly foot bath
- hand and foot lotions or oils
- base coat, top coat and quick dries

- range of coloured polishes and enamels
- range of coloured paints and flexi-brush paints
- nail art tools and brushes
- selection of glitters, rhinestones, decals and other art materials
- nail tips and adhesives
- nail cleansing agents and polish remover
- extras

If you look in our cases, which have been developed over the last seven years, you would be quite surprised to see items like wire cutters, sandwich bag ties and other obscure things that have nothing to do with normal nail treatments but everything to do with nail design!

Your personal portfolio

If you feel this is the area for you, you will need to develop a professional portfolio. This is something that all top hair stylists, make-up artists, stylists, photographers and models have to develop to get work. It is essential that it is constantly updated, as in the fashion industry anything over six months old is old news and will not be considered. Obviously when you first start out you will have no work to show, so how do you go about obtaining photographic evidence? Here are a few suggestions:

- work as an apprentice to an experienced nail artist who will help develop your career
- work locally for newspapers, magazines and fashion shows
- link in with photographers, make-up artists and hair stylists and work for free, but get photographs as payment
- enter nail extension, nail art, fantasy and photographic competitions
- join an agency, but be prepared to work for very little at first until your portfolio has some pictures in it

Technical Tip

It may be a good idea to have a duplicate of all the pictures in your portfolio just in case it goes missing. There is nothing worse than sending out your original work to find that it has gone astray and cannot be replaced. We have had this happen a few times until we learnt our lesson and always have two of everything printed off.

Once you have started gathering photographic evidence, you will need to buy a good, leather bound book. Our portfolio cost us a few hundred pounds, but it has our name imprinted into it and has its own waterproof carrying case. It is important to have a strong book and one with its own case, as your agent, if they are a good one, will be sending your book out regularly by bike messenger to potential clients. We have got to the stage now that we have two portfolios because we represent more than one artist. You will only need around 20 pages maximum; potential clients will stop looking after that so it is a waste. You want quality, not quantity. It is only us nail technicians who are fascinated by lots of pictures and we know that we love to look at nail pictures, the more the better. But our clients are not interested in our history, just that we can provide the best service possible.

Your portfolio should have a selection of various work within it and here is a suggestion of what is normal practice:

- a natural nail shot
- a hand and foot shot
- a hand only shot
- a polished nail shot
- a head and hand shot
- a nail art shot
- a fantasy shot (if you are going to perform this service)
- any existing cover or campaign shots you may have

A good portfolio will have a small selection of shots that vary across the work field, to include natural through to painted and close up to body shots. You will also find that a high profile shot such as a *Vogue* cover will get you work quickly. The only problem with high

Nails for Versace

profile work is that it is usually poorly paid. You will need at least one good high profile shot in your portfolio every six months to keep your name circulating on the photographic circuit.

If you are with an agency you will find that your agent will usually deal with your portfolio for you and guide and advise you on what jobs to accept and which ones are not critical when starting out. We would honestly say that it takes one to two years before your name is well established. For those of us who started over five years ago it took a lot longer and there are a few nail technicians out there who have really paved the way for the rest through sheer hard work and determination to be recognised in what is a tough industry.

Look, listen and learn and you will find you will love it. It takes time to build a relationship, even in our salons, so have patience and you will win through. Do not set your expectations too high at the beginning and be willing to learn from those who have gone that way before. Good luck.

Catwalk and fashion work

Learning objectives

In this section you will learn about:

- **the type of work involved**
- **the kit needed**
- **working as a team**
- **keeping up with fashion trends**

FAKE – Sudo at London Fashion Week

Working behind the scenes at any fashion show can be exciting and rewarding. The atmosphere backstage is always electric and it is much better than being in the audience. You will see a creation in the making. For everyone involved, whether it be a local fashion show or London Fashion Week, it is the culmination of everyone's hard work seeing the catwalk come alive.

If you are working as a photographic nail artist you may find that you are offered work by other artists at London Fashion Week, or it may be that your product company ask you to become involved. We have been doing this type of work for over seven years now and although it is hard work, with little financial return, it is one of the most exciting events of the year. Creative Nail Design have taken steps to ensure that they have some of the UK's top nail technicians working alongside famous make-up artists in London, New York, Paris and Sydney Fashion Weeks. They also liase, if they can, with the designers a few weeks before to design the nails around the colours, textures or overall look of the clothes.

We are occasionally asked directly by the designers to create looks to match their clothes, and in some cases we have had to sign confidentiality contracts with the more famous designers who do not

FAKE – London Fashion Week

want their ideas leaked. For the most part you will be working with the make-up artist who will decide what the colours of the nails will be to match the make-up.

Services behind the scenes

When we first started at London Fashion Week seven years ago we made 22 sets of nails, all different, that took us over three solid weeks to make. Never have we repeated that experience. Only once in Paris Fashion Week were we asked to do anything similar and that was for McQueen and the theme was Rhinestone Cowboy. We made twelve sets of rhinestone encrusted nails that took a few weeks to make, over 400 rhinestones per set!

We have always worked as a team, no matter how simple or complicated a show turns out to be. The kinds of work that you may be asked to perform include:

- basic manicures
- painting of toenails – never full pedicures
- nail repairs on fingers and toes
- polishing
- hand painting on finger and toenails – sometimes extending on to the skin
- using plastic tips with designs already done
- airbrushing
- texturing using materials
- 3D work using various media such as chains and zips

Photograph board – London Fashion Week

Although this type of work is poorly paid, you will gain a great profile for the effort that you put in. It is almost worth taking a week's holiday just to fit it all in! The work is mainly from the list above but usually does depend on the make-up artist. If you are not working under an experienced nail artist then make the main make-up artist your contact and seek out their advice on the colours and looks they require. You may have to attend a meeting a few days or weeks before to sort out just what it is that they want you to do. When you are at the show, make sure that they give you a list of models so that you can tick them off as you do them. It is always difficult to remember who you have done because all of the models come in at different times and the most famous always arrive just before the show starts. It will not do your reputation any good if you allow any models to slip onto the catwalk without their nails being done, so check and double check in your spare moments.

Here are a few questions that you could ask either the designer's stylist or the make-up artist to give you an idea of what kit, colours and ideas to take with you:

- the theme of the show
- colour scheme
- if there are textures
- hair and make-up – simple or avant-garde

- how many models
- fingers, or fingers and toes

Once you know the look that the designer and make-up artist require then you need to ensure that you have your model list. If the make-up artist has a big team with them they will have to be very organised and will usually have a list that includes the following:

- theme
- models' names
- how many models
- the clothes they are wearing
- make-up colours for each
- nail colours for each

List of models – London
Fashion Week

You may find that the theme for the nails is natural and in this case you will just do a mini-manicure and buff the nails to a high shine. It may be that a French polish is required, which sometimes can be worse than doing nail art, as models do not sit still! If you find that they want something artistic that is going to take you or your team some time to create, then you will have to pre-prepare them and adhere them to the models just before the show. As we mentioned in the photographic section, please make sure that you use a method of adhering the nails so that they can be safely removed. Your reputation depends on your working quickly and safely with no damage to the models' nails. Some of the more famous models can do up to five shows a day and if there are five days in each fashion week and New York, London, Paris and Milan all run one after the other, you can imagine what their nails would look like if they had stick-on nails for every show. We have built our reputation totally on how we protect the models' nails and teach them how to use Creative products for their after care.

You will need certain personality traits to survive Fashion Week and some of these are:

- being able to work as a team
- not minding being told what to do
- working well under pressure
- being versatile
- working in the dark
- working in tight corners
- not minding being shouted at – you cannot be sensitive
- being a good timekeeper
- working safely

Backstage – Sudo London
Fashion Week

You need to keep in mind that you could possibly be crawling around on a dirty warehouse floor so do not dress in any designer clothes, unless they are meant to look messy! You may be asked to wear certain clothes, like tee shirts with logos, if you are working alongside a company whose products you are using. The models all

London Fashion Week

turn up with no make-up, looking tired and with their oldest clothes and trainers so you will blend in better if you are in informal clothes. They just make the thinnest person feel fat!

The buzz that you will get is like nothing else that you could possibly do. The atmosphere is brilliant. Fashion weeks are not just for the designers to show off their clothes, but also for the shoe and jewellery designers and the hair, make-up and nail artists and companies to show new trends and products. Use it to your advantage. Make a name at Fashion Weeks and it will guarantee you work for the rest of the year.

The key people you need to liaise with are:

- make-up artist and their team
- hair stylist and their team
- clothes stylist
- photographers
- public relations
- the designers themselves, if you are really lucky

If the show you are working at is for a new young designer, their budget will be low and you may find that the make-up artist has a team of people who are still proving themselves and want the work to put in their portfolio. The team will usually be smaller and the same goes for the hair stylists. If the show is for a famous or very high profile designer, then the budget is larger and the teams are bigger and include more faces well-known in the fashion industry for hair and make-up. It is usually at these shows that experienced manicurists are required. The work is high pressure and not for the faint-hearted. It is the opposite of photographic work, where you will normally have time to relax: at Fashion Weeks you will rarely have a spare moment. The busiest show we have worked at was for Givenchy in Paris where we had 52 models and had to do fingers and toes in just 4 hours, the more famous models such as Kate Moss arriving twenty minutes before the show was due to go on. So hair, make-up and nails were being done at the same time!

You will find that hair and make-up are always the main focus and you will probably have to perform treatments whilst the models are having one of these done. Sometimes this may mean sitting under a table or lying down on the floor. Just be prepared for anything.

Sudo – London Fashion Week

Show kit

It can be exhausting dragging a full kit around the shows, especially if you have more than one in a day. You must make sure that you have everything to hand when working and there have been a couple of occasions when designers have requested on the day a look that we could not produce because we did not have the products available. In this case we sent a taxi across London to pick up what was needed, which took ages because of the show traffic. It is worth checking with the make-up artist before the show. You will need to put enough products in for yourself and for the team if you are heading a group of nail artists. Make sure that you have enough polishes in each colour and always make sure that you have a spare bottle in case of accidents.

The items that you will need in any basic kit are:

- orangewood sticks tipped with cotton wool or cotton buds
- tissues and a towel
- cuticle pusher
- cuticle cream or oil
- hand/foot lotion
- clean files and buffers, including shiny buffers
- the chosen polish colours
- base coat and quick dries
- a further selection of colours and nail art paints

Sudo – London Fashion Week

Once you know what the theme is for the show and what is required of you, you can pack the extra items you may need such as nail art kit, airbrush kit, or your designs already made up on tips. There is no time at a fashion show to be as hygienic as you would normally be, but safety rules always apply.

If you can, find an experienced nail artist who is already doing this type of work and ask if you can assist for free. Working conditions are very different in this environment and it can be quite daunting to be thrown in on your own. Unlike a photo shoot where everything is more relaxed and other artists will have time to talk and help you, it is a different matter altogether at a show and everyone will be fraught and frantic.

Here are a few useful tips that may help:

- always ensure that you have a show pass as you will not get in without one
- ensure that you have the correct items in your kit
- work as quickly as possible, but safely!
- wear old clothes
- try to obtain a list of the models and what they will be wearing on each of their nails
- link in with the make-up artist on arrival if you are not working as part of a team; if you are, find your lead technician and they will have everything arranged for you

Here are just a few of the situations that we have been in that may not have been funny at the time but which we have had a laugh about since.

- Sue always gets searched when we go abroad. It must be the blonde hair. She was duly searched at 5am by customs just before we were to board the Euro-train to Paris. Although

London Fashion Week

we thought we had packed properly, the customs officer opened her case before we had a chance to say 'be careful' and all of the pots of rhinestones fell out and broke open. We had ten minutes to pick up over 5,000 rhinestones and get on the train!

- We were told at one show in London Fashion Week to paint all the models' toes as they were wearing sandals. We had painted around five or six models when the make-up artist told us not to bother as toes were not going to be featured and the models were all in shoes. So we took off what we had put on and from then on just concentrated on the fingers. As the last few models came in, around 20 minutes before the show was due to go on, the stylist came up and asked why had we not done toes. We shouted to everyone to stand still where they were and painted every bare toenail we could find, model or not. We did not lift our heads to even look at whose feet we were painting – no time!

- In Paris, we took one of our young assistants and spent all night finishing nails. We have a photo of poor Kristy knelt down by the side of her bed holding one orangewood stick with a nail on it and another with a rhinestone on it, fast asleep. Just goes to show the young ones have no stamina. Sue and Jacqui stayed awake all night!

Chapter summary

The areas of work within this chapter are the newest in the nail industry and are still being developed. Hopefully, in 2004, we will have new professional qualifications to match these skill areas that will be available for those who want to enter into these areas of work. We would fully recommend finding professional courses that will help you develop your skills. Experience counts for a lot, and learning skills and techniques from those nail artists who are already working in these fields is invaluable. Initially the financial return will be low, but over a period of time and with hard work, determination and skill, you will gain recognition. Always look around you for inspiration – and not just in the nail industry. Never stop learning and always take your skills to the next level.

Knowledge review

1   What are the different types of work covered in this chapter?

2   What steps would you take to plan your own nail shot?

3   What three categories of design are there?

4 What points would you follow on a blueprint?

5 What points would you consider important when choosing your model?

6 How long did it take Sue to make the corkscrew nails?

7 What jobs would you need to ensure that you have done before your photo shoot?

8 Why is it so important to work as a team on a professional photo shoot?

9 What other key professionals might you be working with on a shoot?

10 What qualities will you need to be successful when working with others on professional photo shoots and fashion shows?

11 What treatments might you be asked to perform when attending a photo shoot?

12 Why is it so important to clarify with the photographer or make-up artist what it is they want done?

13 Give five golden rules when attending a photo shoot.

14 What is the benefit of carrying 'colour pops' in your kit?

15 What precautions would you take when using stick-on nails?

16 What type of case is the best to use to carry your equipment in?

17 What key items would you carry in your kit?

18 What pictures should be in your personal portfolio?

19 What ways could you start to get photographs for your portfolio?

20 What can an agency do for you?

21 What type of work could you possibly be asked to do at London, Paris, Milan or New York Fashion Weeks?

22 What questions would you ask of the designer, stylist or make-up artist?

23 The designer or stylist will usually have a list of what?

24 The model list is very important to the make-up, hair and nail artists. Why?

25   What qualities do you need to work as a team during Fashion Week?

26   What items should you have in your show kit?

27   What benefits are there to being sponsored by a product company?

28   Give three very useful tips to a successful fashion show.

29   What happened to Kristy when she was making nails in Paris?

30   What skill areas will you need for this type of work?

7

Competition nail art

Courtesy of Tonia Podimore

Learning objectives

In this chapter we will consider the following aspects of competition work:

- the categories of nail art competitions
- what the judges look for
- marking guides
- the rewards that entering competitions can bring

This chapter covers the nail art competitions that you can enter throughout the world. You will find that these competitions are quite diverse and that each one may be judged very differently, so you need to obtain the specific rules and regulations as we can only guide you through the steps and not quote information from all of the associations and companies that hold these competitions.

The nail art competition circuit is becoming increasingly popular around the world and is very big business in the United States and Japan. In the United Kingdom we have always had some nail art competitions, but over the last three to four years there have been giant leaps forward in this area. One of the biggest competitions we have seen in recent years has been organised on a totally global scale by a nail product manufacturer and has been so successful that it is now organised on a national level by countries such as the USA, the UK, Japan, Russia, Norway and Germany to name a few. The company is Creative Nail Design of Vista California. They launched the Alternative Nail Awards, which was a photographic competition to beat all others. There were three categories:

- Hand and Foot Beauty
- Creative on the Edge
- Total Look

This competition allowed nail technicians to design looks in various ways and incorporated areas such as make-up, costume, props and styling a picture. The competitions run every year and, in the UK, Designer Nails have very successfully turned this event into the 'place to be seen' in the competition world. The images that have been produced are amazing and some of the winners' photographs can be seen in this chapter. The judges each year consist of well-known personalities such as Nicky Chapman of 'Pop Idol', top editors such as Newby Hands of *Tatler*, Hairdresser of the Year and top professional nail artists. Thank you to Christian Knowles-Fitton and Samantha Sweet who, year after year, host this amazing event.

Courtesy of Svetlana Petelova

Courtesy of Elena Gunkovskaya

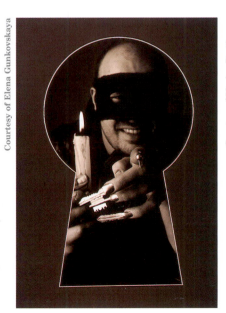

Courtesy of Marina Deetiareva

In the UK, most of the nail art competitions take place at trade shows and are extremely interesting events. If you would like to consider this area of work and are not sure whether it is for you, attend a trade show and make time to have a look at the models from the nail art categories.

Whether you are a complete beginner or an experienced nail artist we hope that you find this section interesting and that it inspires you to take your skills into this very rewarding area of work.

The categories of nail art competitions

Courtesy of Marina Deetiareva

Learning objectives

In this section you will learn about:

- **the different types of competition and how to enter**
- **what to look for in a model**
- **putting a theme together**

The different types of competition

You will find that most competitions are held at trade shows throughout the year, with a few exceptions such as the Alternative Nail Awards. As trade shows can be held by different organisations, who are usually linked to different magazines and trade associations, they may differ from one show to the next. You must always make sure that you have the rules and regulations in print before you set off for the day. Once you register you should be sent these straight away; if they have not arrived a week after registration then contact the person responsible and ask them to send them out to you as soon as possible. You may find that there are products or techniques that you cannot use and it would be devastating to enter, do all that hard work, only to find you are ineligible because of one minor point.

Here are a few of the competitions you can enter:

- hand painting and flat nail art
- basic nail art
- 3D and fantasy nail art
- airbrushing
- mixed media

You will find that all of these competitions will have slightly different rules and regulations. Usually flat or hand painting is just what it says and you will not be allowed to have any build-up of materials or products on the nails. Airbrushing is usually strictly airbrushing with no hand painting or decorations allowed. With 3D, fantasy and mixed media the rules can change from one competition to another. Here are a few points that they will all have in common:

Shar airbrushing

Nail Olympics – Kelly and Michelle

- costume and make-up will be given points
- a written explanation of theme, possibly with written step-by-step instructions may be required
- clarity of design
- originality of design
- colours and good use of nail art media

In a fantasy competition you will need to keep the theme running through the make-up, hair, costume and down on to the nails. Consistency is the key to a good score. In all competitions the originality of the design will be important. If the judges have seen a look over and over again, for example a design with cartoon characters such as Winnie-the-Pooh or Disney, they will not consider this original work, no matter how beautiful your designs are.

If you are unsure about which category to enter then you need to look at your skills in each area. Ask yourself the following questions:

- do I have good hand painting skills?
- am I better with my airbrush?
- am I a good all-rounder who can use a range of different products and techniques?

Model as Fairy – Nail Olympics

Fairy Nails – Silver Medal Nail Olympics

Model in mask

Technical Tip

At the Nail Olympics in Las Vegas we got up at 5am to get our models' hair and make-up done. The costume was made before we flew to America but took two days to make. Our models were great because they strutted around and, by having confidence in themselves, it made everyone look at them rather than them fading into the background.

Model as angel – Gold Medal Nails

- have I got access to the right model for my theme?
- have I got the time to make a costume or do I get someone else to do it for me?
- can I apply the make-up myself or do I need the services of a make-up artist?
- can I work quickly on intricate designs?
- do I need to copy from a picture or can I design from memory?

Only you know your strengths and weaknesses, so decide for your first competition which would be the easiest for you and learn from the experience.

Finding yourself a good model

A good model for a nail art competition does not necessarily imply someone who has a beautiful face, great figure or even the greatest nails. Unlike a nail extension competition your end product does not depend on your model having long slender pink nail beds or even young, healthy, unblemished skin. It does depend on factors such as:

- will they help to set you at ease whilst working?
- does their image reflect your theme?
- do they mind possibly wearing an outrageous costume?
- do they mind lots of make-up and hair accessories?
- are they patient enough to sit there for $2\frac{1}{2}$ hours whilst you are working?
- do they mind sitting for another couple of hours whilst the judging is going on?
- do they mind being stared at and photographed?
- will they converse confidently with the judges on your theme, costume, etc.?
- are they available to practise on before the competition?
- will they support you throughout the whole process?
- are they willing to get up at some unearthly hour for you to prepare them?

Although we have said that your model does not have to have the best nails in the world, for nail art competitions it is important that the nails are very long and sometimes this is difficult on a model with tiny nail plates. Please be aware of this when choosing your model. If you do not wish to put nail extensions on your model beforehand you can adhere long plastic tips to them just before the competition starts. In some cases nail artists work on their tips during the competition and attach them to the model just before the end. Some do not even use a model, but in this case they would lose marks for theme, costume and make-up. If you are using a model who has not got all of the required assets, you need to add them. You can use wigs, hairpieces, false eyelashes, fruit, flowers, just about anything goes! Just remember to keep to your theme.

Kate Rickeard nails – pack of
cards

The picture shown here is an example of a photographic competition entry. Kate Rickeard, one of our Creative Master Technicians, decided to do a picture with a pack of playing cards. She made the nails first by building them as a 3D design with Creative coloured acrylics. The theme was the four different card suits. After the nails had been made, Kate wanted to keep the theme running through the picture but still focusing on the nails. She chose her model to complement the theme: a young pretty girl with a short bob, whose hands were pleasant and who looked quite sophisticated in the make-up and clothes. The model is holding some cards and also has some tucked into her hat. If you look at the whole picture it tells you a story, yet if you just take the hand in itself holding the cards it still tells you the same story. Kate's theme is simple, but clever and put together beautifully.

Have a look in trade magazines, consumer magazines and TV adverts for inspiration for your themes. Always try to come up with something a bit different and find the model to complement your theme.

How to put a theme together

First decide on the nails you want to do. It can be a mistake sometimes to decide on a theme and then try to decide what nails will complement this. It is much easier as a nail artist to design a set of nails and then build your look or picture around them.

There are a few points to consider when thinking of a theme:

- colour – will it be easy to carry the colours onto the costume and make-up?
- the products you need to do your nails – will they be easy to use in the competition?
- how long will it take to make your nails if it is a nail art competition? – remember you will normally have a maximum of $2^1/_2$ hours
- how long is it going to take you to do make-up, hair and costume?
- if you are using natural or fresh props will they last all day in the competition arena, or under studio lights?

If you have chosen your model and have not yet made your nails make sure that you measure your model's nails for the size of tips you need. There is nothing worse than judging nails that have been applied to a model that are three sizes too big or two sizes too small. It just does not look professional. You may even need to pre-tailor the tip to match the model's cuticle area if you are using plastic tips on the day.

Remember that you will gain extra marks if you have made the costume yourself instead of buying something already made up or hiring it. You may want to look in theatre or make-up books for inspiration, or even take a trip to a fancy dress hire agency to get ideas.

What the judges are looking for and a marking guide

Learning objectives

In this section you will learn about:

- **floor judging**
- **what judges look for in general**
- **the specific areas judges look for in different categories**
- **competition set-up**
- **your kit**

It is very important to be aware of what the judges are looking for in each nail art competition whether it be a college competition, a national nail art competition or even one on a global scale such as the Alternative Nail Awards. You should be give the opportunity as a contestant in any competition to have the rules and regulations laid down for you. If you have not got these, make sure that you obtain them before the competition day to ensure that you make maximum use of all the rules and regulations.

Competition Arena – Nail Olympics

Floor judging

This is something that should happen in all nail competitions, whether it be nail art or nail extensions and it is there to protect your model as the client and yourself, as well as those other professionals around you. It may not necessarily be just to do with the treatments going on but also areas such as health and safety, safe techniques and possible cheating. Believe it or not, it does happen! Sometimes contestants have misunderstood the rules and do not realise that they are breaking them.

The points that a floor judge would take into account are:

- the competitor's working area is neat and tidy with no bottles uncapped or left in a hazardous position
- all working materials should be in good condition
- all equipment is safe and if it is electrical that it has been tested within the last year
- models should never be put at risk
- all products and equipment are accessible for ease of use
- all hygiene rules apply throughout the competition
- all competition rules are adhered to
- all models start with clean nails with no product, paint or polish on them
- throughout the competition, they will check that there is no cheating going on, such as using pre-prepared art designs

If any competitor is found to be contravening any of the above rules they could risk being disqualified from the competition immediately. Although the floor judges are only observers, they will report their concerns to the competition organisers. You may wish to ask a question but are not allowed up from your nail station and in this case you can use the floor judge to ask these questions for you.

During the competition the floor judges are your point of contact if you need anything. They are not there to judge you, just to check that you are working within all the rules and regulations.

What judges look for in general

The competition judges will be looking for specific areas of artistry and expertise in each competition. You will be allowed around $2-2\frac{1}{2}$ hours for most competitions. You will find that in the majority of nail art competitions you will be expected not only to do a set of beautifully creative nails but also to have a strong theme, a good costume and hair and make-up to match, if appropriate. You will need to find out before the competition what is required of you on the day and what to take. All judges will be looking for a theme that is very different to anything that they have seen before. You could take a design that has been done before but put it over in a totally different theme. Try to be as original as possible. Most judges are very experienced artists and are familiar with what has gone before. Sue and Jacqui have judged nail art competitions in the past where a technician has copied not only their nail design but also the picture. If you need inspiration then look at your scrapbook, ask friends and family, go to the library and look at children's books, art books or even science fiction books, but then be creative.

Here are a few points that the judges will be looking for that are general to most nail art competitions:

- originality of theme
- originality of nail design
- hand made costume and make-up
- legible written or typed step-by-step instructions for the design
- a legible written or typed explanation of the theme
- that the theme is carried though all ten nails
- clarity of designs
- a diverse use of nail art tools and products
- good use of colour
- the complexity of the design
- how difficult it was to do in the time allocated

If you are unsure about any of the above points then contact the organisation running the competitions and ask for advice. You could also seek the advice of a friend or colleague who has already entered a competition and look at their judging sheet. All judges should be available for feedback at the end of the competition, so if you are unhappy or confused seek them out. They should also be able to give you feedback on your nails, the theme, and how they felt you could have earned extra points. This advice can be invaluable, so do not be afraid to ask. Most judges are usually competition winners themselves, so they have a broad range of experience that they can pass on to you. There are sometimes competition workshops run by previous competition winners and these can be a valuable source of help. The Untouchables put on courses called 'Playdays' each year around the UK – fun workshops that not only look at technicians' personal skills but also pass on ideas on new techniques. In some cases nail artists can be encouraged to look at their work in a totally different way. It is always worth continuing your education in any area of the professional nail industry and nail art is an important area of work for those wishing to enter fields such as fashion and photographic work.

Alternative Nail Awards/Hands and Feet

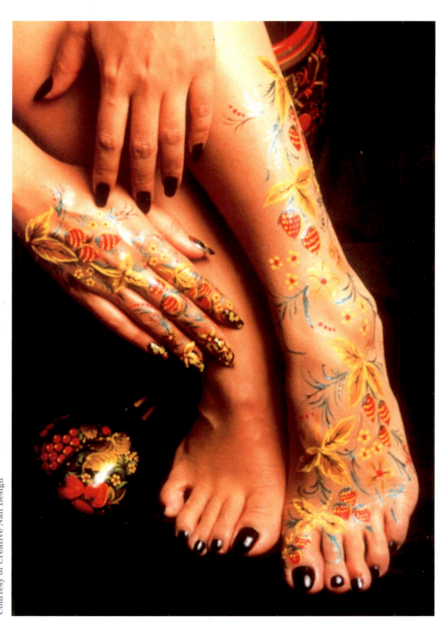

Courtesy of Creative Nail Design

Specific areas that the judges will be looking for

The advice we are giving in this chapter is as near as we can get to what most competition judges will be looking for. Remember to always obtain the rules and regulations before starting out on your competition planning.

We have mentioned that there are competitions in the different nail art media. One of the most versatile and Jacqui's personal favourite is airbrushing. For all three of us this area has become one of great development and excitement since we joined forces with Sudo Simair Graphics, an airbrush company that not only offers airbrush nail training but also tanning, make-up, body art and hair art. This has allowed us to take our photographic and fashion work to another level. We are in constant demand by editors, stylists and designers to use our airbrush skills in all five of these areas. In the past we designed a set of nails and then applied make-up in the traditional way; now we can provide our clients with a total look, using our airbrushes for nails, body art and extending it into the hair.

If you are entering a nail airbrush competition, you will usually find that you are not allowed to use any other medium other than airbrushing on the nails. There can be no hand-painting or additions such as rhinestones to finish off the design. The judges will want to see your skills as an airbrush artist. It will probably gain you some points to have some airbrushing on the costume, hair or make-up as well, just so that they can see that the theme is running through your whole design.

If you are entering a *nail airbrush competition* a judge may look at the following points:

- your use of masking or frisket
- handmade stencils
- the shading and contouring in your design
- the blending and use of colours
- your control over the airbrush
- the difficulty of the design

The judges' marking sheet will give you more idea of what it is they expect from you. You will certainly gain marks for the clarity of your design and the difficulty involved. Try to make each nail a little different, there is nothing that puts a judge off more than looking at the same design on eight nails!

If you are entering a *mixed media competition*, you will find that the rules state that you have to use a minimum of 3–5 different nail art products. These could be:

- airbrush
- hand painting
- glitters
- fabrics

Jacqui Jefford
Gold Medal Nails

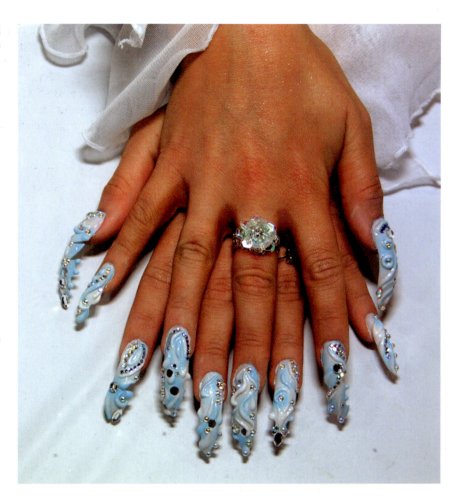

- coloured acrylics or gels
- foils
- flat-stones or rhinestones
- embellishments – this could mean lots of things!

There may be more items on the list, but if you are unsure contact the competition organisers to clarify what it is they want. You will find that all work has to be done within the competition and not bought into the arena and applied. For instance, we judged a competition where a competitor had applied screws and nails to the nails; they would have earned a few more points by making these items within the competition and applying them rather than using real screws and nails and painting over them.

Since the launch of Creative Nail Designs mosaic powders, we have found the work that nail artists are designing is much more creative. Using coloured acrylics allows you the diversity to create works of art. We have already shown you pictures of Sue's fairies and Jacqui's dragons, all made with the mosaic powders. These can be made within competitions and would earn you top marks for skill. If you do not have time to make ten nails to this level of complexity, then make one and reduce the work on the other nine to much simpler designs.

Although every competition organiser will have different rules and regulations and maybe the judges will have their own agendas, there will still be a general rule to a judging sheet. We illustrate here an example of a judging sheet that was written by ourselves for the Nails Plus Roadshow Grand Championships. This is a competition circuit that is taken around the country to technicians rather than them having to attend major trade shows, and so far it has been a huge success.

FANTASY NAIL ART COMPETITION SCORE SHEET		
Competitor Number _____ Judge _____ Total Score _____ Placement _____	Point Guide 0 = Below average 1 = Average skills 2 = Good more complex skills 3 = Very good 4 = Excellent skills 5 = Flawless cannot be improved	
Marking Criteria	**Maximum Points**	**Points Given**
1. Work Area: – The work area is safe, neat and tidy?	5	
2. Costume: – Does the costume reflect the theme?	5	
3. Use of Colour: – Was colour theory applied? Are there enough contrasts to see the different parts of the design? Do the colours complement one another?	5	
4. Control: – Does the technician have control over the various nail art mediums used?	5	
5. Blending and Shading: – Are blending and shading techniques used effectively within the design?	5	
6. Graphics: – Are the components of the nail flat or dimensional? Do they complement one another?	5	
7. Clarity of design: – Can you tell what the design is meant to be? Are all the various nail art mediums distinguishable?	5	
8. Composition: – Is the design well balanced on each nail?	5	
9. Continuation of Design across Nails: – Does the design flow from nail to nail and the theme continue throughout?	5	
10. Difficulty: – What is the complexity of this design? Look at the steps and tools it took to create.	5	
11. Originality of Design: – Is the design new and innovative?	5	
Maximum Points	**55**	**Total Points**
Judge's Comments		

Competition set up and kit needed

When you are packing for the competition make sure you check, double check and triple check all of your kit, costume and any props you will need. We have seen many a nail artist forget something crucial to their entry and because nail art is so individual they have not been able to buy or borrow from another technician or product stand.

Obviously if you are entering a specific competition like airbrushing you will need to take your airbrush and compressor, but you may need to check if you will have to take items like extension leads and lamps with you. When Jacqui entered the Nail Olympics in June 2002 it would have been a nightmare to take all of the airbrush equipment to Las Vegas, plus there was no guarantee that it would work. Simon Everingham of Sudo Simair Graphics, who was our sponsor, provided all the equipment for us and it was waiting in our hotel room. If you use a company's products and are entering a competition abroad, find out whether your company will help you with equipment. Most large companies have distributors in Europe and the States.

Here are a few general items that you may want to put on your list for the day:

- lamp and extension lead – remember an adaptor if working abroad
- your nail art kit
- all your tools
- compressor, hose and airbrush, with a spare airbrush just in case!
- copies of your theme and step-by-step instructions
- your model's costume and props
- spare nails just in case things go wrong
- water bottles for you and your model; they may be sat still for a long while

When you are packing your nail art kit remember to include spares of everything that you are using just in case your design goes wrong. It is always a good idea to have a few spare colours of paint whether you are hand painting or airbrushing, just in case you wish to change the colours or theme slightly.

Here are a few technical tips to help you on the day

- always take spare tips, paints and products
- always have plenty of pre-cut stencils in case you go wrong
- get your model to have a watch next to them so they can pace you
- set yourself time targets allowing 10 minutes spare at the end to clear up

- make sure your model goes to the toilet before the competition; it can be a long wait!
- be clear about the design you are doing rather than leaving it to chance
- check that all equipment is in good working order before you leave

The rewards that competitions can bring

Competition winners at the Nail Olympics

Entering competitions is not for the faint-hearted and you must have confidence in your work and abilities. If your friends, family and clients keep telling you how talented you are then give it a go. Be prepared to compete against yourself and make each competition you enter better than the last. Nail art is one of the hardest competitions to judge, because you are not just judging an artist's skill level, but also their artistic integrity as well. Every individual has an idea of what they like, the look and colours that they are attracted to and this can be very difficult when judging nail art. Judges have to keep an open mind and stay impartial to their own tastes.

If you do decide to enter competitions you will find there are great rewards such as:

- cash prizes
- trophies to display
- free advertising and profiling in local and trade magazines
- a stretch of your capabilities
- making new friends and contacts
- learning new skills and ideas
- being motivated by other artists
- seeing your work in a magazine or as a cover shot

There are many other benefits and also some downfalls as well, especially if you lose and you know that you have put your heart and soul into your competition nails. You must be prepared to enter a few competitions before winning, it is very rarely that any artist wins their first competition and some slog away for years never winning, but just enjoying the competition atmosphere. Some people are just naturally competitive and thrive on the whole experience whilst others have to be cajoled and coaxed into it. Whichever type of person you are does not matter: at the end of the day it is your skill that will win for you.

This section has featured a few of the finalists for the Alternative Nail Awards, courtesy of Designer Nails. You will see that each picture tells a story. The pictures have been styled around the nails of each artist and all have a great impact on the person looking at them. We are all drawn towards a certain picture because it is in our favourite colours, or the picture appeals to us, but look beyond that and see how the pictures have been very carefully thought out.

Entering competitions is a good way of learning, gaining experience and using your experience towards areas of work such as fashion and photographic work. If you are a student at college, ask your lecturer to set up a mini-departmental competition before you go on to enter national competitions. Whichever route you decide to take, we wish you the best of luck.

Bubble nails

Courtesy of Amanda Revell

Chapter summary

We hope that this chapter will inspire you to take your skills on to the competition circuit. Remember that you are only competing against yourself and that entering competitions will allow you to network with other artists, look at new ideas and techniques as well as maybe winning some prizes! Competitions should be fun, and if you enjoy the experience you will be more relaxed and have a better chance of winning. This chapter shows you all of the various categories of competition and what the judges are looking for. The competition circuit is different to your normal day-to-day work and as long as you prepare yourself as we have suggested you will always have a chance of winning. The profile of being placed in a competition will only enhance your business. We have all entered competitions so all three of us can write about the competition circuit. Nail art competitions are a way of being allowed to express your artistic abilities that no client would want to wear! Try it and see.

Corkscrew nails

Knowledge review

1 What is the name of Creative Nail Designs Photographic Competition?

2 What type of nail art competitions can you enter?

3 Where would nail art competitions be likely to be held?

4 Where could you find out about the competitions available?

5 What five points will most categories of nail art competitions have in common?

6 What questions should you ask yourself before entering competitions?

7 Give ten points you would look for in a good nail art model.

8 Where could you look for inspiration for ideas and designs?

9 What was Kate Rickeard's theme for her photographic nails?

10 What points would you consider when putting your theme together?

11 How could you gain extra marks besides your nail designs?

12 How and when would you prepare your model for competition day?

13 Give the main points that a floor judge would look at.

14 When should you register and obtain the rules and regulations?

15 Most nail art judges will be looking at general points within every competition. Name five of these.

16 What is a 'Play Day'?

17 What points would a judge cover when giving you feedback on your competition work?

18 What specific points would a judge of an airbrush competition be looking for?

19 What products could you use in a mixed media competition?

20 What skill areas would you see on a judging sheet?

21 What would you need to plan when registering to enter a competition?

22 What general equipment do you need for competitions?

23 What special requirements might you need for an airbrush competition?

24 How could your airbrush supplier help you, if you are entering a competition overseas?

25 Give five important technical tips that could help you on the day.

26 Why are you competing against yourself in competitions?

27. Give six rewards that entering competitions can bring.

28. What downfalls are there to competition work?

29. How can entering competitions help you get other types of work?

30. What does a nail art competition allow you to express?

Bibliography

Elaine Almond (1994) *Manicure, Pedicure and Advanced Nail Techniques*, Thomson Learning, London

Jacqui Jefford and Anne Swain (2002) *The Encyclopedia of Nails,* Thomson Learning, London

Milady's Art and Science of Nail Technology (1997) Milady Publishing, New York

Marian Newman (2001) *The Complete Nail Technician*, Thomson Learning, London

K. Sa-Ra (1999) *All You Need to Know about Nail Art*, Oceana Books, London

Glossary of terms

Abrasive Material used to shape and redefine nails

Absorption One of the routes of entry into the body, of liquids through the skin

Acetone A solvent that is very efficient in removing nail extensions

Acrylates Family of monomers used in light curing gel products

Activator Speeds up a reaction in the fibreglass system

Adhesion When molecules on one surface are attracted to molecules on another

Adhesive A chemical that causes two surfaces to stick or bond

After care advice Information for clients to maximise their investment through products and care

Allergic reaction Adverse response by the human body caused by contact with a substance to which that body is sensitive

Allergy In nails, reaction caused by repeated contact

Apex The high point of the nail just above the stress area

Arteries Vessels in the body that carry oxygenated blood from the heart around the body

Bacteria A single cell organism capable of causing disease

Bacterial spore A dormant state of some bacteria, spores can become active under certain conditions

Blood A nutritive liquid circulating through the blood vessels

Breathing zone 1m sphere extending around your head and mouth that contains all the air you breathe

Carpel tunnel A small passage in a wrist bone which houses a nerve that runs from the fingers into the arm

Catalyst Substance that activates or controls a chemical reaction

Cell The smallest and simplest unit capable of life

Chemical Everything that you can see and touch except light, sound and electricity. One of the building blocks of all matter

Chemical reaction The process of combining two or more chemicals into a new substance

Consultation The process of gaining information on clients' needs and requirements

Contact area The well area of the tip just above the stop point

Contact dermatitis Inflammation of the skin caused by touching certain substances

Contamination To make impure, infect or corrupt a substance

Contra action A possible adverse reaction caused by a treatment

Contra indications A reason why a treatment should not be carried out

Corrosive Substance that can cause visible and sometimes permanent damage to skin

COSHH Control of Substances Hazardous to Health

Cure The process of turning a liquid into a solid

Cuticle The seal at the base of the nail plate

Cyanoacrylates Family of monomers that can be used with low light gels and instant adhesives

Dehydrate To remove water from the surface

Dermatitis Inflammation of the skin

Dermatology The study of the skin

Dermis The deeper layer of skin under the epidermis

Disinfectant A substance capable of removing or reducing disease-causing organisms

Disinfection The process of removing or reducing disease-causing organisms by using a disinfectant

Distal The farthest attached end

Effleurage A stroking movement during massage

Epidermis The top layer of skin

Eponychium The seal of colourless skin on the underside of the cuticle attached to the nail plate and cuticle

Ethyl Methacrylate (EMA) The monomer most commonly used in acrylic nail systems; causes significantly fewer allergic reactions than MMA

Exhaust A ventilation system that removes vapours and dust to the outside of the workplace

Extension Artificial addition enhancing the length of the natural nail

Fibreglass The weave or material within the wrap system

Formaldehyde A substance that causes the nail plate to stiffen

Free edge The portion of the nail that extends beyond the nail plate

Free radical A excited molecule responsible for many chemical reactions

Fumes Tiny solid particles suspended in smoke

Furrows Ridges, horizontal or vertical

Gels Thickened liquids (oligomers)

Glues Adhesives made from proteins (normally animal)

Habit tic Nervous disorder; picking at nail plate

Hang nail Small tear or split in the cuticle

Hapalonychia Soft nails

HASAW Act Health and Safety at Work Act

Histamine Chemical released by the body to protect against harm from an unwanted substance or irritation

Home care advice Recommendations given to clients to ensure they continue to benefit from a treatment once they are at home

Hygiene Standard of cleanliness intended to prevent cross infection and secondary infection

Hyponychium The protective seal at the distal end of the nail unit

Ingestion One of the routes of entry into the body, by eating or drinking

Inhalation One of the routes of entry into the body, by breathing

Initiator A molecule that starts a reaction

Irritant A substance capable of causing inflammation of the skin, lungs, eyes, throat and nose

Keratin A group of fibrous proteins found in the skin, hair and nails

Koilonychia Spoon-shaped nails

Lamellar distrophy Flaking and peeling of the nail plate layer

Lateral To the side

Lateral nail fold Creates a seal at the side wall

Leukonychia White spots on the nails

Lifting Separation of product from the natural nail bed

Liquid When talking about nails this term normally refers to monomer

Lower arch The curve of a nail extension from the side wall to the edge of the tip

Lunula (half moon) Proximal end of the nail plate, a white area formed by immature keratin cells

Lymph A clear straw-coloured liquid circulating in the lymph vessels and lymphatic system of the body

Mantle The area of skin that covers the matrix, the proximal nail fold

Matrix The area below the proximal nail fold where keratinisation takes places

Methacrylates A family of monomer used in several types of nail systems

Methacrylic acid A commonly used acid found in primer

Methyl methacrylate (MMA) A monomer no longer used by responsible manufacturers due to severe allergic reactions

Micro-organisms Term used for microscopic living creatures

Mix ratio The mix of powder and liquid when creating nail extensions

Molecule Basic chemical building block of all matter

Mono Meaning one

Monomer Single molecule chain, in the nail industry normally used for the liquid in liquid and powder systems

MSDS Material Safety Data Sheets, providing information on safety used in the US.

Muscle Contractile tissue responsible for the movement of body parts

Nail bed The area under the nail plate

Nail plate The hard layers of keratinised skin at the tips of the fingers and toes

Nail tip A plastic tip used to extend the length of the natural nail

NVQ National Vocational Qualification

Odour Caused by vapours in the air

Onychia Infection in or on the nail plate

Onychoclasis Broken nail, normally at the free edge

Onychocryptosis Ingrown nail

Onychogryphosis Claw nail

Onycholysis Separation of the nail from the nail bed

Onychomadesis Loss of the nail plate at the proximal nail fold

Onychomycosis A fungal infection normally present under the free edge of the nail

Onychophagy Nail biting

Onychorrhexis Split or brittle nails

Overlay A thin coating applied to the natural nail or an application over the natural nail and tip

Paronychia Bacterial infection in the side of the cuticle or nail wall

Pathogens Disease-causing micro-organisms

Perionychium Lateral nail fold which creates a seal at the sidewall

Petrissage A compression movement during massage

Poly Meaning many

Polymerisation A chemical reaction that converts monomers to polymers

Polymers Many units of molecules, or monomers joined together to make a polymer chain

Powder In the nail industry, a finely ground polymer powder

Preparation To prepare the natural nail for a nail treatment

Pre-tailor Adjustment of tip before fitting

Primer Substance that makes the nail plate more compatible to certain overlays

Proximal The nearest attached end

Psoriasis A skin or nail disorder

Pterygium Excessive forward growth of the cuticle

Resin A cyanoacrylate adhesive used in the fibreglass system

Risk assessment The procedure of ascertaining and controlling for any potential hazards

Routes of entry Passageways by which chemicals can enter the body

Sanitation To reduce pathogens from a surface, e.g. hair, skin, nails

Sculpting form Paper or metal aids placed at the end of the free edge to lengthen nails without the use of a tip and then removed once an application has taken place

Sculptured nail Nail extension extended beyond the free edge without the use of a tip

Ski jump A nail plate that curves upwards as it leaves the free edge

Smile line The natural nail area where the nail leaves the nail plate; free edge. When referring to the extension this is the clean white line in zone one

Solvent Substance capable of dissolving another substance

Splinter haemorrage Tiny longitudinal streak of blood under the nail plate

Sterilisation Total destruction of all micro-organisms

Stop point The thicker part of the tip under the stress area where the free edge will fit

Stratum corneum Surface layer of skin within the epidermis

Stratum germinativum Where cell division takes place within the epidermis

Stratum granulosum Outermost living layer within the epidermis

Stratum lucidum Clear layer of skin found in the second layer of the dermis

Stratum spinosum Where the keratin is made, also within the epidermis

Stress area Zone two, the area that has to withstand the wear and tear of everyday life; this should be the thickest part of the nail

Subungual Under the nail

System In this context 'system' refers to the three media; fibreglass, UV gel, liquid and powder

Tapotement A percussion movement during massage
Toluene A substance used to dissolve ingredients into nail enamels
Trachyonychia Extreme roughness of the nail surface
Upper arch The curve of nail from the cuticle to the free edge
UV (ultra violet) Invisible light above violet in the spectrum
Vaporisation The process by which a liquid is converted into a
  gaseous state
Vapour A gas; usually liquid at room temperature
Veins Vessels in the body that collect deoxygenated blood from
  capillaries and return it to the heart
Ventilation The process of replacing stale air with fresh air
Volatile A substance that evaporates rapidly
Wrap The term used in the fibreglass system for the material used
  to overlay natural nails
Zone one The area that extends from the nail plate
Zone three The thin area around the cuticle
Zone two The stress area

Index